```
HN        Wireman, Peggy.
90
C6        Urban neighborhoods,
W47         networks, and
1984        families
```

DATE		
7-86	MAY 15 1980	
NOV 16 1987		
LW 18		
JUN 6 1988		
JUL 12 1988		
MAR 11 1989		

© THE BAKER & TAYLOR CO.

Urban Neighborhoods, Networks, and Families

Urban Neighborhoods, Networks, and Families

New Forms for Old Values

Peggy Wireman
U.S. Department of Housing and
Urban Development

LexingtonBooks
D.C. Heath and Company
Lexington, Massachusetts
Toronto

The views expressed in this book are those of the author and do not represent official opinions or policies of the U.S. Department of Housing and Urban Development.

Library of Congress Cataloging in Publication Data

Wireman, Peggy.
 Urban neighborhoods, networks, and families.

 Bibliography: p.
 Includes index.
 1. Neighborhood—United States. 2. Community development, Urban—United States. 3. Family—United States. 4. Social interaction—United States. 5. Community life. I. Title.
 HN90.C6W47   1984   307'.3362'0973   80-9016
 ISBN 0-669-04503-9

Copyright © 1984 by D.C. Heath and Company

All rights reserved. No part of this publication may be reproduced or transmitted in any form or by any means, electronic or mechanical, including photocopy, recording, or any information storage or retrieval system, without permission in writing from the publisher.

Published simultaneously in Canada

Printed in the United States of America on acid-free paper

International Standard Book Number: 0-669-04503-9

Library of Congress Catalog Card Number: 80-9016

*To my mother, Margaret Russell Blumberg,
and to my late father, Raoul Blumberg, for
sharing their intellectual curiosity and
respect for knowledge*

Contents

	Figures and Tables	xi
	Foreword *Sylvia F. Fava*	xiii
	Preface and Acknowledgments	xvii
	Introduction: The Concept of Community	xxi
Chapter 1	**Intimate Secondary Relationships**	1
	Primary and Secondary Relationships	2
	Dimensions of Intimate Secondary Relationships	3
	Networks of Intimate Secondary Relationships	6
	Comparison with Other Types of Relationships	7
	Functions of Intimate Secondary Relationships	9
Chapter 2	**The American Household: Its Support Needs**	15
	Households Likely to Be At Risk	17
	Individuals At Risk	19
	Types of Support for Households	23
	Implications	25
Chapter 3	**Community in the 1980s**	29
	Psychological Aspects of Community	29
	Social Network Analysis	33
	Institutional Aspects of Community	36
	Functions of Neighborhoods	38
	Varieties of Neighborhoods	40
	Neighborhood Involvement	42
	Neighborhood Support for Households and Families	44
	Implications for Policymakers	46
Chapter 4	**Resident Involvement in Community Life**	51
	Types of Resident Involvement	51
	Supports That Are Also Spillover Effects	60
	Politics and Power	66
	Conclusions	69

Chapter 5	**Spillover Benefits: The Federal Urban Gardening Program**	75
	The Program	75
	Spillover Effects	77
	Conclusions	84
Chapter 6	**Columbia: Accomplishments and Limitations of a Private Community Association**	87
	Columbia Association	87
	Support for Social Networks	90
	Support for Community Development	91
	Support for Pluralism	92
	Accomplishments	93
	Limitations	93
Chapter 7	**The Dynamics of Integration**	99
	Columbia, Maryland	99
	Reston, Virginia	107
	Other Integrated Communities	111
	Conclusion	112
Chapter 8	**Community Design for Families with Children**	115
	Physical Environment	115
	Basic Services	118
	Community Atmosphere	119
	Community Relationships	120
	Alternate Housing for One-Parent Families	122
	Conclusions	125
Chapter 9	**Community Supports for the Elderly**	129
	Physical Environment	129
	Social Environment	131
	Case Studies	136
Chapter 10	**Conclusions**	145
Chapter 11	**Postscript: Relevance of the American Experience for Other Countries**	153

Contents ix

Bibliography	161
Index	189
About the Author	195

Figures and Tables

Figures

2–1	American Households Living with or without Relatives	19
2–2	American Households Living with or without Children	20
2–3	Chances of Being At Risk	21
2–4	Persons over 65 in At-Risk Situations	23

Tables

1–1	Intimate Secondary Relationships Compared with Other Relationships	10
3–1	Neighborhood Commitment and Neighborhood Satisfaction: Statistically Significant Findings	43

Foreword

This book is a fresh, new look at some enduring concerns in the United States: family, neighborhood, and community. The changes in these components of society have been so rapid that their decline and death have been announced solemnly, frequently—and prematurely. Dr. Wireman's work shows that family, neighborhood, and community have not died, but have been transformed.

Her analysis is fine-grained and far-reaching, reflecting both her practical experience with community organizations and her training in academic sociology. The case materials presented include an analysis of the federally funded urban gardening program; the community association in the new town of Columbia, Maryland; the relative success of race and class integration in the new town of Reston, Virginia, and in Columbia; the effectiveness of Warren Village in Denver, Colorado, in helping low-income single mothers cope with the outside world when they leave the special housing; and programs for the elderly such as the mutual help project in Benton, Illinois, and the shared housing program in Washington, D.C. Her penultimate chapter deals with the parts to be played by public and private efforts to maintain community. Some, but by no means all, of Wireman's case data derive from government-supported projects.

Simply put, Wireman proceeds from the thesis that *the* family has now become many types and that neighborhood support systems must be designed and implemented for these new types: working couples, single parents, and the elderly. However, the neighborhood has also been transformed; Wireman uses the network approach in addition to a traditional spatial analysis, enabling her to conclude that community is alive and well in the United States at the close of the twentieth century. She goes beyond these general points to the specifics, using the case materials noted previously. One of the difficulties in obtaining support for community-based programs is conveying the importance of sometimes mundane activities and minor logistical supports to those who lack personal experience with local groups. Often community support is not even an explicit goal. One of the contributions of this book is in providing a "gut" understanding for those not involved, as well as some practical ideas and a better theoretical framework for those who are involved. Several chapters conclude with detailed lists of things to check for determining whether a neighborhood serves particular constituencies well. Happily, a whole chapter is devoted to the support systems needed for children in various family arrangements. Another chapter, based on Wireman's visits to neighborhoods in various countries, notes how widespread the family changes described for the United States have become, and raises the possibility that similar neighborhood support strategies may be effective overseas. While I am not an exponent of easy comparability and transferability across cultures, I find Wireman's analysis provocative, and detailed enough to avoid sweeping "portability."

The arguments linking the changing family, neighborhood, and community are not phrased in terms of gender, although this is in effect what Wireman has done in describing changing families and the need to change neighborhood strategies to accommodate them. For far too long, urban sociology and planning have been cast into the mold of unacknowledged male models. Much more work needs to be done to link geography with gender and the family cycle.

In my view, the most important contribution Wireman makes is the introduction and application of the concept "intimate secondary relations." Studies of cities and communities have failed to develop concepts appropriate to describe the urbanization of whole nations such as the United States, where all places—of whatever density and distance—are involved in a many splendored and often unperceived interdependence. How do the resulting bureaucratization and proliferation of formal organizations affect the individual? With anomie, disorganization, and the decline of local attachment? No, because new associations have arisen (or at least we now recognize and name them) that allow people to participate in formal organizations without becoming depersonalized.

Wireman describes intimate secondary relationships as having elements of primary relationships in that there is warmth, rapport, and intimacy; yet the relationships occur in formal settings and with specific, limited goals. She defines intimate secondary relationships as involving "intense involvement, warmth, intimacy, sense of belonging, and rapport; mutual knowledge of character; minimal sharing of personal information; minimal socializing; involvement of the individual rather than the family; a commitment that is limited in time and scope and with a relatively low cost of withdrawal; a focus on specific rather than diffuse purposes; consideration of public rather than private matters; and a preference for public meeting places."

She developed the concept from her observations of the participants in the community association of Columbia, Maryland. While she describes the concept as an ideal type, just as are primary and secondary relationships, intimate secondary relationships fit better into the reality of modern metropolitan life. Who does not know people (especially women) who derive a large share of personal identity and psychological sustenance from specialized local groups? Who does not know others (especially men, or does this reflect only the traditional family division of labor) who derive much of their identity and psychological sustenance from intense involvement with nonlocal specialized groups?

Foreword

Wireman also examines the potential of the federally funded Urban Gardening Program to create a variety of supportive relationships. Her analysis shows that when local efforts were consciously directed to social ends, contacts with the elderly, intergeneration relationships, and leadership development were strengthened. Unfortunately the data were collected indirectly and therefore did not include interviews with the participants; thus a test of the intimate secondary relationship concept was not possible. Applying the intimate secondary relationships concept in conjunction with the geography of the groups (local versus nonlocal) and with gender and family type is an approach I would recommend for dissertations and research projects. This is the stuff of which well-grounded urban sociology is made.

Wireman's book does not provide all the answers, but it is asking the right questions, as indicated in her summary:

> The concept of family needs to be broadened to include a variety of household types and those kin who provide support to its members. The concept of neighborhood must include not only the neighborhood's resources and relationships but also its ability to draw on external relationships and resources. Within a neighborhood, various forms of relationships from nodding recognition to intimate secondary relationships need to be recognized as valid. Varied informal and voluntary groups should be recognized, supported, and explicitly valued. Governments need to recognize the value of neighborhood organizations, support them, involve them in decision making, and foster coproductive activities. The value of less-than-perfect integration needs stating and affirming. These are part of the current American search for new forms and meanings of family, supportive networks, and community.

Sylvia F. Fava
Brooklyn College and
The Graduate Center,
City University of New York

Preface and Acknowledgments

The immediate impetus for this book was my experience working with developers of new towns and on the development of a national urban policy during the 1970s. As a staff member for what was then called the New Communities Administration of the U.S. Department of Housing and Urban Development, I reviewed prospective developers' plans to see how they provided for the social aspects of community life, including such services and facilities as schools, child care, and recreation. At that time the prevailing assumption of the developers was that new community residents would be young, upwardly mobile couples with two young children. I remember pondering one day what the reaction would be if I said, "Assume that 40 percent of the families that move in will get a divorce. Now give me a social plan." This experience started my inquiry into what the typical American family is really like and what types of supports they need.

Later I provided staff support for the development of an urban policy under the Carter administration. My frustration in trying to explain quickly to someone one night what a neighborhood is and why its needs cannot automatically be met through regional economic development led to a desire to spell out the functions of neighborhoods for those lacking personal grass-roots experience.

The longer impetus for this book goes back to my work as a community organizer in the 1960s in the Hyde Park-Kenwood neighborhood in Chicago. I drew on that experience in developing ideas about integration and the concept of intimate secondary relationships that evolved when I compared observations in the new towns of Columbia, Maryland, and Reston, Virginia, with my earlier experiences.

The intellectual foundations of this book lie in my efforts to integrate my experiences as a community organizer into the academic curriculum in the graduate program in community development at the University of Missouri where I was employed as an assistant professor. That led promptly to Roland Warren, whose book *Community and America* I used as a text. My interest in networks evolved after I developed the idea of intimate secondary relations. Barry Wellman and Eugene Litwak were especially important in introducing me to the work in that field.

Networks were also responsible for leading me to use urban gardening as a case illustration of the implementation of the concepts in the book. Allison Brown kindly shared insights from her study of the Urban Gardening Program. Special thanks are due to Ricardo E. Gomez, program leader, Urban Gardening Program, and to the coordinators and staffs of the programs in the sixteen cities studied.

William Michelson kindly invited me to explore some of the international implications of these ideas with colleagues at a symposium entitled "Managing Urban Space in the Interest of Children," held in Toronto in 1979 under the sponsorship of UNESCO in connection with the Man and the Biosphere Programme and the International Year of the Child hosted by The Child in the City Programme at the University of Toronto. Noboru Kobayashi arranged a conference "The Child and the City" in Tokyo, Japan, in 1981 sponsored by the Japanese National Institute for Research Advancement, the Japan Pediatric Society, and the International Pediatric Association.

This book attempts to marry theory and practice, to make the insights of both types of expert accessible to the other. It also attempts to integrate findings from a number of fields of knowledge. To the extent it has succeeded, it will provide workers with concepts and data from several fields.

The first part of this book examines the facts behind some of the stereotypes of family and neighborhood. The introduction raises questions about the reality of some of the more common stereotypes. Chapter 1 presents a new concept of how some relationships in neighborhoods actually work. The next two chapters examine what today's households look like, how today's neighborhoods work, and the relevance of neighborhoods for meeting the needs of various types of households. Chapter 4 examines four types of resident involvement that can provide neighborhood services and strengthen resident networks.

The second part of the book presents case material on local programs, and considers what aspects made the programs helpful—or not helpful—in building community institutions and supporting households. The first case shows how a national program to encourage urban gardening varied in its indirect effects on households and neighborhood development. The second case examines a community association in the new town of Columbia, Maryland, and considers its limitations in providing a broad range of supports to residents. This is followed by an analysis of the dynamics of race and class in Columbia and another new town. Since the interactions of members of different groups in our pluralistic society have major effects on the development and dynamics of our neighborhoods, this chapter raises issues applicable to neighborhoods with Hispanic, Asian, and other ethnic groups, although the cultures and problems of these groups are not treated in any detail.

The next section examines how some of the concepts discussed earlier can be applied to designing neighborhoods and neighborhood programs that meet the special needs of the groups most likely to spend most of their time there: children and the elderly. Policy implications are presented in the conclusions. This is followed by a short postscript on Asia that indicates how some of the concepts presented might be usefully examined by other nations undergoing changes in traditional family and residential patterns. This postscript is based on personal observations during a six-month lecture-study trip to nine countries and does not encompass the extensive literature on Third World development. My observations should be considered only as questions to be raised in the context of specific cultural, economic, political, and social conditions and traditions.

Personal thanks are due to a number of other people who encouraged me in writing this book. Gary Hack, head of the Department of Urban Studies and Planning at MIT, spent an afternoon listening to my ideas and telling me they were worth pursuing. All of my friends have asked the needed encouraging question, "How's the book going?" A number of them, as well as colleagues, have read parts. Most of the chapters were rewritten in the light of their perceptive suggestions (although I take full responsibility for any inaccuracies). Many thanks go to Roger S. Ahlbrecht, Robert A. Aldrich, Edwin W. Baker, Mark Beach, Vivian T.R. Berry, Allison Brown, Lynne C. Burkhart, Phyllis Ehrlich, Rona Feit, Ricardo E. Gomez, Janet Gutkin, David S. Harre, Douglas S. Hill, Susan Hodges, James Kretz, H. Beth Marcus, Howard Millman, Charles Mowry, Milcah Mrema, Joan M. Nelson, Richard C. Rich, Carol Schreter, Jack Smit, Norma Turner, Victor Wilburn, and Sabra F. Woolley. I also appreciate the assistance of Freeman Adv., Inc., with picture layouts and the courtesy of Printing and Visual Arts, U.S. Department of Housing and Urban Development, for the loan of photographs. My debt to Morton Leeds goes beyond his reading this manuscript to his urging me to pursue the Ph.D. and providing innumerable hours of professional guidance.

Margaret Pearson, with patience and tact, assisted with the tedious task of checking the numbers in tables, the pages of references, scattered facts and figures, putting the notes and bibliography in proper form, and finding missing references. My gratitude goes to Delorah "Dee" Arnold for her unfailing pleasantness, professional competence, ability to read my handwriting, and cheerful retyping of what she had already typed ten times before. Jean Rhodes bore patiently the major burden of typing the notes and bibliography, competently assisted by Doris L. Lesesne and Areatha S. Davis. Kay Hill helped with final proofreading.

Noëlle Blackmer Beatty edited the final manuscript, eliminating repetition, reorganizing sections, and tactfully forcing me to clarify what I meant. The entire book is more readable thanks to her ability to rewrite clearly and her patient attention to detail.

Warm appreciation for generous sharing is due to those listed in chapter 11, especially Yukiko Kada, Kirtee Shah, M. Dishmar, Wismu Ardjo,

Winnie Tang, Chua Beng Huat, and Nini Kusumaatmadja and participants and staff of the UNICEF training program for regional planners held in Bali, Indonesia, in the summer of 1981.

Finally, my thanks to persons in many communities who shared insights, friendships, and intimate secondary relations with me.

Introduction: The Concept of Community

A number of scholarly and popular authors have claimed that community no longer exists in the United States—that American families have fallen apart and that neighborhoods are no longer relevant to their residents. These authors consider urban neighborhoods merely as a collection of dwellings that house individuals who carry on their important business elsewhere. A look at the facts, however, shows that a large number of Americans continue to receive companionship and tangible support from their families and from their neighborhoods. Whether they are meeting everyday obligations or are undergoing a major life crisis, many residents of urban communities actively participate in social networks that contribute positively to the quality of their daily lives.

The concept of neighborhood has a number of complex dimensions. Decisions about location of businesses—and thus jobs—about health care, social security, and many other services are made by large corporations and federal and state government, not at the neighborhood level. America's family makeup is changing and creating new kinds of family structures. At the same time, many Americans now live far from close kin. Finally, neighborhoods differ, and residents show varying degrees of commitment to their well-being and survival. This book examines that complexity and, in so doing, argues the need for a wider understanding of the communal aspects of neighborhoods and of the value of neighborhood-centered social networks. It demonstrates ways in which innovative neighborhood programs have proved to be beneficial to residents and encourages planners to design institutions and support systems that will promote the development of community groups and activities. Most important, it attempts to expand traditional views of American households and neighborhood relations to meet the needs of contemporary society.

Central to this study is an analysis of the wide range of informal networks and support systems set up among families, neighbors, friends, coworkers, and members of voluntary organizations. Primary and secondary relationships as traditionally defined continue to exist within the neighborhood setting. But because these terms do not adequately describe some aspects of neighborhood relations, I introduce here a new concept: that of intimate secondary relationships. My explanation of this type of relationship, which exists among people working together around a joint enterprise,

xxi

will, I hope, bring new life to discussions of the dynamics of neighborhood relations.

All Americans, even those who treat their neighborhoods as a hotel, are affected by the appearance and safety of their environment. Some, however, are closely tied to their communities—particularly children and those who care for them. Others, the elderly or poor, for example, lack the mobility or money to go elsewhere and are dependent on their neighborhoods. My analysis of those households likely to need community-based support includes suggestions for developing such support systems.

An approach to the vitality of American life that assumes that the family has died is as unrealistic as one that assumes that the family alone can handle all the social problems created by a changing society. Although it is true that families are no longer necessarily made up of a husband, wife, and two children, it does not follow that families no longer love, care about, or support each other. Caring families may consist of a single adult with two children, an elderly widow living alone but near a child, or other combinations. Empirical data about household composition are presented along with ways to provide support for these new patterns of family life.

We need to enlarge our definition of a good community relationship so that it no longer means only one that might have been considered typical in a nineteenth-century small town. An attempt is made here to demonstrate ways in which neighborhoods work. The empirical data from a number of studies are presented, as well as illustrations of the successes and failures of individual community endeavors.

It is essential that planners and neighborhood residents understand the potentials and limitations of their communities if they are to work together to encourage neighborhood development. Even if these groups jointly acknowledge the potential of community institutions to make residents' lives easier and happier, they cannot ignore the realities of political, business, and institutional power.

Many of those working for neighborhood improvement do so as volunteers. The American tradition of self-help and volunteerism first noted by de Tocqueville in the 1800s is valuable and should be supported. Unfortunately much volunteer work in our country is a substitute for social services for which society is unwilling to pay. (Volunteer work of business persons is often done on company time as part of public relations efforts or as a self-improvement project important to career advancement.) This is not intended to denigrate the important humanistic contributions of volunteers but to point out the socioeconomic and even political realities that affect the underlying problems. I urge all those involved in neighborhood planning to seek also the changes in laws and institutions that will bring long-lasting improvements to their neighborhoods, as well as the services and support for basic necessities needed by their residents.

Although the communal aspects of American life are intrinsically valuable in ameliorating some of the adverse effects of social inequalities, strengthening communal supports is not a solution to structural economic and political problems. Nor is it a substitute for national approaches to dealing with major social and technological change. For example, local community programs cannot address the question of why so many of our elderly are poor or why so many of today's middle-aged adults are likely to face poverty when they become old. This requires examination of issues such as policies that require people to retire at age 65, regardless of their health, inclination, or economic situation; pension plans that discriminate against women; and discrimination that has and continues to limit the income and savings ability of minorities and women.

In his book *Megatrends,* John Naisbitt claims that Americans are fed up with big government and centralization and are moving toward decentralization, local initiative, and self-help. He suggests that the movement in this country toward a high tech society must be accompanied by what he calls "high touch," or warm communication and mutual support, among individuals involved in personal networks. He considers the traditional family and neighborhood to be largely irrelevant to the new forms of supports he foresees for Americans.

I see an alternative possibility where new forms and expressions of traditional relationships and values will continue to provide many of the "high touch" contacts for numerous Americans. Although high tech society is clearly the America of the future, it does not spell the death of American family or neighborhoods. It is salutary to remember in this regard that the decline of community in America was first noted in connection with the Boston of John Winthrop in 1650.[1] It is the aim of this book to indicate ways in which urban community planners, officials, organizers, and residents can continue to support the traditional values often found in neighborhoods and families within the new forms taken by today's households, families, networks, and communities.

Note

1. Thomas Bender, *Community and Social Change in America* (New Brunswick, N.J.: Rutgers University Press, 1978), pp. 47-48.

1 Intimate Secondary Relationships

In the middle of the nineteenth century the German sociologist Ferdinand Tönnies developed a theory that put into perspective the societal changes taking place during the upheaval caused by the industrial revolution. It was his view that humanity was moving from a period of *Gemeinschaft* (community) to that of *Gesellschaft* (society).[1] Tönnies's term *Gemeinschaft* has been used by sociologists to represent an idealized precapitalistic, preindustrial, homogeneous rural village united by overlapping ties of kinship, economic interdependence, and common values. *Gesellschaft* represents urban, capitalistic, industrial society where individuals relate only in contractual relationships for specific and limited purposes, primarily to further their individual economic goals. The impact of size, according to Georg Simmel, causes urban man to react "with his head instead of his heart," forces an emphasis on punctuality, exactness, impersonality, and produces ennui.[2] Moreover, the use of money causes him to become more calculating in his relationships with others.

The growth of bureaucracy also influences relationships among people. Its essence, as characterized by Robert K. Merton, is a "spirit of formalistic impersonality."[3] The individual, Merton says, is considered to be interchangeable with any other individual of a similar type. Decisions are based on rules created to further the goals of the organization, not on emotional response to the needs of a particular individual.

In his book, *Community and Social Change in America,* historian Thomas Bender criticizes American historians for accepting the *Gemeinschaft–Gesellschaft* dichotomy without acknowledging that Tönnies considered it possible to have *Gemeinschaft* relationships in cities or examining the actual extent to which people in American small towns were embodied in *Gesellschaft* relationships.[4] Bender shows that American society for well over one hundred years has fostered a variety of social relationships, some of which reflect values of *Gesellschaft* and others of which reflect values of *Gemeinschaft*. Individuals participate in both kinds of relationships. Institutions primarily held together by one type of relation also incorporate some aspects of the other, as when colleagues in a bureaucracy become friends.

1

Primary and Secondary Relationships

Primary relationships, a term first used by Charles H. Cooley, are associated with *Gemeinschaft* and describe the kinds of relationships found within families, children's play groups, in rural villages, and in ethnic urban neighborhoods.[5] People in primary relationships are concerned about each other. A mother, for example, has a primary relationship with her child; she is concerned with everything affecting her child's development. In contrast, a doctor is concerned only with the child's health. Groups in which primary relationships generally occur are homogeneous, rather small, relatively permanent, and offer continued face-to-face relationships.

In many primary situations, the entire family participates in an activity. Often membership in several primary groups overlaps, as in cases where individuals have relatives in their neighborhoods who are part of their social circle. When such individuals participate separately from their families, as in the case of men in a neighborhood ethnic bar or women in a rural church sewing circle, they still often know each other's families and exchange personal data.

Individuals involved in secondary relationships meet only for specific purposes of a limited nature. Such relationships are typical of *Gesellschaft*. Secondary relationships occur, for instance, between the modern businessperson and a customer or between the bureaucrat and client and are considered to be typical in a modern urban area. In secondary relationships, the overall personalities and lives of the individuals involved are irrelevant to the encounter.

Observers of community activity can be expected to identify some relationships as primary and others as secondary. This chapter presents data about observed relationships that combine identifiable traits of both primary and secondary relationships. In an attempt to characterize this combination, I developed the term *intimate secondary relationships*.[6] Like the concepts of primary and secondary relationships, this term describes an ideal type, an abstraction from the major characteristics of actual relationships.

The concept was developed to describe relationships observed among members of the Oakland Mills Village Board, part of the community association in Columbia, Maryland. Columbia is a racially integrated new town, predominantly middle income, but with a substantial lower-income population. The concept was tested further in interviews in a similar new town, Reston, Virginia, and by comparison with relationships in a number of community organizations in a racially and economically integrated inner-city neighborhood, Hyde Park-Kenwood in Chicago. Discussions with observers of other communities have indicated that similar patterns of relationships have been observed in a number of other communities in the United States and in other nations.

Dimensions of Intimate Secondary Relationships

The term *intimate secondary relationship* at first appears to contradict itself. This seeming contradiction was a deliberate choice; the concept describes relationships that have the dimensions of warmth, rapport, and intimacy normally connected with primary relationships yet occur within a secondary setting and have some aspects of secondary relationships. The dimensions are: intense involvement, warmth, intimacy, sense of belonging, and rapport; mutual knowledge of character; minimal sharing of personal information; minimal socializing; involvement of the individual rather than the family; a commitment that is limited in time and scope and with a relatively low cost of withdrawal; a focus on specific rather than diffuse purposes; consideration of public rather than private matters; and a preference for public meeting places.

As participants in an intimate secondary relationship work together around a joint enterprise, as in the case of the community association in Columbia, they experience the warmth, intimacy, sense of belonging, and rapport (or intense arguments and hostility) often associated with primary groups. Unlike members of primary groups, however, members of an intimate secondary group are not concerned with the personal backgrounds, family relationships, or even necessarily the tastes of the other individuals. Although the personal information shared varies from individual to individual and among groups, generally it is limited and in no case is considered central to the relationship. One man, for instance, described a group in Toronto, Canada, where the chairwoman of a neighborhood council suffered from epilepsy. This might never have been known except that she suffered a seizure and could not chair the annual meeting. Fellow board members were shocked to realize that they had known her for several years yet had been unaware of a recurrent serious physical disorder. Intimate secondary relationships can have the intensity of involvement normally associated with primary groups but still lack the sharing of personal information or socializing usually found in primary group situations.

Intimate secondary relationships differ from secondary relationships in that participants know each other's characters in sufficient depth to be able to develop trust or to determine whether trust is warranted. One Columbia resident commented that he was not asked where he came from or about previous activities and jobs. The board members, however, did know his character and how he would act under circumstances that concerned all of them.

Another dimension of intimate secondary relations has more in common with secondary relations. The individual rather than the family group tends to be involved. One former chairman of a community group in Falls Church, Virginia, commented that husbands and wives were never active in the same group at the same time. The chairman attributed this separation to a desire to avoid competition between spouses and to provide each a separate opportunity for growth. Columbia residents particularly noted the opportunity that participation in the community association gave to non-employed women to develop skills and confidence in their abilities to function as individuals, separate from their roles as wives and mothers.

An intimate secondary relationship differs from both primary and secondary relationships in terms of commitment. In most primary group settings, such as friendships or family relations, the activities and time commitment tend to be open-ended and diffuse. Attempts to establish stricter limits or to withdraw involve considerable cost and frequently personal hostility. Leaving a primary work group can be accomplished without personal hostility by changing jobs, but this is not always possible without substantial other costs. Even withdrawing one's children from a neighborhood play group or oneself from a circle of friends may not be easy. No long-term commitment is required in a secondary relationship.

The commitment experienced by members of the Columbia board is characteristic of intimate secondary relationships. They were intensely involved in the group's activities but were not necessarily close friends. One community activist reported being very careful about socializing with people he met through community association activities. He avoided getting close to families in his cul-de-sac, because "once you let someone into your personal life it is difficult to get them out if you turn out to have different tastes or values." When people got tired of their fellow board members, they could simply resign or not run for a second term.

Although many people in Columbia remain active on the same board or with the same organization for a number of years, another common and accepted pattern is intense involvement for several years followed by a period of withdrawal into personal and family affairs or membership in another organization, frequently one covering a larger geographic area. Withdrawal from intimate secondary groups because of family, work obligations, or other personal reasons is an accepted part of the commitment pattern. From time to time former members will be asked to perform specific tasks and also will demonstrate continued loyalty through participation in fund-raising events or annual meetings. Thus, intimate secondary relationships have some secondary characteristics in terms of their limited duration of commitment but some primary characteristics in terms of the intensity of commitment during the period of involvement. Members of the Oakland Mills Village Board estimated that they spent from ten to twenty hours per week on board business.

Intimate secondary relationships arise when people work together to perform specific public tasks. The reason for the interaction is public business rather than private friendship or business. Board participants, for instance, saw themselves in a public role carrying out a public responsibility. One group in Hyde Park-Kenwood met for years without engaging in personal social relations. Once a month members came to a community meeting to fulfill their role obligations as neighbors. This distinction between being a good neighbor and being a friend was made clear by one active Columbia respondent who indicated that he liked his cul-de-sac because there were seventeen families who respected his privacy.

Instant intimacy is rarely part of intimate secondary relationships, although immediate liking between members might occur. In another sort of a situation, such as a singles' bar, individuals might well develop immediate rapport and conversation might also exclude personal data. The crucial difference, however, is that presence in a singles' bar does not involve either personal commitment or a community role. Intimate secondary relationships clearly involve both because they combine some degree of personal intimacy with a secondary role obligation. This is what makes them unique. Members have clear roles and obligations determined by the secondary setting rather than by the personal tastes of the individuals.

Intimate secondary relationships not only form around public business but also generally develop in public places such as a community center. When asked whether the Columbia community centers were necessary, one person explained that although many of the meetings were small enough to be held in peoples' homes, holding them in the community center made it clear that everyone had a right to attend. Another respondent suggested that a person might think, "I might like to drop in on that meeting but I don't feel free to drop in at somebody's house." If the meeting were in the community center, they could just wander in and sit down. But if the meeting were in a home, they would "have to go up and knock on the door and say, 'May I come in to your meeting?'" When meetings are at the center, "You don't have to ask someone's permission." People are also freer to leave without explanation or apology. A respondent from another village board said that "you could get up and walk out of boring meetings, but I would feel terribly rude walking out of a private home." Thus the use of public space avoids establishment of a host-guest relationship, including nuances of deference owed to a guest or a host. It also avoids problems of expectations of reciprocity, especially important where great economic or social distances exist.

A black block group in Hyde Park-Kenwood, a neighborhood of Chicago, had been extremely successful over a number of years in creating solidarity, maintaining the block's appearance, and preventing their homes from being condemned by urban renewal through initiating a renovation project. Their meetings were always held in public places. The chairman said that attendance dropped whenever the meetings were held in homes. While racially homogeneous, the block contained both single-family homes and apartments and persons of a variety of ages, family compositions, incomes, and life-styles. The block leader had enabled the neighbors to establish block norms and to obtain resources and recognition from outside institutions. Neighbors also offered each other mutual support by maintaining surveillance over potential criminals and sending cards to hospitalized members. However, none of the group's social events had been successful in its ten-year history. By using public meeting places, the leader was able to include all of the diverse residents of the block in their public roles as neighbors yet still permit them freedom in individual selection of friends for more intimate primary relationships. Only by meeting in a public place did people overcome social distances so that they met as equals, neighbors temporarily setting aside any differences in status, tastes, or values.

Networks of Intimate Secondary Relationships

Once formed, intimate secondary relationships persist even after an individual leaves the group in which they were formed. The result can be a network of such relationships throughout a community among persons who have had previous group affiliations. Barry N. Crump suggests that an essential characteristic of networks is that they emphasize linkages among actors rather than the characteristics of the actors.[7] The concept of intimate secondary relationships describes a particular type of linkage.

Some networks deal with the close-knit ties found in primary groups, kin structures, and friendships.[8] Others are characterized by weak ties between people who are not intimate and may see each other rarely, such as former classmates who meet at a reunion.[9] Intimate secondary relationships are too secondary in nature to be called close-knit ties. Members have definite role obligations derived from their performance of other secondary group tasks. The essence of the trust relation that develops in an intimate secondary relationship is not that of personal friendship but trust in the other participants' character and confidence in one's own ability to rely on or at least judge the accuracy of information given. For example, one respondent noted that one man continually asked her about the opinion of the Jewish congregation on certain matters. When she asked why he did not call the congregation leaders directly, he responded that he trusted her information because he knew her.

Another respondent, who was black, worked on a village matter with a white person now active in county affairs. That individual continues to refer non-Columbians requesting information about racial matters in Columbia to the black with whom he had formed an intimate secondary relationship. Thus, a network does not merely continue a friendly relationship; it continues communication on matters of public concern and is based on a knowledge of a person's judgment and areas of competence. The crucial quality is not personal friendship but credibility based on a prior relationship. The network revolves around public rather than private business and involves more important fulfillment of role expectations than is involved in weak ties.

Comparison with Other Types of Relationships

The nature of these empirically observed relationships, their theoretical significance, and potential importance for neighborhoods may become clearer through comparison with other relationships that also combine primary and secondary traits. The kinds of relationships formed in John Irwin's "scenes" and those formed in therapy or encounter groups will be considered briefly. Each combines some traits of the ideal type of primary and secondary relationships, and each is formed as a means of coping with conditions of modern mobility, heterogeneity, or rapid change. They differ, however, in the traits they combine and in the extent to which they are embodied in or connected with a set of social relationships involved in community institutions. In each of the relationships considered, the individuals are members of a group, although in the case of the scene, the group may be only a loosely defined reference group.

Irwin describes scenes as events during which groups of individuals congregate for pleasurable activities.[10] The purpose, whether surfing, taking drugs, attending a rock concert, or some other activity, is strictly for pleasure and self-expression. Participants are conscious of themselves as actors and of their impression on the audience, which consists primarily of other participants. Scenes occur in public places, such as beaches, and are open to anyone who decides to participate. Scenes attract both an inner group, which has some knowledge, skills, and equipment, such as surfboards or drugs, and those who wander by because of the action. Clearly a variety of different relationships may exist among the various individuals who are "making the scene," but these do not typically include the rapport, sense of mutual community obligation, and knowledge of character developed through performance of shared public tasks.

The group observed in Columbia and many of the other groups I considered were not organized spontaneously. They were elected boards. Although establishing a role as a participant was not difficult, much activity occurred in meetings at which only elected members or regular participants were allowed unrestricted participation. Also much activity occurred outside of meetings in conversations between individual members about task accomplishment or group dynamics. These, of course, were not open to casual participants.

Although the controversies and theatrical personalities of some community endeavors may have the drama of one of Irwin's scenes, much of the activity of community boards involves bureaucratic and political intricacies that are difficult for an outsider to follow and are likely to be considered dull. Participants do tend to be self-conscious about their role and their audience. Their success as community leaders, however, depends to a large extent on instrumental task accomplishment. Board members who are perceived as not producing can be defeated in the next election.

Most of the participants observed in intimate secondary relationships developed in community associations were middle class—either actually or in orientation. Their participation was in addition to their major pursuits, not expressive of a desire for an alternative life-style. Both men and women seemed to feel an obligation for community service.

The type of relationship found in group therapy or encounter groups has more in common with an intimate secondary relationship: the commitment is voluntary and limited in time and scope; participation often is by individuals rather than family groups; intense personal relationships are formed rapidly and in sufficient depth to reveal important aspects of each other's characters and develop mutual trust or distrust; and there is an emphasis on equality within the group and deemphasis of status based on outside job roles, personal wealth, race, age, or sex.

Therapy or encounter groups differ from intimate secondary groups, however, in the amount of personal information shared, particularly about family matters, and in the focus on private rather than public matters. The latter involves more than a lack of public tasks. There is a subtle difference crucial to understanding the essential public and community basis of intimate secondary groups. In the case of elderly persons attending a therapy group, the relevant data about their age probably would revolve around such matters as declining health, relationships with children, and loss of status due to retirement. The focus would be on individuals' feelings, others' reactions to their problems, and listeners' concerns with the same matters. In the case of a neighborhood-based intimate secondary group, the emphasis would be on the public response necessary to accommodate the individuals' needs. The focus would therefore be on the ways individuals in a certain category, such as the elderly, could make known to others special needs that should be met by a public response, such as constructing ramps to buildings. For example, in Columbia, the elderly expressed their need for public transportation by testifying at a public hearing.

The concept of intimate secondary relationships was developed to describe observed relationships and also can be conceptualized as an ideal type. This discussion does not mean to imply that all board members of voluntary associations display the cluster of behavioral patterns that here are called intimate secondary relationships. Nevertheless, the concept does describe a behavioral pattern displayed by some and does provide an ideal

Table 1-1
Intimate Secondary Relationships Compared with Other Relationships

Characteristic	Primary	Therapy Group	Making the Scene	Intimate Secondary	Secondary
Intense personal involvement	yes	yes	yes	yes	no
Mutual knowledge of character	yes	yes	no[a]	yes	no
Knowledge of personal life	yes	yes	no	no	no
Socializing	yes	no	yes	no	no
Involvement with family	yes	no[b]	no	no	no
Diffuse commitment	yes	no	no	no	no
Focus on specific purpose	no	yes	yes	yes	yes
Public purpose of business	no	no	no	yes	yes
Public place for interactions	no	no	yes	yes	yes

[a] Except perhaps among some inner groups.
[b] Unless it is couple or family therapy.

type lying somewhere between primary and secondary. Table 1-1 presents a comparison of characteristics of different types of relationships.

Functions of Intimate Secondary Relationships

Communities with Population Mobility

In the new town of Columbia and other communities with considerable mobility, intimate secondary relationships can permit newcomers to experience warm relationships yet make commitments to friendships slowly. Newcomers' fears of unwanted obligations may be especially great in apartments or areas of high density where physical protection of privacy is limited. Irwin Altman has called privacy the "selective control of access to the self or to one's group" and emphasizes the importance of achieving the desired balance between feelings of crowding or intrusion and feelings of loneliness or isolation.[11]

Intimate secondary relationships may also encourage a feeling of belonging, thus adding to community integration as well as to personal satisfaction. One of Columbia's board members commented that he felt as if he had lived in Columbia a long time, although he had been there only a year. Many of those involved had become active in community affairs within six months of arriving.

In brief, intimate secondary relationships allow newcomers to come to know a number of persons before forming individual friendships, experience some warmth and intimacy without commitment to personal friendships and with protection of privacy, learn about community resources and norms, identify with the community, and join with others on projects or mutual problems. The relationships in the Oakland Mills Village Board in Columbia fulfilled each of these functions.

Families

Intimate secondary relationships are also helpful in some family situations, particularly where family patterns are changing. A minister in Reston, Virginia, indicated that these relationships have special relevance for women in unhappy marriages. Frequently women enter into such relationships to obtain the support needed to face dissolving their marriage. In other instances women use such relationships to help their personal growth, to promote close relationships with men without having a sexual affair, and to develop new interests and skills. Some of these women are able to change the dynamics of their marriages by assuming new outside roles. Joining a voluntary group and forming intimate secondary relationships is, for some, a preliminary step to obtaining a job and entering into a secondary relationship.

Although intimate secondary relationships can provide support to people undergoing marital stress, the support offered is more a reflection of the secondary nature of these relationships than of their primary aspects. One Columbia resident explained that members of several different village boards had undergone marital conflict or separation during their terms of office. The group was supportive in the sense of offering sympathy and, more important, in its continuation of the existing warm relationship on a business-like but intimate basis. Information about the problem was conveyed initially not so much in terms of the trauma involved, which might have been shared with a personal friend, but as a matter of status change that fellow board members needed to know to avoid embarrassing comments or incidents. Board members might sympathetically inquire, "How's it going?" leaving the individual free to accept sympathy without discussing details. The importance of the continuation of an intimate secondary relationship on a business-as-usual basis can better be understood by considering that marital difficulties frequently cause severe strain on primary relationships. Friends may ally with one partner or feel awkward about inviting a single person to a gathering of married friends. Relatives are concerned but may be angry or critical as well as sympathetic, and their inquiries may infringe on private matters.

Even apart from situations of divorce, intimate secondary relationships can fulfill a function for members of modern American families. The limited intimacy they offer may still be more than the participants experience in actual interactions within their own family group. The modern American nuclear family generally consists of two to five persons, of whom only two are adults. Frequently this is too small a group to act as the main source of emotional support for all family members. Eugene Litwak has suggested that the isolated nuclear family lacks sufficient resources to fulfill all of the functions of the traditional primary group; it is especially difficult for the family to serve as the sole base for common interests and experiences in a rapidly changing society.[12] Instead this function is fulfilled by friendships and by intimate secondary relationships, which are able to provide some degree of intimacy around areas of mutual interests. Since married social relationships generally involve other couples, involvement is limited when all four persons do not share the same interests. Intimate secondary relationships can provide spouses with an opportunity to have relationships that are not part of the dyadic relationship yet are relatively unthreatening to it because of limited expectations and public meeting places.

In summary, intimate secondary relations can help relieve stress in family relations by providing support for individuals having marital difficulties, support for women developing skills and relationships outside of traditional roles, opportunities for individuals to establish personal relationships beyond their small nuclear families, and opportunities for marital partners to have relationships around interests not shared by their spouses.

Heterogeneous Populations

Intimate secondary relationships perform several important functions in heterogeneous populations. The first, and perhaps most vital, is to enable persons who might feel uncomfortable with each other because of differences in race, age, income, or life-style to meet on a neutral, limited basis. People who meet in a situation of status uncertainty can reserve more intimate overtures of friendship for those with whom they find status compatibility. Intimate secondary groups may enable residents in an integrated community to socialize with whomever they wish, yet avoid total geographic or social isolation of any group.

Even the limited contact in intimate secondary relationships may be sufficient to increase understanding and empathy among different groups or at least public recognition of the groups' needs. Blacks in Columbia tended to socialize among themselves and participated only minimally in village board activities. Their limited participation nevertheless created some sensitivity to issues that might otherwise have been overlooked.[13]

In Hyde Park-Kenwood, residents of a middle-class, racially integrated street shared a common back fence with black lower-class apartment dwellers. One summer, residents of both groups met outdoors weekly to discuss painting the fence and other block problems. The group dispersed when winter came; there was no public place indoors for meetings, and the social distance between the residents was too great for them to feel comfortable in each others' homes. Nevertheless, a year later residents still felt differently about their neighbors and more comfortable about living on their block because of the joint experience.

In both Hyde Park-Kenwood and Columbia, intimate secondary relationships enabled residents of different backgrounds to feel comfortable with each other and to tackle community problems jointly. It also enabled the middle class to maintain their belief in equality, which was a well-publicized community goal, yet largely continue patterns of social stratification in their social lives. Herbert J. Gans suggests that segregation by class is desirable at the microlevel, the area of elementary school attendance, with heterogeneity at a high school level.[14] An alternative to segregated neighborhoods may be to design neighborhoods in a manner that facilitates formation of a range of different relationships, including intimate secondary ones.

Intimate secondary relationships in heterogeneous neighborhoods can fulfill several functions: permit a degree of intimacy and knowledge of others without commitment to friendship; permit common action on joint projects or mutual problems; facilitate acceptance of persons from different incomes, races, ages, life-styles, and housing tenure (home owners and renters, apartment dwellers, and single-family residents) as legitimate members of the community; encourage understanding of the differing needs of persons in the various categories; help define a community's responsibility to meet the needs of various groups; and create a community network of trust relationships available for community business.

Community Integration

Intimate secondary relationships promote an intangible spirit of community, a feeling of being connected at least indirectly to many members of the community, not just one's own friends and neighbors. They also provide an informal mechanism for community-wide information exchange and for creating, disseminating, and enforcing community values and norms. The trust and understanding established in intimate secondary relationship networks are especially important if a person wants to sound out opinion on a sensitive issue or test a position on a potentially controversial subject. In both Hyde Park–Kenwood and Columbia, such networks played an important part in the intricate dynamics of public attitudes about race and low-income residents. Several former village board members now work in county agencies or are members of the county council. They continue to maintain their networks of intimate secondary relationships as a means of staying in touch with community sentiments.

These relationships facilitate building coalitions among diverse interest groups. The manager of a subsidized Columbia housing project gradually became active in several community organizations, each of which gave him increased contacts and credibility as a spokesman for the low-income residents.[15] Later, a woman who had known him through her work on a village board urged him to run for the community association governing board and actively supported his campaign.

Networks of intimate secondary relationships can be especially important to low-income or low-status individuals or groups, members of a racial or ethnic minority, and women. They provide links across class and racial boundaries. They also can provide access to political and social centers of power that otherwise would be totally closed and to resources and institutions outside the immediate neighborhood, which may not otherwise be known to some.

Notes

1. Ferdinand Tönnies, *Community and Society,* ed. Charles P. Loomis (New York: Harper and Row, 1963).

2. Georg Simmel, "The Metropolis and Mental Life," in *Classic Essays on the Culture of Cities,* ed. Richard Sennett (New York: Meredith Corporation, 1969), p. 48.

3. Robert K. Merton, *On Theoretical Sociology: Five Essays, Old and New* (New York: Free Press, 1957), p. 27.

4. Thomas Bender, *Community and Social Change in America* (New Brunswick, N.J.: Rutgers University Press, 1978).

5. Charles Horton Cooley, *Social Organization* (New York: Schocken, 1962).

6. Most of this chapter is a revision of material originally presented in Peggy Wireman, "Meanings of Community in Modern America: Some Implications from New Towns" (Ph.D. diss., American University, 1977); Peggy Wireman, "Intimate Secondary Relationships" (Paper presented at the Seventy-third Annual Meeting of the American Sociological Associa-

tion, San Francisco, September 4-8, 1978); Peggy Wireman, "The Functions of Intimate Secondary Relationships" (Paper presented at the Ninth Congress of Sociology, Uppsala, Sweden, August 1978). The quotations are from my dissertation.

7. Barry N. Crump, "The Portability of Urban Ties" (Revised version of paper presented at the Seventy-second annual meeting of the American Sociological Association, Chicago, 1977), p. 12.

8. Elizabeth Bott, *Family and Social Network* (London: Tavistock Publications, 1957), p. 12.

9. Mark Granovetter, *Getting a Job* (Cambridge: Harvard University Press, 1974).

10. John Irwin, *Scenes* (Beverly Hills, Calif.: Sage Publications, 1977).

11. Irwin Altman, *The Environment and Social Behavior* (Monterey, Calif.: Brooks/Cole Publishing Company, 1975), p. 18; Irwin Altman, "Privacy Regulation: Culturally Universal or Culturally Specific?" (Paper presented at the Werner-Reimers-Stiftung Symposium on Human Ethnology, Bad Homburg, West Germany, 1977).

12. Eugene Litwak and Ivan Szelenyi, "Primary Group Structures and Their Functions: Kin, Neighbors, and Friends," *American Sociological Review* 34 (1969):465-481.

13. Wireman, "Community," pp. 113-150.

14. Herbert J. Gans, "The Possibility of Class and Racial Integration in American New Towns: A Policy-Oriented Analysis," in *New Towns: Why and for Whom?* ed. Harvey S. Perloff and Neil C. Sandberg (New York: Praeger, 1973), pp. 137-158.

15. Lynne C. Burkhart, *Old Values in a New Town: The Politics of Race and Class in Columbia, Maryland* (New York: Praeger, 1981).

2 The American Household: Its Support Needs

Until quite recently the typical American household was usually described by the media as consisting of a husband, a wife who was not employed outside of the home, and children, all living in a single-family house with a lawn. There is some historical truth in this picture; many adults now in policymaking positions grew up in that type of household. Today, however, the changed makeup of American families makes this a misleading image on which to base policy. Indeed, even if the detached single-family house is eliminated from the picture, only 15 percent of American households currently fit the stereotype. Thus, a wide range of individuals and families may need to rely on their communities for certain supports; all are considered households at risk. The case of a young woman who was living alone and became ill with a high fever is illustrative. She visited the doctor for tests and went home to bed. The next day, the doctor telephoned with a diagnosis of infectious hepatitis, and instructed the woman to remain at home and not to allow any visitors. In her groggy state, she forgot to mention that she had little food in the house. At that point she was at risk; she needed food she could not purchase herself and had no one in her household to supply it. She could have ordered food from Meals on Wheels but thought that service was only for low-income elderly persons.

Although the example concerns meeting health needs, the use of the term *at risk* in this book describes households with differing kinds of needs that could be met through expanded locally based relationships or services. There is no implication that having unmet needs will necessarily lead to physical or emotional illness, although some research indicates that this occurs in some cases.[1] The idea here is simply that people are more likely to have more satisfying lives in numerous ways if their needs are met.

In a study of high-risk communities, Susan Hodgson has divided the needs of individuals into core needs and coping needs. People feel basically secure and valued when core needs—the need to be attached to others in an intimate relationship, to be told we are loved and valued, to have a special role in a valued group, and to feel a sense of affirmation that comes from liking others and sharing values with them—are satisfied. Hodgson suggests that core needs probably are more fundamental than coping needs and not having core needs met is probably more disruptive to an individual's ability to function.

Twenty-five years ago this American family of husband, wife-at-home, and children comprised 32 percent of all U.S. households; today, less than 15 percent conform to this stereotype.

Coping needs are satisfied by help with day-to-day living. Assistance with such tasks as babysitting can fulfill a coping need. So would providing information needed to solve a problem. Those who provide emotional support in specific, trying situations—listening to someone who is angry at the boss, giving someone encouragement in tackling a new job, or sitting with a friend whose spouse has died—are satisfying coping needs tied to specific situations. The adequacy of a person's network to meet coping needs depends on the availability of specialized types of information and support. An ethnic neighborhood of low-income people may be capable of providing general emotional support to its members but may lack specific knowledge about how to deal with the agency responsible for providing a widow's pension benefits or how to counsel a youth entering an Ivy League college. Hodgson points out that the quantity of contacts does not always determine whether an individual's needs are met. This depends on the quality of the relationships, the type of assistance that the contact can provide, and the individual's perception of his or her own needs.[2]

This chapter examines demographic data on the structure of American households in order to consider what kinds of households have unmet needs for support. This national data about who potentially is at risk provide the basis for hypotheses about the needs of a particular community. Program design should be undertaken only after research on local conditions and after consultation with those affected.

The American Household

Donald Warren found that adults experiencing problems normally use relationships with a network of people for support. Seventy percent of those interviewed said that in the past several months they had experienced at least one of nine concerns that Warren was probing (e.g., losing their temper at work, experiencing a wish to change jobs). Forty-six percent had experienced two or more recent concerns. Sixty-five percent of the respondents had experienced at least one of fourteen identified life crises (e.g., birth of a child, a new job) within the year, and one-third had experienced more than one. Those who did not turn to members of their social networks for help with these problems were more likely to experience ill health and other forms of stress. People who used more than one type of help—for example, both their spouse and a neighbor—were more likely to be healthy than those using only one helper.[3]

The psychological, social, and other costs of not having needed support are greater for some people than for others. Many factors can make a family or individual especially dependent on the community. Anyone living alone, for instance, is more at risk than a person living in a household with other adults. The amount of risk, or inconvenience, increases if the person is subject to ill health, has physical handicaps, or has a limited income, which precludes ordering food from a restaurant or even buying needed medication. A family with two adults employed full time outside the home is more at risk for after-school care for an eight year old than a family where one adult is home. Single parents are at risk for assistance with children. Anyone without access to an automobile is at risk unless services are located nearby or easily accessible by public transportation. This category includes all children under sixteen, many elderly, many low-income adults, and wives in one-car families whose husbands use the car to commute. Those people whom Claude S. Fischer found to have small networks—the elderly, the poor, minorities, and women with small children—are likely to be at risk in several ways.[4]

Households Likely to Be At Risk

How many Americans live alone or live with children but no other adult? Almost one-third of American households are in this situation. People who live alone make up 23 percent of the households. About 8 percent of the households are single parents, 90 percent of these headed by women.[5] These groups are dependent on community resources in emergencies and for a variety of social and physical needs on a daily basis.

Other categories of households are generally considered to be less at risk. In 40 percent of total U.S. households, adults live with other adults but no children. Thirty percent of the total households are married couples. Six percent consist of adults living with other family members such as parents, adult children, or siblings. Four percent are adults living with other adults, either roommates or unmarried couples.[6] Although these groups would seem to be self-sufficient, many of these households consist of elderly couples with varying needs for community assistance. Sometimes the care provided by such community resources as visiting nurses or shopping assistance can eliminate the need to move one partner to a nursing home and therefore allow the couple to continue to live together.

Two-parent families with children under eighteen also might appear to be households not likely to need help. Here, however, consideration must be given to the fact that the majority of mothers work outside their homes. In 1983, two-thirds of the women with only school-age children in the United States were employed, and thus needed after-school care for their children. Half the mothers with preschool children worked and needed all-day care.[7] Good care for very young children is difficult to find and expensive because the adult-to-child ratio must be high. Furthermore, many women have children of different ages and therefore need more than one kind of assistance.

Clearly the old stereotype of the typical household as a self-reliant nuclear family does not fit. A large portion of the population is potentially at risk in terms of community support. The amount of risk varies according to household type and factors such as age and presence of children. Data on household composition are presented in figures 2–1 and 2–2.

Figure 2–1 shows who lives with family members and who does not. Slightly over one-quarter of American households do not include at least two members of a family. Most of these (23 percent) are adults living alone; 4 percent of the households contain adults living with other adults to whom they are not related. Almost three-fourths of all households consist of individuals living with at least one family member. Almost 60 percent are married couples, half of whom have children under eighteen. Not shown in figure 2–1 but relevant to the discussion is the fact that 11 percent of all households are headed by a female. Of these, 7 percent are women raising children, and 4 percent are women living with another family member (probably an elderly parent). Only 2 percent of all households are headed by a man with no female present and less than 1 percent of these contain children.[8]

Figure 2–2 shows that 63 percent of the American households do not contain any children under eighteen years old. Forty percent of the households consist of adults living with other adults, and another 23 percent are adults living alone. Eight percent of the households are single-parent families with children. Only 29 percent of the total households consist of husband, wife, and children, and in half of these, wives are employed outside the home.[9] Thus less than 15 percent of the households fit the stereotypical American family of husband, wife at home, and children.

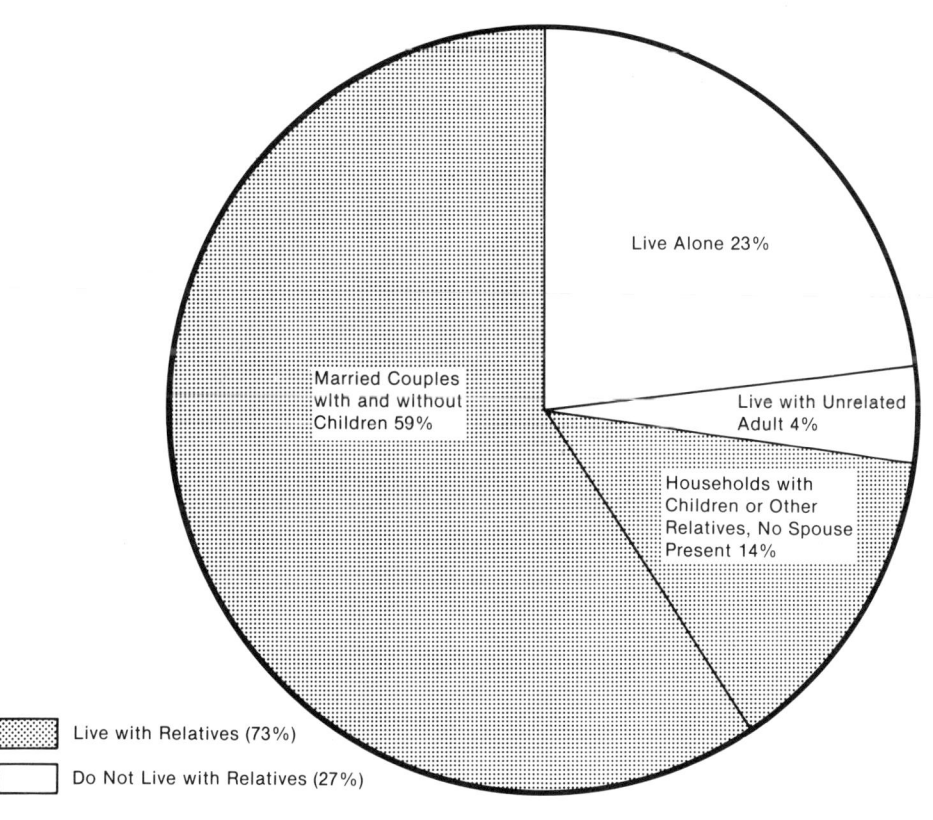

The American Household

Live Alone 23%

Married Couples with and without Children 59%

Live with Unrelated Adult 4%

Households with Children or Other Relatives, No Spouse Present 14%

▓ Live with Relatives (73%)
☐ Do Not Live with Relatives (27%)

Source: U.S. Department of Commerce, Bureau of the Census, *Household and Family Characteristics: March 1982,* Current Population Reports, Series P-20, no. 381 (Washington, D.C.: Government Printing Office, 1983), table A.

Note: The base is 83.5 million households

Figure 2-1. American Households Living with or without Relatives, 1982

Individuals At Risk

Some individuals are more dependent on community resources than others. Factors likely to be related to risk are race, Spanish origin, sex, income, and age. These factors have an influence on dependence on community quite apart from household type. For example, the most serious problem for female heads of households is not the lack of a male parent to help raise children but the poverty that results from the lack of a male income.[10] Wealthy people who live alone can buy home nursing care and cleaning services, as well as use taxis to shop or visit friends. As we shall see, minority status, older age, female sex, and low income are highly correlated.[11]

20 Urban Neighborhoods, Networks, and Families

- Two-Parent Families with Children 29%
- Adults Living with Other Adults 40%
- One-Parent Families with Children 8%
- Adults Living Alone 23%

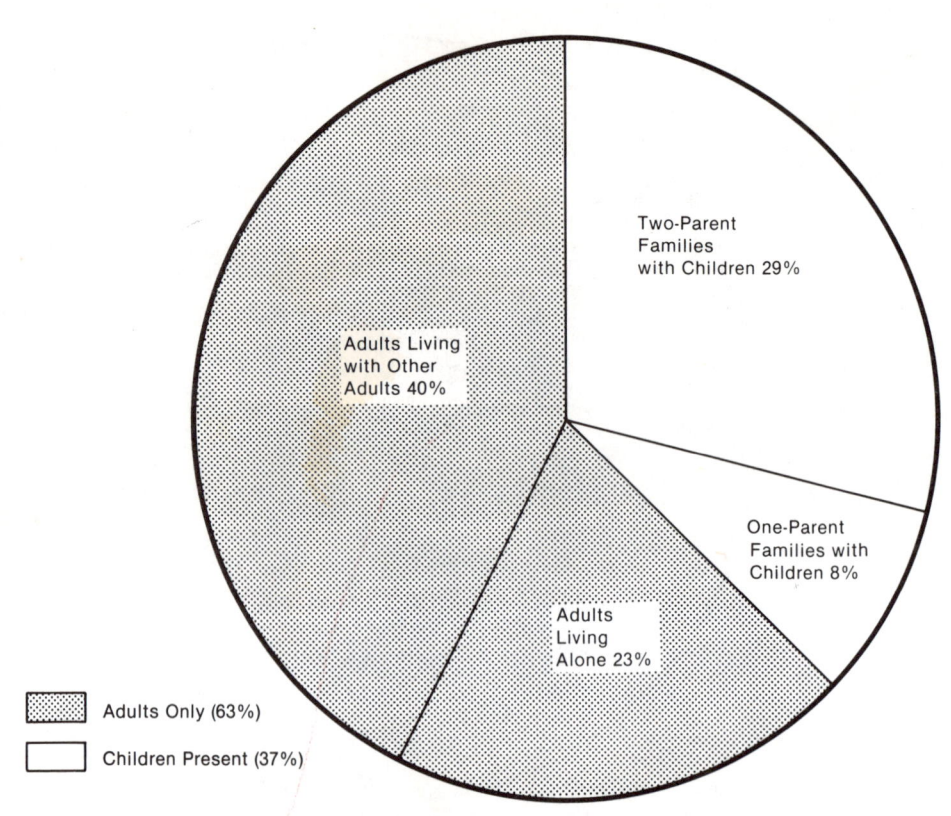

Adults Only (63%)
Children Present (37%)

Source: U.S. Department of Commerce, Bureau of the Census, *Household and Family Characteristics: March 1982,* Current Population Reports, Series P-20, no. 381 (Washington, D.C.: Government Printing Office, 1983), table A.
Note: The base is 83.5 million households
Figure 2-2. American Households Living with or without Children, 1982

Figure 2-3 shows that black persons are most likely to be in at-risk situations. Blacks are more likely than whites or persons of Spanish origin to live alone, head a family alone, or have an income below the poverty level. In 1982 almost 30 percent of all black families were female-headed households with children, in contrast to 7 percent of white families. Black households are three times more likely to be poor than white ones; approximately one-third of all black households have incomes below the poverty line. Many black families are both female headed and poor.[12]

In their study of families headed by women, Heather L. Ross and Isabel V. Sawhill state that the most important reason that female blacks are more likely to head families is the lower remarriage rate of divorced women.[13] They suggest this may be correlated with the less stable job market for black men since the high separation rate among black couples is directly corre-

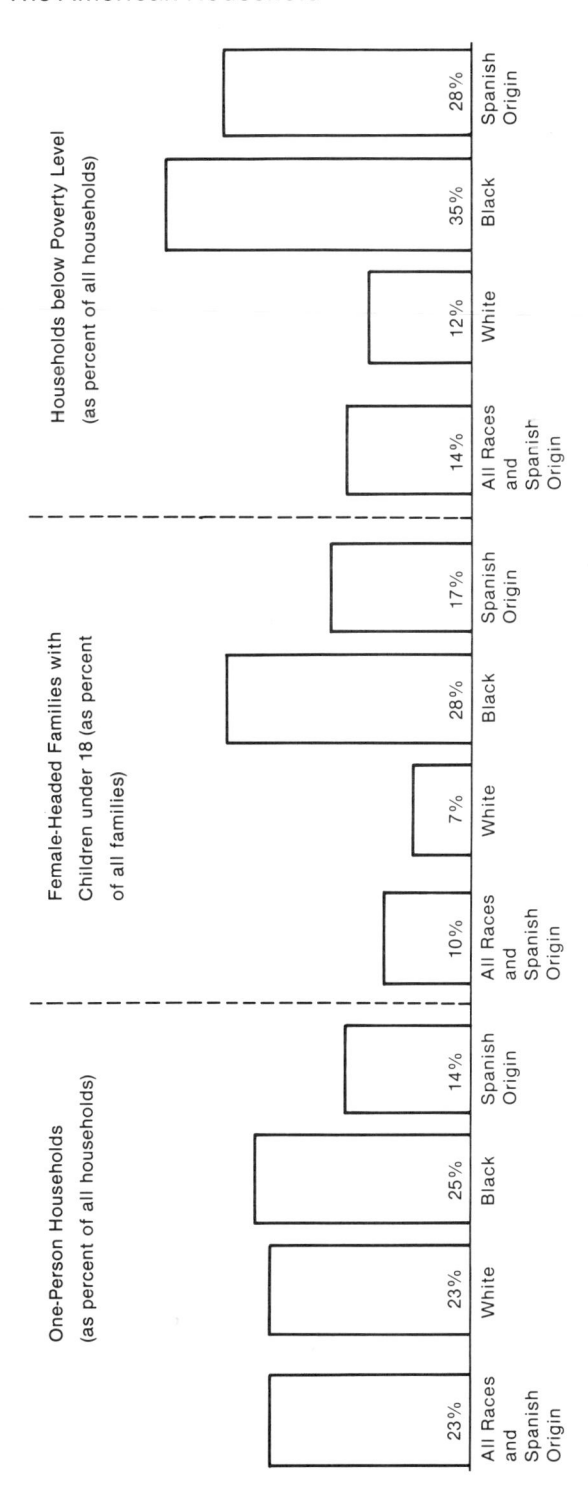

The American Household

Figure 2-3. Chances of Being At Risk (1982)

One-Person Households (as percent of all households):
- All Races and Spanish Origin: 23%
- White: 23%
- Black: 25%
- Spanish Origin: 14%

Female-Headed Families with Children under 18 (as percent of all families):
- All Races and Spanish Origin: 10%
- White: 7%
- Black: 28%
- Spanish Origin: 17%

Households below Poverty Level (as percent of all households):
- All Races and Spanish Origin: 14%
- White: 12%
- Black: 35%
- Spanish Origin: 28%

Sources: U.S. Department of Commerce, Bureau of the Census, *Household and Family Characteristics: March, 1982*, Current Population Reports, Series P-20, no. 381 (Washington, D.C.: Government Printing Office, 1983), table 21; *Characteristics of Households and Persons Receiving Selected Noncash Benefits: 1982*, Current Population Reports, Series P-60, no. 143 (Washington, D.C.: Government Printing Office, 1984), table 1.

Note: Persons of Spanish origin can be any race.

lated with this less stable job market. Blacks also have a longer lag between separation and divorce. Another reason may be that a greater proportion of black female-headed households than white are likely to raise an out-of-wedlock child.[14]

As figure 2-3 shows, persons of Spanish origin are less likely than either blacks or whites to be living alone, possibly because of a cultural tradition of three-generation families. They are considerably more likely than whites but less likely than blacks to be poor or heading a single-parent family with children.

Figure 2-4 shows that 30 percent of the elderly live alone, which places them at risk. *The Surgeon General's Report* indicates that almost half of persons over sixty-five must limit their activities because of chronic health problems; some 20 percent are limited in their ability to move about freely.[15] In 1982, 15 percent of the elderly had incomes below the official poverty line. Here again the chances of being poor when old were highly correlated with race and Spanish origin. Over one-third of the elderly blacks and one-fourth of those of Spanish origin are poor compared with 12 percent of whites.[16]

The data in figure 2-4 provide a somewhat overly optimistic picture. Being below the poverty level does not mean that one simply lacks the amenities of life. It means being poor in the sense of lacking adequate food, medical care, heat, and clothes. A number of individuals and government agencies have stated that the poverty level is set unrealistically low.[17]. In 1984, for example, the maximum amount the food stamp program provided to a couple was only $1.55 per day each for food. The calculations on which that amount is based do not take into account the fact that the elderly often need to pay more for food because they have restricted diets, usually must buy in small quantities, and often must use small expensive grocery stores to which they can walk. One analysis calculated that of the persons following the food plan used as the basis for the poverty index, only 10 percent were properly nourished.[18]

The situation of many elderly becomes worse as they grow older. Since women as a group outlive men, most eventually become widows living alone. At that point they have lost not only the companionship and practical assistance of their husbands; they also lose income because their social security payments as widows are less than the joint payments. In addition, many pension funds do not provide for widows.[19]

In all but one of the situations discussed, women are worse off than men: they are more likely to be poor, more likely to be living alone, and more likely to be heading a single-parent household.[20] The only exception is that black and Spanish-speaking men are as likely to be living alone as are women.[21]

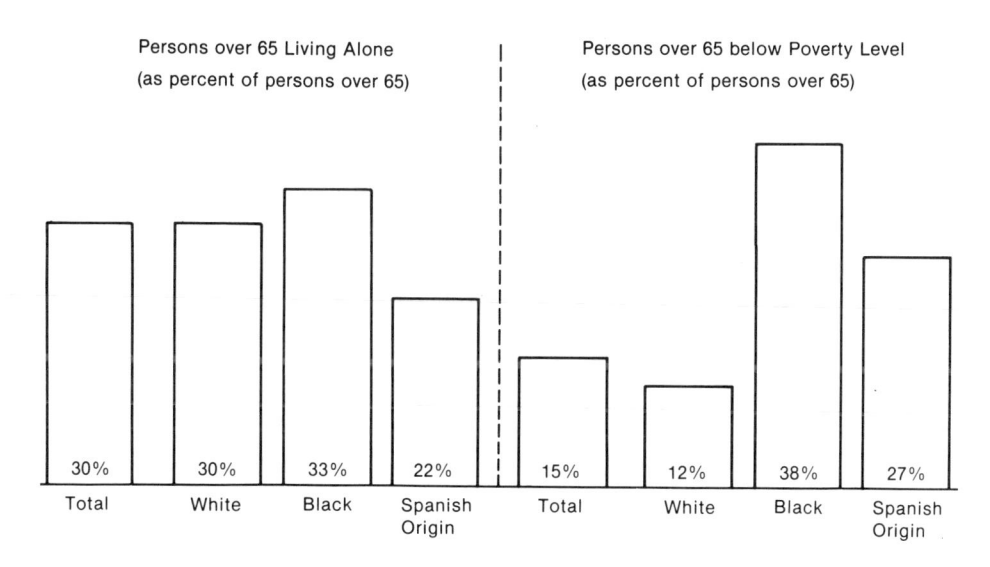

The American Household

Persons over 65 Living Alone (as percent of persons over 65)				Persons over 65 below Poverty Level (as percent of persons over 65)			
30%	30%	33%	22%	15%	12%	38%	27%
Total	White	Black	Spanish Origin	Total	White	Black	Spanish Origin

Sources: U.S. Department of Commerce, Bureau of the Census, *Marital Status and Living Arrangements: March, 1982,* Current Population Reports, Series P-20, no. 380 (Washington, D.C.: Government Printing Office, 1983), table 2; *Characteristics of the Population below the Poverty Level: 1982,* Current Population Reports, Series P-60, no. 144 (Washington, D.C.: Government Printing Office, 1984), table 11.

Note: Persons of Spanish origin can be any race.

Figure 2-4. Persons over 65 in At-Risk Situations, 1982

Types of Support for Households

There is considerable evidence that the family continues to provide major support to American households. A number of studies have noted the importance of extended kin support among black families. Most of the health care of all elderly persons is provided by their daughters or daughters-in-law. About three-fourths of the 80 percent of the elderly who have living children have at least one child within easy driving distance. An extensive study by Claude Fischer of personal networks in fifty northern California communities of varied sizes found that 42 percent of those named as members of all individuals' social networks were relatives. Relatives constituted 48 percent of those to whom people confided their personal problems and 67 percent of those to whom they would turn to borrow money.[22]

The extent and type of support households obtain from their family depend partly on how close they live. Eugene Litwak has developed a theory to explain what happens to the supports traditionally provided by primary groups, including the family, in modern society with its geographic and social mobility. His theory of shared functions maintains that the traditional primary groups of family, friends, and neighborhood are particularly well adapted to solving three kinds of problems: those that do not require technical knowledge, those that require technical knowledge that is either nonexistent or so complex that no decisions can be reached quickly, and those that are idiosyncratic. For example, it does not require any technical skill to grab a child dashing in front of a car. When knowledge about how to solve a problem is both complex and incomplete, the usefulness of the experts is limited: "The experienced mother may be more effective for the everyday problem of rearing a child than the expert, since in fact they raise their children equally well."[23] A nurse at an alternative birth center in a San Francisco hospital described a solution to the idiosyncratic food desires of mothers from Mexican-American, Philippine, Japanese, and traditional American backgrounds. The hospital turned to the primary group for a solution. Maternity patients were given home-like rooms, and their families were encouraged to bring them meals.[24]

As society has become more specialized and more mobile, the conditions have changed under which the traditional primary groups of kin, neighborhood, and friend operate. Litwak found that tasks that were traditionally performed by different types of primary groups have now become differentiated or separated. A small nuclear family, for instance, is not well equipped to provide twenty-four-hour-a-day nursing care since family members need time for sleep or other responsibilities. Since many people do not live near their kin, they must depend on neighbors for those tasks that must be performed quickly or on a daily basis, such as borrowing minor items, calling an ambulance, or watching their house while they are on vacation. On the other hand, kin continue to be relied on for tasks that require a long-term commitment since people do not expect to have permanent relations with their neighbors. Litwak found that in cases of ill health lasting more than several weeks, people turned to their kin, who substituted modern means of communication and transportation for proximity. They called, they sent money, and they came. The elderly used kin to handle finances, a trust that requires a permanent interpersonal connection. Friends were intermediate. They were used to share personal interests, which sometimes could not be shared with kin who might be of a different social class or have different tastes. Friends were relied on for assistance in short-term emergencies of several weeks. But kin, rather than even very close friends, were asked to rear children in case of death.[25]

Litwak's theory of shared functions is supported not only by his own research but also by Fischer's study. Fischer found that people obtained companionship from their friends, went to their friends or immediate relatives for advice about personal problems, and sought practical help from either neighbors or relatives, depending on the type of assistance needed.[26]

The nuclear family is most suited to those primary group tasks that require only one or two adults and the extended kin to those primary group tasks that "require low face-to-face contact, long-term commitments and more than two people."[27] Friends are used when agreement of tastes or interests and relatively long-term involvement are needed. Neighbors best perform primary group tasks that do not require long-term commitment but do require everyday contact and the availability of more than two adults. Primary groups are not well suited to tasks that require large numbers of people, specialized training, or large investments of capital.[28] Whether the bureaucracies that provide these services are responsive to people's needs sometimes depends on the pressures brought by family members, groups of neighbors, or formal neighborhood organizations. Neighborhood organizations can also provide services directly.

Implications

Many American households need assistance from outside the household for everyday tasks and emotional support and satisfaction. The help likely to be needed varies by size and composition of household, race, ethnicity, age of household members, and income. Households do get support from non-household family members and from relationships with people near where they live. The amount and types of support from family and neighborhood vary and can be adversely affected when people move. The effect of moving on a household's support system will vary according to the reason for and extent of the move, the nature of the relationships left behind, and the ease with which the household members find satisfactory relationships at their new locality. The impact of relocation when companies transfer employees should be studied to determine potential negative spillover effects, ways to evaluate costs to the employee and their families, and ways to reduce negative effects.

These facts have a number of implications for policymakers who need to recognize that many—if not most—households are not by nature self-sufficient for services or emotional well-being. Recognition of this would enable the public to stop thinking of services or external support as needed only by individuals or families that are in some way inadequate. Instead thought needs to be given to how to make a wide variety of formal and informal supports available to all households on a regular basis.

The ability of families to provide assistance to kin not living in their home needs to be strengthened. A number of local, state, and national laws, regulations, and agency operating practices currently inhibit this. One example is local zoning codes that prohibit building "granny flats," a small unit for a parent-in-law on a couple's single-family lot. Planners could start by examining federal government policies and regulations that encourage or discourage families to assist their members. Incentives could also be provided to encourage developers to locate housing for the elderly and nursing homes near existing family housing. Nonfamily members who share a household should be able to provide assistance to each other if they so wish. This can be done by eliminating barriers such as those that reduce certain federal assistance payments if two nonrelated individuals share a household. Actions that encourage volunteer and neighborhood programs will also help. The ability of neighborhoods to offer informal and formal assistance needs support.

Notes

1. Susan Hodgson, "Research and Progress Report: Interviewing to Support Parents in High Risk Communities," mimeographed (Toronto, Canada: The Child in the City Programme, University of Toronto, July 1981).
2. Ibid.
3. Donald I. Warren, *Helping Networks: How People Cope with Problems in the Urban Community* (Notre Dame, Ind.: University of Notre Dame Press, 1981), pp. 25–54, 121–131.
4. Claude S. Fischer, *To Dwell among Friends: Personal Networks in Town and City* (Chicago: University of Chicago Press, 1982), pp. 135–137.
5. U.S. Department of Commerce, Bureau of the Census, *Household and Family Characteristics: March 1982,* Current Population Reports, Series P-20, no. 381 (Washington, D.C.: Government Printing Office, 1983). All statistics from table A.
6. Ibid.
7. Unpublished data, March, 1983. Conversation with Howard Hayghe, Division of Employment and Unemployment Analysis, Bureau of Labor Statistics, U.S. Department of Labor.
8. Bureau of the Census, *Household and Family Characteristics,* table A.
9. Ibid.; U.S. Department of Commerce, Bureau of the Census, *A Statistical Portrait of Women in the United States: 1978,* Current Population Reports, Series P-23, no. 100 (Washington, D.C.: Government Printing Office, 1980), table 6-6.
10. Heather L. Ross and Isabel V. Sawhill, *Time of Transition: The Growth of Families Headed by Women* (Washington, D.C.: Urban Institute, 1975).

11. In considering the material following, readers will notice that some of the numbers do not match those cited earlier and that there are some inconsistencies in the numbers. This is because the data are taken from different studies, done in different years, and written for different purposes. Some of the definitions and categories vary slightly. Some of the data presented were based on families and some were based on households. The general points made in the discussion are valid, but readers should be careful not to add data from one page to data from another without checking the original sources and statistical bases for the numbers.

12. Bureau of the Census, *Household and Family Characteristics,* tables 1 and 21; *Characteristics of Households and Persons Receiving Noncash Benefits: 1982,* Current Population Reports, Series P-60, no. 143 (Washington, D.C.: Government Printing Office, 1984), table 1.

13. Ross and Sawhill, *Time of Transition.*

14. Ibid.

15. U.S. Department of Health, Education and Welfare, *Healthy People: The Surgeon General's Report on Health Promotion and Disease Prevention* (Washington, D.C.: Government Printing Office, 1979), p. 74.

16. U.S. Department of Commerce, Bureau of the Census, *Characteristics of the Population below the Poverty Level: 1982.* Current Population Reports, Series P-60, no. 144 (Washington, D.C.: Government Printing Office, 1984), table 11.

17. Center for Community Change, *Beyond the Numbers: The Failure of the Official Measure of Poverty* (Washington, D.C.: Center for Community Change, 1979).

18. Ibid.

19. Helena Znaniecka Lopata, *Women as Widows: Support Systems* (New York: Elsevier, 1979).

20. U.S. Department of Commerce, Bureau of the Census, *Characteristics of Households and Persons Receiving Selected Noncash Benefits: 1980,* Current Population Reports, Series P-60, no. 131 (Washington, D.C.: Government Printing Office, 1982), table 1; Bureau of the Census, *Household and Family Characteristics: March, 1982,* Current Population Reports, Series P-20, no. 381 (Washington, D.C.: Government Printing Office, 1983), table A; Bureau of the Census, *Marital Status and Living Arrangements: March, 1982,* Current Population Reports, Series P-20, no. 380 (Washington, D.C.: Government Printing Office, 1983), table 6.

21. Bureau of the Census, *Marital Status and Living Arrangements: March, 1982,* Current Population Reports, Series P-20, no. 380 (Washingtion, D.C.: Government Printing Office, 1983), table 6.

22. Elaine M. Brody, "Women's Changing Roles, and Care of the Aging Family," in *Aging: Agenda for the Eighties* (Washington, D.C.: Government Research Corporation, 1979), pp. 11-16; Lawrence E. Gary,

Support Systems in Black Communities: Implications for Mental Health Services for Children and Youth (Washington, D.C.: Mental Health Research Center, Howard University, 1978), p. 35; U.S. Department of Health and Human Services, Federal Council on the Aging, *The Need for Long Term Care: Information and Issues: A Chartbook of the Federal Council on the Aging* (Washington, D.C.: Department of Health and Human Services, 1981), p. 68; Fischer, *To Dwell.*

23. Eugene Litwak with Josefina Figueira, "Technological Innovation and Theoretical Functions of Primary Groups and Bureaucratic Structures," *American Journal of Sociology* 73 (January 1968):474.

24. Interview with Rosemary Mann, Nurse Midwifery, Education Program, San Francisco General Hospital, San Francisco, June 1980.

25. Litwak, "Technological Innovation"; Eugene Litwak and Ivan Szelenyi, "Primary Group Structures and Their Functions: Kin, Neighbors and Friends," *American Sociological Review* 34 (1969):470.

26. Fischer, *To Dwell.*

27. Litwak, "Primary Group Structures," p. 471.

28. Ibid.

3 Community in the 1980s

A number of authors of scholarly and popular works have claimed that community no longer exists and that American neighborhoods are not important to their residents or for government policy purposes. Many scholars who have studied American neighborhoods disagree. Examination of their data will provide understanding of how communities and neighborhoods work, what they might do, and their strengths and limitations as a focus for alleviating societal problems.

Psychological Aspects of Community

Sociologist Barry Wellman has identified three approaches to community theory: "community lost," "community saved," and "community liberated."[1] He contends that those who ascribe to the Tönnies *Gemeinschaft-Gesellschaft* dichotomy are adopting the community-lost approach, which assumes that we have lost community during the process of urbanization and industrialization. Accompanied by rapid geographic mobility and a trend toward small, nuclear families, these changes are said to create transient people, living isolated from kin, lonely, and alienated. High rates of mental illness, alcoholism, drug abuse, and crime are seen as typical and almost inevitable results of a society that has lost its sense of community.[2]

The community-lost approach dominated sociological and popular literature for over a hundred years. More recently sociologists have studied particular areas within cities and have discovered some "saved" communities. One of the most important studies is Herbert Gans' *The Urban Villagers,* which details the life-style of working-class Italians in Boston's West End. Gans found that the residents' lives focused on relationships among an extended kin group of siblings, aunts, uncles, and cousins. Most members of the community knew each other well, were members of the same church, exchanged local gossip, and used the same bars, corner grocery store, and other institutions. They had a strong attachment to the area and their way of life. They used the streets and local institutions as extensions of their homes: as a place to meet friends, gossip, and observe each other. They were in fact participants in a type of village life within a

30   Urban Neighborhoods, Networks, and Families

*Four slices of
urban life.*

Photos: U.S. Department
of Housing and Urban
Development

large ctiy.³ An English study by Michael Young and Peter Wilmott identified a similar pattern in Bethnal Green in East London. There life revolved around the wife's "mum" who lived nearby and was available for companionship, gossip, babysitting, and help in times of illness, childbirth, or financial trouble.⁴ The close relationships and interdependence of both the Boston and London communities were seriously disrupted by outside interference. The area Gans described was torn down by an urban renewal program, which dislocated the residents and disrupted their relationships. Marc Fried found that some of the dislocated people suffered symptoms of grief for a prolonged period.⁵ Contacts with the many former residents of Bethnal Green who had moved to new public housing outside London revealed that most respondents found that they lacked the time and money to travel to town and could not maintain the close relationships they previously had enjoyed.⁶

Recently residents of ethnic neighborhoods have banded together to revitalize and preserve their communities. The resurgence of ethnic consciousness seems to have been partly a reaction by white working-class people to the civil rights movement. In many cases it also reflects a desire of children and grandchildren of immigrants to discover their roots. The expansion of the U.S. Census to include questions on ethnicity, the increase of titles on ethnicity in scholarly journals, the emphasis on heritage during the national bicentennial celebration, and the concern with ethnic food and fashion in the popular press all suggest an increased recognition of the value of ethnicity.⁷

Wellman's community-liberated concept considers the idea of community in terms of networks of individuals.⁸ Social network analyses undertaken by a number of researchers have concentrated on tracing all of the relationships carried on by one individual or family. These studies trace direct relationships—contacts with those individuals the person knows—and indirect relationships—contacts with individuals the person does not know but who are known to people he knows. The individuals in a network do not necessarily share characteristics such as ethnicity or common residence in a neighborhood, but they do share a relationship with the person whose network is being considered.⁹

Wellman suggests that individuals in urban areas can have a variety of network relationships over which they have considerable control. An individual may maintain relationships in more than one network whose members do not know each other, such as one network in the neighborhood and another at work. In community liberated, therefore, the individual has a freedom of behavior and choice unknown in either the old-fashioned rural village or in a community saved.¹⁰

Claude Fischer also emphasizes the element of choice in patterns of social relationships available to modern urbanites. He suggests that friendships are made and maintained somewhat rationally. The actual friendships an individual maintains depend on opportunity to meet people, whether a particular friendship satisfies particular needs, and the cost of maintaining that relationship. In a study of Detroit men, Fischer found that although the men did make friends with neighbors, for the most part these friendships were not very intimate. He concluded that they were relationships of convenience rather than commitment.[11] If the individual moved, he probably would not choose to expend the extra effort needed to continue the relationship and instead would form a similar connection with a neighbor in his new location.

A fourth approach to community is that of the community of interest; for example, close ties based on shared ethnic or racial status or membership in a profession. These approaches share the orientation of network theorists in deemphasizing the importance of a territorial base.[12]

Each of the concepts of community has limitations. The community-lost approach has been criticized because of its functionalist bias. Functionalism considers communities to be composed of integrated parts, each of which performs a function in the whole. Change is considered to be disruptive to the normal condition of stability. The system is held together by mutual values.

This approach has been criticized by conflict theorists, who consider conflict and change within societies to be normal. Societies, they believe, are held together, not by agreed-upon values, but by power that operates for the advantage of the privileged.

Similarly, the community-lost approach overlooks the realities of rural villages, which are frequently characterized by competitiveness, hostility, mental illness, and exploitation.[13] It also ignores the existence of strong kin ties and other relationships among persons in cities. The community-saved approach tends to ignore the extent to which many ethnic communities retain their identity as a result of prejudice and poverty rather than positive cultural identification. Moreover, most Americans do not live in a truly ethnic community. Indeed Gerald Suttles has noted that the Chicago neighborhoods generally considered by sociologists to be prototypes of culturally homogeneous immigrant areas were rarely exclusively occupied by one ethnic group. Nevertheless, these areas have maintained their neighborhood identity over periods as long as thirty-five years despite a succession of different groups and ethnic heterogeneity. The longevity of these neighborhoods was due not just to close cultural ties but also to the ability of a few groups in the area to maintain neighborhood boundaries and a public stance of a neighborhood unity.[14]

In its stress on the somewhat voluntary networks of individuals as the basis of urban relationships, the community-liberated approach seems to ignore the extent to which individuals are affected by the structural characteristics of the socioeconomic groups to which they belong and the institutional arrangements of the neighborhoods and cities. People are affected by the functioning or nonfunctioning of their neighborhood as an environment regardless of the extent to which they have relationships there. In order to consider the relative value of these ideas of community, it is useful to review theoretical and empirical studies of the varied nature of the social relationships and networks that exist in today's communities.

Social Network Analysis

Close-knit and loose-knit networks were first described by Elizabeth Bott in her pioneering study of marital roles in East London.[15] In a close-knit network, relatives, friends, neighbors, and coworkers all know each other, provide various kinds of mutual support, and also serve as a reference group for norms and values. Close-knit networks describe the type of relationships that occur in a saved community. Geographic proximity seems to be necessary to maintain such networks, at least when they function as daily support systems. If a highway is run through a neighborhood, making it impossible for a young child to walk to a grandparent's house, demolishing the local bar or church, or dislocating people from the area, the network is destroyed. Not all residents in such a neighborhood wish to maintain close-knit networks. Instead they may have formed networks that do not depend on frequent communication among families, friends, and relatives. Geographic closeness is less important for maintaining these loose-knit networks.

Geography is not the only consideration. Melvin Webber's concept of community without propinquity suggests that modern technology in the form of fast transportation and telephones may help people to maintain relationships even if they do not live close together.[16] Litwak and Szelenyi described how distant kin respond to fulfill long-term needs: they come, they telephone, and they send money for purchasing services that they are too far away to provide, such as nursing care.[17]

Mark Granovetter uses the concept of weak ties to describe relationships among people who do not necessarily maintain regular communication and who in some cases did not know each other at all before a chance casual meeting. Granovetter, in a study of middle-management men, found these ties to be more useful for finding jobs than were more intimate ties with kin or others.[18] The logic is that the jobs known to one's kin and friends are often the same jobs one already knows about; therefore relationships with people one does not know well are more likely to provide new job leads. Sometimes these weak ties are between people who once were close but have lost touch for various reasons, such as between college classmates who meet at a reunion. In some cases, however, they are friends of friends with whom the individual has had no previous relationship. One man, for example, obtained a job he had heard about through someone he met at a picnic.[19]

Weak ties are potentially very important to low-income or minority residents of a neighborhood because they can provide access to outside resources for themselves and their children. Intimate secondary relationships also can provide such access, as well as supportive relationships within the neighborhood.

Fischer's research showed that networks vary widely. Generally people with more opportunities tend to have larger social networks. For example, not only were educated people able to meet people in college or at professional conferences, they were also more likely to have the money and other resources needed to maintain a large network. Urban residence encouraged large networks partly because people with the other characteristics likely to result in large networks—those with more education, income, younger people, employed people, or couples without children—are also likely to live in cities. In addition, cities have sufficient numbers of persons of the same subgroup to enable them to have a subgroup social and organizational life.[20]

Popular theory has often claimed that people with large networks have only superficial contacts rather than deep friendships. Fischer's study indicates the opposite. Persons in these large networks did not take the place of close friends but were included in addition to them. Moreover, it was the number of companions, people available to do something with, that was related to a better psychological mood, not the number of confidants. The number of people who could be counted on for practical support was also irrelevant to people's feeling of psychological well-being.

Fischer found that those who were most involved with their neighbors tended to be those who had the fewest opportunities to develop relationships elsewhere. Thus people in small towns, low-income respondents, minorities, women with small children, the elderly, and nonworking people tended to be more dependent on neighbors as part of their social networks. These same categories of people were those most often lacking in social support. People who were employed and had money for transportation tended to name greater proportions of nonneighbors as members of their network. When those with greater opportunities for selectivity among relationships did name neighbors, however, they were more likely to consider those neighbors to be friends rather than just neighbors.

In an extensive study of Detroit and surrounding areas, Donald Warren found that many people relied on their neighbors for help with a variety of problems. Over half of those interviewed had used a neighbor to help them during a life crisis, such as the loss of a spouse. A third of those who did not consider their neighbors to be friends used them in a time of crisis. One in four of the respondents used a neighbor to help solve what Warren calls a recent concern, such as wanting to find a new job. Warren found that the use of neighbors varied by sex, race, and marital status and with the respondent's perceptions about the extent of neighborhood interaction and people's feelings about it.[21]

He also determined that people's use of social networks in times of crisis or concern affected their perceived health. Their at-risk level generally dropped with the number of helpers used. Certain types of help were more useful than others. Just listening was not very helpful, but asking questions and referring the individual to other sources of assistance was helpful. Warren suggests that one way of strengthening support systems may be to provide increased knowledge of outside resources to the informal helpers within the neighborhood.

Some neighborhoods function as traditional primary groups with overlapping bonds of kin and friendship. It is important that such neighborhoods not be disrupted by inappropriate revitalization. In neighborhoods where relationships are not close-knit, certain physical and organizational arrangements can assist neighbors to perform appropriate neighboring roles. The neighborhood also can function in a manner that increases people's opportunities for forming friendships and other relationships. Neighborhood organizations, for example, can serve as means for individuals to become integrated into the community quickly. Neighborhood support networks can provide emotional and practical support to families and, especially, to individuals living alone and single-parent families.

Policymakers and community planners need to consider carefully which form of network will provide the kind of support needed by different individuals and family groups. Consider, for example, the ways in which different kinds of networks fulfill two kinds of functions: meal preparation and career counseling.[22] The nuclear family usually has the main responsibility for both shopping and preparation of meals, although kin living nearby may assist regularly in some cases. Neighbors generally assist with these functions only in emergencies. Intimate secondary relationships have no direct role but may be useful in facilitating joint action to obtain a local grocery store, community garden, or nutrition programs through enabling neighbors of different racial, socioeconomic background, or interests to work together and through providing links with city and outside institutions.

Effective career counseling, on the other hand, assumes the existence of a variety of role models for children, access to good basic education, vocational counseling and training, and knowledge of job possibilities. It includes white collar choices for the low-income child, and also blue collar options for any child who does not have academic ability or an interest in college. It includes knowledge of and access to part-time, summer, and entry level jobs as well as advanced educational possibilities.

A child's nuclear family and kin may provide support varying from sensitive exploration and realistic assessment of a wide variety of choices based on the child's abilities and interests to a narrow focus on limited possibilities. Neighbors' assistance generally is limited, but they can serve as role models and/or provide weak ties to other outside resources. Intimate secondary relationships also help indirectly through contribution to creating strong community groups which can obtain vocational programs for the area. Both weak ties and intimate secondary relationships have the potential for being very important because they can provide access to opportunities different from those of kin or the immediate neighborhood.

Thus, in considering how to create programs to support individuals and families, attention needs to be given to the range of existing family and network resources. Regardless of the type of network relations within a community, the specific services and facilities available and the environmental impact of the physical design are determined not only by the individual relations among the adults living there but also by a variety of forces external to the area that affect its institutions.

Institutional Aspects of Community

Roland Warren has described a great change in American life characterized by an "increasing orientation of local community units toward extra-community systems of which they are a part, with a corresponding decline in community cohesion and autonomy."[23] Some aspects of this change are increased division of labor, closer ties between local institutions and the larger society, bureaucratization, transfer of various activities formerly performed by families and neighbors, such as nursing care, to profit enterprises and to government, urbanization, suburbanization, and changing values. Warren distinguishes between the community's vertical pattern, "the structural and functional relation of its various social units and subsystems to extra-community systems," and its horizontal pattern, "the structural and functional relation of its various social units and subsystems to each other."[24] The local school district and local parks department might have horizontal relations with each other, but each would have stronger vertical relations with various state and federal agencies.

Warren has listed a number of criteria that can be used to measure the extent to which an institution is able to deliver services in a manner suited to the needs of a particular community: psychological identification, autonomy, coincidence of boundaries, and horizontal integration. A church whose members live nearby, for example, is more likely to have staff psychologically identified with the neighborhood and its needs than would a local branch of the post office. Autonomy refers to the extent to which the institution establishes its own goals and policies. Without this autonomy an institution cannot adapt to local needs; a franchise fast-food chain, for example, cannot change its menu to include ethnic snacks.

Coincidence of boundaries is a term used to indicate that an institution's boundaries coincide with those of a particular neighborhood or with those of other institutions serving that neighborhood. People living on opposite sides of a street can find themselves in different congressional districts, different school districts, the same park district, and different police and fire service areas. In addition, each federal and state program has different guidelines and different requirements for citizen participation in its programs. This lack of coincidence of boundaries and program requirements makes rational planning and coordination of services extremely difficult. For every aspect of life, neighborhood residents must deal with different people playing different games with different rules and different umpires. Services not only are divided functionally into such areas as education, health, and recreation but also are delivered through different agencies, depending on the age, geographic location, income, and other special categories of the individual. Stories of mothers having to take children to three different agencies for health care are legion.

Horizontal integration is the extent to which an institution has strong bonds to other institutions in the neighborhood or community as opposed to the strength of its vertical relationships with outside institutions. For example, local retail merchants may be very concerned with their relationships with a neighborhood group. An office that stores records and does accounting for a large national firm is less dependent on local goodwill. Moreover, an employee of the branch office of a national organization will not be promoted on the basis of contribution to local community good.

What does the increase of communities' vertical ties mean for individuals and families? Since national organizations make major decisions affecting a community member's employment, educational trends, and health practices, neighborhood residents lack control over many aspects of their environment and the institutions that provide them with services. Why, then, is there a concern with neighborhoods? Retired persons, married women not employed outside their homes, and individuals whose employment is in their homes or neighborhoods still spend most of their time there. Most important, this is where children grow up. Although people use neighborhoods in different ways and for different purposes, it is important for planners to recognize that all neighborhoods are capable of performing several basic functions.

Functions of Neighborhoods

A neighborhood provides residents with a place to rear children, housing, a delivery point for a variety of administrative and political services, an economic base, and social relationships. Some of these functions can be performed elsewhere. Children, for example, spend considerable time in school, which may be located outside the neighborhood. The neighborhood, however, often offers the most logical and convenient place for many daily and regular activities. It is necessary, therefore, to consider the spatial, economic, social, and political functions of neighborhoods.

The population base needed to support each function varies. A small suburban tract may be a good place to raise children but cannot fulfill many economic functions for its residents. An area performing all of the neighborhood functions described here probably would need a population between 50,000 and 100,000, the same population as a moderate-size city. A city area with such a population may be called a district rather than a neighborhood, but it is performing neighborhood functions. Areas with much smaller populations can provide some of these functions to their residents. In this discussion, the concepts of neighborhood and neighborhood functions are used as ideal types. A particular neighborhood may perform only some of the neighborhood functions considered here.

Spatial and Personal Identification Aspects

A neighborhood is the area named by residents when asked, "Where do you live?" The concept of neighborhood includes buildings, housing, parks, streets, and other infrastructure and such environmental factors as street cleanliness, air and noise pollution, and factory odors. Its physical aspects also include boundary maintenance. When evaluating a neighborhood, one must ask if the spatial area has clear boundaries separating it from other spatial units and if physical structures such as major roads or warehouses divide the area internally in a way that supports or hinders personal identification and neighborhood social relations.

Economic Aspects

Whatever size spatial unit is to be considered a neighborhood, it is unlikely to be economically self-sufficient in the manner of the nineteenth-century isolated rural community. Neighborhoods performing all of their potential economic functions would have the following aspects:

1. Sufficient economic base to support local services seriously wanted by residents.
2. Sufficient credit to maintain and rehabilitate existing housing, build new units, and support desired local businesses.
3. Sufficient economic power to obtain the appropriate level of services from city and other external institutions.
4. Sufficient jobs to provide adequate income to residents through location of jobs in the area and/or rapid, convenient, affordable transportation to centers of employment.
5. The ability to capture some of the economic advantages created by local institutions.

Social Aspects

Regardless of what other functions have been taken over by other institutions or performed in other geographic areas, by default, if nothing else, neighborhoods are still the place where children grow up. The ideal neighborhood would provide the following social functions:

1. Effective schools responsive to neighborhood needs.
2. Attractive, clean, safe play places close to home for casual, unstructured play. (For small children, these areas must be within sight or calling distance.) Places and appropriate supervision for more formal play, including cultural activities.
3. Adult control over neighborhood children's behavior.
4. Fast access to emergency health care.
5. Locally available or convenient transportation to other support services—normal health care, family counseling, special educational services, and so on.
6. A variety of provisions for child care, including preschool, after school, and care during summer vacations.
7. An opportunity for children to know a variety of adults as friends, neighbors, and role models.
8. An environment relatively safe from crime, physical hazards, and racial or ethnic tensions.

Opportunities for adults to participate in neighborhood activities and to form a variety of relationships and networks ranging from close friends to mere visual recognition are also needed. These include local organizations for social, recreational, political, cultural, and mutual support purposes.

Political Aspects

The boundaries of the various administrative and political units affecting the neighborhood will rarely be identical to the spatial ones. Neighborhoods should be able to obtain needed services from a variety of external institutions and tailor them to the particular needs of the residents and/or to create and maintain appropriate neighborhood-based institutions that provide services.

Neighborhoods should also have the ability to set and enforce norms for behavior of neighborhood residents and of outsiders who enter the neighborhood for business or pleasure or who merely pass through on their way elsewhere. These include behavioral standards for teenagers, police officers, and school teachers and for others working for neighborhood institutions or delivering services in the neighborhood.

Varieties of Neighborhoods

Rachelle Warren and Donald Warren have presented a typology of seven types of neighborhoods: integral, parochial, stepping-stone, mosaic, diffuse, transitory, and anomic. The neighborhoods are defined according to the amount of identity with the area found among residents, the amount of interaction among residents (both as neighbors and as members of local organizations), and the extent of the links between residents and the outside world. An integral neighborhood ranks high on all three counts. Its members feel strongly positive about living where they do and are active within both their neighborhood and the larger community. Such neighborhoods can be found in white-collar suburbs, inner cities, and blue-collar industrial areas. They may have heterogeneous populations and are structured to handle high population turnover easily.[25] Hyde Park-Kenwood in Chicago and Oakland Mills in Columbia, Maryland, are integral neighborhoods.

Residents of parochial neighborhoods also feel strong positive identification with their area and have considerable interactions with their neighbors and local organizations, but they may be quite isolated from the larger community. The model ethnic neighborhood with ethnic churches and many close-knit networks among kin and neighbors fits this model. These neighborhoods are quite stable; people do not move out even if they can afford to.[26] This neighborhood provides strong social supports for its individual members but may be weak when threatened by pressures from outside institutions. The Italian neighborhood Gans studied was destroyed by an urban renewal project that the residents did not have enough power to prevent.[27]

In the stepping-stone neighborhood, there is still a lot of interaction and participation in neighborhood organizations, and there are strong links with outside institutions. Indeed these links often are more important than the neighborhood ones. Residents lack long-term commitment to their neighborhood. They intend to move up as soon as their income permits or transfer out as their job changes. Their neighborhood activity is part of an effort to get ahead. It provides opportunities for direct recognition by their companies and/or for practicing social and organizational skills. This neighborhood can absorb newcomers easily.

In the mosaic neighborhood, people consider their neighborhood to be only their immediate neighbors. Residents of such areas may or may not have patterns of close ties among neighbors and show few ties to the neighborhood as a whole.[28]

The next three types of neighborhoods lack much interaction among residents. Diffuse neighborhoods include many single-income subdivisions or public housing projects where many families move in at about the same time and have similar socioeconomic characteristics. Residents have common values and could exercise influence but are not organized to do so. There is little neighborhood interaction either among residents or by local organizations. Identification with the area tends to be strong but may be either positive or negative.[29]

In the transitory neighborhood, residents tend to be divided between old-timers and newcomers, who often are of a different race or economic status. Although there is considerable communal activity, it tends to be within each of the two groups, with little consensus or communication between them. Cliques emerge whose claims to speak for the neighborhood can easily be discounted by other cliques, making success in influencing outside institutions difficult. There are no institutionalized means of helping newcomers enter community life.

In anomic neighborhoods, residents do not interact much. There is little local leadership or organizational activity. These neighborhoods can exist in a transitory heterogeneous slum or in homogeneous luxury condominiums.

Warren and Warren warn against using their typology as a classification system into which all neighborhoods should be forced. Rather, it simply illustrates clusters of characteristics that have been observed to characterize a number of neighborhoods. For our purposes, it illustrates that planners must expect neighborhoods to vary in terms of primary groups and networks, local organizational capacity to provide support for individuals and families, and ability to obtain aid from external institutions. Thus, regardless of the theoretical potential of all neighborhoods, all will not have the individual and organizational skills and resources to provide all functions.

Neighborhood Involvement

Several studies have attempted to measure residents' relationships to their neighborhoods. In the late 1960s, Albert Hunter undertook participant observation and interviews in seventy-five Chicago neighborhoods. He found that lower-income residents and blacks often defined their neighborhoods in terms of a small area, such as a street, while whites and higher-income persons more often named large areas with widely recognized boundaries. In some cases, people expressed positive attachment to more than one area of the city. The most likely to do this were higher-income people whose city activities and interests did not indicate withdrawal from local attachment but merely an identification with more than one level of community.[30]

Hunter also found that people's evaluations of their neighborhoods generally were correlated with race and class. This is to be expected since the communities of higher-income persons and those of whites are likely to have more amenities. Attachment to the area, however, was independent of income and was independent of race if length of residence was controlled.[31]

Analysis by Roger S. Ahlbrandt, Jr., and James V. Cunningham of six middle-income neighborhoods in Pittsburgh found that residents' attitudes varied along a number of dimensions related to the functions of neighborhood as spatial unit and as social unit. They found a high correlation among commitment to the neighborhood, a sense of community, social fabric (as measured by social relationships in the neighborhood), the availability and use of neighborhood facilities, and several other variables shown in table 3-1. Those who ranked high on measures of social fabric were more likely to be committed to their neighborhoods and to be satisfied with them. They chatted with their neighbors more frequently and were more likely to visit, to perceive their neighbors as similar to themselves and as interested in neighborhood problems, and to believe that their neighbors know each other. They were also more likely to have relatives and close friends in the neighborhood and to assist them with small favors. They used neighborhood facilities more often, doing grocery shopping, participating in recreation, and attending church in their neighborhood more frequently.[32]

The authors found that satisfaction with a list of public services, which did not include schools, and neighborhood conditions was not significantly related to commitment. Thus people could be committed to their neighborhood yet judge its physical condition and public services to be poor.

These factors were, however, highly important as indicators of residents' satisfaction with their neighborhood. In fact, two of the higher-income neighborhoods with the highest proportion of satisfied residents also had the lowest number who were committed. An increase in the quality of public services therefore might easily lead to higher satisfaction with the neighborhood but would lead to increased commitment to the neighborhood only if social fabric increased.

Table 3-1
Neighborhood Commitment and Neighborhood Satisfaction: Statistically Significant Findings

	Commitment to Neighborhood	Satisfaction with Neighborhood
Social fabric (relationships with people in the neighborhood)	Yes (second most important)	Yes (one of two most important)
Neighborhood conditions	No	Yes (one of two most important)
Neighborhood facilities (availability and use)	Yes	Yes
Satisfaction with public services (not including schools)	No	Yes
Sense of community (perception as a small community, as having specific activities solely for residents, loyalty)	Yes (most important)	No
Age of residents	Yes	No
Small household size	No	No
Household income	No	No
Home ownership	Yes	No
Satisfaction with dwelling unit	Yes	Yes

Source: Compiled from Roger S. Ahlbrandt, Jr., and James V. Cunningham, *A New Public Policy for Neighborhood Preservation* (New York: Praeger, 1979), pp. 46-60.

These findings are consistent with Fischer's findings on attachment to neighborhood based on length of residence. Fischer found that the longer people had lived in a neighborhood, the more likely they were to be happy with it and to feel sad at the prospect of leaving. This was true, however, only for those who had local ties. Those who neighbored and were involved in local organizations were likely to be unhappy at the thought of leaving. Having local friends was even more highly correlated with positive feelings about the neighborhood. Since both neighborhood and organizational involvement were correlated with local friends, it is possible that these factors contribute to attachment to the neighborhood both directly and indirectly through increasing local friendships.[33]

Hunter reached similar conclusions. He found no relationship between people's evaluations of their area and whether their friends lived inside or outside. But only one-third of those whose friends lived outside the area expressed positive attachment to it, while more than half of those whose friends lived inside the area were positively attached to it. Both attachments to the area and having friends there were positively correlated with membership in local organizations. People's evaluation of their local area was also positively correlated to local organizational membership, although to a lesser degree. It is impossible, of course, to draw cause-and-effect conclusions since those with more attachment may be more motivated to join local organizations. Hunter suggests that there probably are mutually reinforcing effects.[34]

Neighborhood Support for Households and Families

For some tasks, the proximity provided by neighborhoods is a necessity.[35] Only someone standing nearby can snatch a child out of the way of a truck. A person whose heart has stopped must receive emergency treatment quickly. Neighbors frequently respond in emergencies and perform such tasks as watering plants or caring for a pet during vacations. Many people do find their friends among their neighbors. For those who are not mobile, including children, many elderly, and wives or low-income persons without access to cars or public transportation, proximity is also necessary for friendship and companionship.

Another function that a primary group such as a neighborhood can perform well is that of personalized attention. Because the group is small, members know each other well and care about each other's feelings. Thus they can accommodate individualized needs and desires. The question of personalized attention affects neighborhoods in three ways. First, neighbors can and do provide sensitive and individualized services for their neighbors, especially during crises. Second, neighborhoods establish patterns of accepted behavior for their members. This applies to both standards of upkeep for housing, especially the outdoor area, and patterns of behavior among residents. Clearly some of the neighborhoods in the Warrens' typology would be more successful at establishing and maintaining community norms than others. Third, neighborhoods have different degrees of success in obtaining personalized treatment from institutions, both those based in the area and city-wide institutions serving it. Many of the battles of the War on Poverty during the 1960s and the neighborhood movement during the 1970s revolved around this issue of obtaining treatment from institutions sensitive to the individualized and personal needs of its residents.

The members of a neighborhood, or any other primary group, are not selected because of specialized skills. Therefore, they cannot be depended on to perform tasks that require specialized training. Most neighbors can watch a child for a short period, stop by to ensure that an elderly person is well, perform minor household repairs, call the police, assist with an alley cleanup, or plant bulbs in the park. Most of the tasks of daily maintenance of households and neighborhood do not require skills beyond those of the average resident. Many neighborhoods also contain individuals who have a wide diversity of specialized skills that they will make available for neighborhood projects, often on a volunteer basis. Neighborhoods obviously differ in the range of skills available and in their ability to organize and channel their volunteer resources. The Warrens' integral neighborhood would be more able to use the skills of its residents than would their anomic neighborhood.

The size of a primary group is a critical factor. Larger neighborhoods have more resources of people. This gives them potentially more political power and a greater variety of skills and contacts. As evidenced by the Warrens' typology, the ability to mobilize that potential power varies with the neighborhood. Homogeneous low-income ethnic neighborhoods, for example, are more likely to have close-knit networks that might provide for child care by relatives or neighbors but are less likely to have the skills and contacts outside the neighborhood needed to obtain an agency-operated child care center.

A second aspect of long-term commitment is residents' commitment to an area, which affects their willingness to invest in it both financially and emotionally. As the Warrens indicate, however, it is a mistake to assume that residents who expect to move will not be willing to participate in community activities. Some residents expect to be transients but are fully active during their stay.[36] Often the home owner-versus-renter discussion masks a class, life-style, or racial difference rather than a commitment-to-the-neighborhood difference. I was a community organizer in a university area where the faculty home owners involved with the community organization complained about the lack of interest of tenants in community affairs. Yet many of the tenants had lived in the same building for thirty years and had a stake in what happened to it. Even the students were sometimes around more than the off-and-on sabbatical faculty. Many students entered as freshmen and had children in the schools by the time they finished advanced degrees ten years later. The nonparticipation of these groups was at least partially due to lack of appropriate outreach by home owners who assumed they would not be interested.[37]

The question of long-term commitment also applies to institutions. Consider the difference between the commitment of churches that remained in changing neighborhoods and devoted their staff and building space to operating programs for new residents and that of many local banks that stopped loaning money in the same areas. Institutional commitment to an area is relevant to support for families and individuals because committed institutions are more likely to consider the needs of the various groups in the neighborhood. Committed institutions also are more likely to contribute space, money, and staff time to assisting neighborhood projects and to involve residents as members of advisory or governing groups. Participation in these groups can be important in creating intimate secondary relationships among residents.

Neighborhoods differ in their physical and institutional characteristics and the amount of resident involvement in neighborhood affairs. Some functions, however, continue to be performed within neighborhoods because they are an integral part of the physical setting, because everyday proximity is necessary, for convenience, or because of strong neighborhood structure. The challenge for policymakers is to identify the specific types of program delivery that may strengthen the networks and neighborhood institutional structures and, in addition, assist them in supporting individuals and families.

Implications for Policymakers

Americans experience different degrees of community identification. Individuals' desires to have communal experiences where they live vary. Neighborhoods vary in the extent of communal relationships available and the institutional services provided. Nevertheless all Americans are dependent on their immediate neighborhoods for some things, if only for the quality of the physical environment and public services. The variations that exist and the factors that influence the ability of neighborhoods to provide a pleasant living environment with suitable supports for the resident households have a number of important implications for policymakers.

First, the basic societal forces, private and governmental, that operate to create new housing and rehabilitate existing stock should be examined to determine incentives for providing the physical environment and institutions needed for strong community life. Second, anyone planning services for a neighborhood should study the structure and dynamics of that neighborhood to be certain that the services are needed, appropriately designed, and do not disrupt existing networks and institutions. Third, no one should assume that a particular neighborhood can or will provide certain supports; empirical data are necessary. Nor should anyone expect neighborhoods to solve problems caused by factors beyond their boundaries or institutional control, such as juvenile delinquency or racial prejudice. And fourth, neighborhood efforts to eliminate such problems from their areas or alleviate their effects and to develop positive programs and networks should be carefully researched. The research should be widely disseminated in practical language.

The following questions, based on Roland Warren's discussion of vertical and horizontal integration, should be asked by neighborhood residents and policymakers planning programs that affect neighborhoods.

1. What is the neighborhood orientation of the organization charged with delivering the proposed program? Is the organization psychologically identified with the neighborhood? Do the organizational goals address the

needs of the specific neighborhood? Is there an ongoing organizational effort to ensure that staff know the community and have positive identification with it? These efforts might include recruiting neighborhood residents for staff, placing neighborhood residents on policy boards, providing neighborhood residents with an opportunity to review or control budget decisions, or requiring staff to live in the community. For example, many police forces now require their officers to live in the city served. How much autonomy does the organization have? Is it local or part of a larger body? If it is part of a larger body, where are major policy, budget and staffing decisions made? How do the boundaries of this organization coincide with those of the neighborhood? Does the organization provide services only to this neighborhood? If services to this neighborhood are delivered as part of those delivered to a larger unit, how responsive will the organization be to the needs of this particular area? Does the organization serve the entire neighborhood or only a geographic part or certain types of individuals or families? Does more than one organizational unit deliver services to this neighborhood? If so, what kinds of coordination and cooperation exist among these units? How well does the organization relate horizontally?

2. Which neighborhood functions will the proposed program fulfill? Will the functions of the neighborhood as a spatial unit be strengthened? Will the service or the manner in which it is provided help to increase residents' identification with their neighborhood? Programs that recruit residents as volunteers or members of advisory boards do this, but so do special activities such as art festivals, annual parties or walking tours, and support of local teams in city-wide competitions. Provision of certain kinds of physical facilities, signs, or plantings also helps. Neighborhoods become known for their cherry trees or are identified by a certain monument.

Will the proposed service add to a neighborhood's attractiveness or detract from the coherence of the neighborhood as a physical area? The most obvious negative example is a highway that dissects a neighborhood. Does the service provide jobs or enable neighborhood residents and institutions to claim a greater share of city, state, or federal resources or increase the neighborhood's chance of obtaining grants or other funds from government or private institutions? Is the neighborhood strengthened as a social unit?

3. How does the proposed program affect the desirability of the area as a place to raise children? Will the program appropriate any vacant lands now used for informal play or informal travel routes? Will it affect any group or gang rivalries? Will it affect schools or health services? If so, will it make them more or less responsive to requests from neighborhood parents? Will it affect the opportunities for adults to have informal social relationships with neighborhood children? Recreational programs that involve neighbors as volunteers, places for informal community picnics, and parks

that include activities for all ages have positive effects. Will the program help adults to deal with conflict within the family or neighborhood conflicts? This includes services such as family counseling and hiring staff capable of dealing with racial tensions, crime, and gang problems.

4. Will the proposed program increase opportunities for social participation? Will it involve adults as volunteers or in policymaking positions? Are public spaces provided for meetings connected with that program or other community activities? Will outdoor activities and spaces promote casual interaction among neighborhood residents? For example, to encourage mothers to chat, play areas for small children should provide benches arranged perpendicular to each other rather than in parallel rows. Ballparks should have benches or a grassy area for nonplayers to watch.[38] Will the program promote a wide variety of local organizations? Such a variety not only can provide services that meet the needs of different classes or lifestyles but also can provide more opportunities for direct participation and leadership opportunities.

5. Will the proposed program strengthen the neighborhood as an administrative and political unit? Will the result of the program be to increase or decrease the neighborhood's control over the service delivered or its ability to enforce local norms? For example, some neighborhoods have developed conflict-resolution systems to help resolve local controversies.[39] Others have neighborhood juvenile crime prevention programs, calling in police only as a last resort.[40]

6. Will the proposed program strengthen the neighborhood as an economic unit? Will the neighborhood receive some of the benefits of the institutions to be located there? Often institutions do not recruit or train local persons for jobs. Sometimes the wealth produced by institutions flows out of the neighborhood to stockholders or central offices. For many years, for example, banks took the deposits of inner-city residents but refused to make loans to inner-city neighborhoods.[41] Can the neighborhood support the business or service it needs and wants?

The challenge for policymakers is to identify the specific types of program delivery that will strengthen the networks and neighborhood institutional structure and assist them in supporting individuals and families.

Notes

1. Barry Wellman, "The Community Question: The Intimate Network of East Yorkers," *American Sociological Review* 85 (1979):1201–1231.

2. Joe R. Feagin, "Community Disorganization: Some Critical Notes," in *The Community: Approaches and Applications,* ed. Marcia Pelly Effrat (New York: Free Press, 1974), esp. pp. 126–127.

3. Herbert J. Gans, *The Urban Villager: Group and Class in the Life of Italian-Americans* (New York: Free Press, 1962).

4. Michael Young and Peter Wilmott, *Family and Kinship in East London* (London: Routledge and Kegan Paul, 1957).

5. Marc Fried, "Grieving for a Lost Home," in *The Urban Condition,* ed. Leonard J. Duhl (New York: Basic Books, 1963), pp. 151-171.

6. Young and Wilmott, *Family.*

7. Conversation by Margaret Pearson with John Kromkowski, president of the National Center for Urban Ethnic Affairs, Washington, D.C., April 1983.

8. Wellman, "Community Question."

9. J.A. Barnes, "Networks and Political Process," in *Social Networks in Urban Situations,* ed. J. Clyde Mitchell (Manchester: Manchester University Press, 1969), p. 355.

10. Wellman, "Community Question."

11. Claude A. Fischer et al., *Networks and Places* (New York: Free Press, 1977), p. 53.

12. Marcia Pelly Effrat, "Approaches to Community: Conflicts and Complementarities," in *The Community,* ed. Effrat, pp. 1-32; Ralf Dahrendorf, *Essays in the Theory of Society* (Stanford: Stanford University Press, 1968).

13. Jessie Bernard, *The Sociology of Community* (Glenview, Ill.: Scott, Foresman, 1973).

14. Gerald D. Suttles, *The Social Construction of Communities* (Chicago: University of Chicago Press, 1972), pp. 21-43.

15. Elizabeth Bott, *Family and Social Network* (London: Tavistock, 1957), and *Family and Social Network,* 2d ed. (London: Tavistock, 1971).

16. Melvin M. Webber, "Order in Diversity, Community, without Propinquity," in *Cities and Space: The Future of Urban Land,* ed. L. Wingo (Baltimore: Johns Hopkins Press, 1963), pp. 23-54.

17. Eugene Litwak and Ivan Szelenyi, "Primary Group Structures and Their Functions: Kin, Neighbors and Friends," *American Sociological Review* 34 (1969):465-481.

18. Mark Granovetter, *Getting a Job* (Cambridge: Harvard University Press, 1974).

19. Mark Granovetter, "The Strength of Weak Ties," *American Journal of Sociology* 78 (May 1973):1360-1380.

20. Claude S. Fischer, *To Dwell among Friends: Personal Networks in Town and City* (Chicago: University of Chicago Press, 1982), pp. 135-137.

21. Donald I. Warren, *Helping Networks: How People Cope with Problems in the Urban Community* (Notre Dame, Ind.: University of Notre Dame Press, 1981).

22. Peggy Wireman, "But That's Where the Children Have to Live:

Using Urban Social Fabric in Support of Children" (Paper delivered at Managing Urban Space in the Interest of Children, an international UNESCO symposium, Child in the City Programme, University of Toronto, Toronto, 1979).

23. Roland L. Warren, *The Community in America* (Chicago: Rand McNally, 1963), p. 53, and Roland L. Warren, *The Community in America*, 2d ed. (Chicago: Rand McNally, 1978).

24. Warren, *Community,* pp. 161-162.

25. Rachelle B. Warren and Donald I. Warren, *The Neighborhood Organizer's Handbook* (Notre Dame, Ind.: University of Notre Dame Press, 1977); Warren, *Helping Networks.*

26. Warren, *Neighborhood.*

27. Gans, *Urban Villager.*

28. Warren, *Helping Networks.*

29. Warren, *Neighborhood.*

30. Albert Hunter, Symbolic Communities: The Persistence and Change of Chicago's Local Communities (Chicago: University of Chicago Press, 1974).

31. Ibid., pp. 122-123, p. 136.

32. Roger S. Ahlbrandt, Jr., and James V. Cunningham, *A New Public Policy for Neighborhood Preservation* (New York: Praeger, 1979), pp. 41-61.

33. Fischer, *Networks,* pp. 152-158.

34. Hunter, *Symbolic Communities.*

35. This section draws on Litwak's concept of shared functions.

36. Warren, *Neighborhood.*

37. Personal experience as community organizer, Hyde Park-Kenwood, Chicago, 1961-1965.

38. Central Mortgage and Housing Corporation, "Design Guidelines: Play Opportunities for School Age Children, 6 to 14 Years" (Ottawa, Canada: Central Mortgage and Housing Corporation, 1979).

39. Janice A. Roehl and Royer F. Cook, "Evaluation of the Urban Crime Prevention Program," mimeographed (Reston, Va.: Institution for Social Analysis, 1983); Citizens Planning and Housing Association, *CPHA's Baltimore Neighborhood Self Help Handbook* (Baltimore, Md.: Citizens Planning and Housing Association, 1982), p. B88.

40. Citizens Planning and Housing Association, *CPHA's Baltimore Neighborhood Self Help Handbook,* p. 93.

41. Karen Kollias with Arthur Naparstek and Chester Haskell, *Neighborhood Reinvestment* (Washington, D.C.: National Center for Urban Ethnic Affairs, 1977).

4 Resident Involvement in Community Life

Residents of American neighborhoods have been involved in a vast number of local improvement activities over the past two decades.[1] These activities benefit a neighborhood directly—through specific improvements such as the installation of a traffic light—and indirectly—through the formation of relations and networks that strengthen their support systems and the cohesiveness of the community. Since neighborhood activities are potentially important, it is helpful to examine the range of types of participation that have occurred and some of the conditions that facilitate them.

There is a vast literature on citizen participation, self-help projects, community development, community organization, and neighborhood development.[2] For the purposes of this discussion, resident involvement activities will be classified into four types: self-help activities, community development, program operation, and citizen participation. Two related aspects of neighborhood resident involvement will also be discussed: information flow and coproduction.

Types of Resident Involvement

Self-Help

Self-help activities are actions taken by several individuals or a large group to help themselves solve some problem. Often the problem is relatively simple; perhaps the alley is dirty. The solution in this case is also relatively simple: distribute flyers inviting the neighborhood residents to bring their brooms for a morning cleanup. This type of activity enables people to meet new neighbors and their children, as well as to renew old acquaintances. In many neighborhoods in American cities, the alley or street cleanup is an annual spring event, usually accompanied by refreshments. Similar types of self-help activities include giving parties for neighborhood children and for holiday celebrations, building a small play area, holding a dance or festival to raise money for some other neighborhood purpose, and planting trees or flowers in a common area. Somewhat more complicated examples of self-help activities are operating a cooperative nursery school for neighborhood

52   Urban Neighborhoods, Networks, and Families

A community-building block party planned by residents to provide something to involve everyone.
Photos: Peggy Wireman.

children, jointly hiring a contractor to help rehabilitate a number of houses in the area, and creating a community vegetable garden on a vacant lot.

Depending on the activity and the inclination of the participants, self-help groups can facilitate the growth of individual friendships and various types of relationships. The support needed for such activities from anyone other than the participants is generally minimal but nevertheless important and sometimes crucial for success. The resources needed will vary with the group but may include use of a typewriter, minimal funds for paper, postage, and reproduction of flyers, and access to a public meeting place. The amount of outside help necessary is related to the resources and skills of the individuals involved. In some cases, persons skilled in human development, generally community organizers or social work staff, visit people to encourage their participation and to teach simple management and organizational skills to participants.

Community Development

Self-help activities, especially simple ones, can develop spontaneously. They can also be consciously stimulated as part of a community development program. Community development is both a philosophy and a field of practice. Abroad it was used, for instance, by the British for village development in colonial areas in Africa and India. The idea later was adopted by the United Nations and U.S. organizations concerned with Third World development. Domestically the idea has been fostered as part of the work of the Cooperative Extension Service of the Agriculture Department and several universities.[3]

The community development philosophy holds that members of a local village or neighborhood can and should identify their own needs, set their own priorities, and use their own resources to create and carry out programs to develop their own community. In American neighborhoods, community development occurs when there is an organized effort to assist community residents to identify their needs and organize to meet them. The role of the community organizer is to help residents to talk together, to advocate their taking a holistic approach to problems rather than focusing on one area of community life, and to bring in outside technical assistance and resources as necessary.[4] Needs might be met by establishing self-help activities, starting local programs, urging private social service agencies or the government to initiate programs, or encouraging citizens to redirect existing government efforts to suit local situations. Community groups recently have become increasingly aware that neighborhood improvement often requires active participation by private businesses. Changes in the policies of a local business can greatly affect a neighborhood.

Community development is open-ended and democratic. The specific action goals will change if new neighborhood problems develop or residents identify new needs. Most community development organizations are open to everyone who lives in the neighborhood at no cost or for a nominal fee.

Often community development organizations have staff hired to promote self-help activities and to involve as many residents as possible in consideration of a proposed government action. These functions, which can be time-consuming, are often in conflict with a third staff responsibility: the efficient operation of programs. Measuring success can be difficult since part of the goal is the self-development of individuals or groups. Maintaining an ongoing forum for citizens to give their views on government programs is also difficult, especially if the residents do not believe the bureaucrats will listen. Generally obtaining financial support for community development is much harder than obtaining support for program operation. Many times, in fact, community groups operate funded programs partly as a means of paying for overhead, sometimes surreptitiously. The groups know what the funding sources may not realize: the ongoing community organizing efforts are necessary for the long-term survival of the organization and any individual programs it operates. Without these efforts, incoming residents will not be asked to participate or made to feel welcome, and the organization's base and credibility will shrink. Unless new leadership is developed continually, the organization may become dominated by cliques or die. Older members, especially those volunteering year after year for the same tasks, eventually may become tired and quit or become rigid and ineffective in the manner in which they approach new problems.

The conditions most favorable for community development include a community tradition of democratic involvement rather than one of domination by a few leaders, paid staff with a community development approach, at least minimal organizational resources such as office space, operating funds, and seed money for new projects, a democratically organized governing board, and a structure that permits participation by a variety of people with different skills and interests. The Hyde Park–Kenwood organization in Chicago had block clubs that organized self-help activities and were a conduit for citizen comment on proposed government actions. In addition, it had a number of neighborhood-wide committees that encouraged citizen participation and developed programs for specific problem areas. One was the youth committee that developed a teenage employment program, which was operated with separate staff but used the block clubs for recruiting potential employers and volunteers.

The philosophical assumptions behind the concept of community development are similar to the approach of the 1960s War on Poverty, especially during its earliest period. The most striking example was the Community Action Program, which Congress required to be developed with "maximum feasible participation" of those affected.[5] The federal government directly funded nongovernmental community-based organizations to run those programs the community believed would be most helpful in meeting its needs. In community after community, "maximum feasible participation" translated into asking the poor what they thought about their problems and listening to and acting on the answers. Low-income persons were hired to work in and administer programs. Meetings were run in a participatory manner that encouraged everyone to speak, even if the process was not orderly and went on long into the night. All of the needs of the community were analyzed to see how they were interrelated, and solutions were devised. There was enthusiasm among participants, volunteers, and staff.

Congress quickly limited the extent of uncontrolled participation by giving local governments greater authority over the Community Action Program and earmarking the major part of funds for programs designed at the headquarters in Washington, D.C.[6] Nevertheless, a variety of programs adopted in the 1960s as part of the War on Poverty contained some aspects of the community development philosophy. One legacy of those programs was the involvement of many individuals and communities in some form of community development. Many of the efforts introduced low-income persons, minorities, and women to political activity and gave them jobs and experience that led to employment within government bureaucracies or in politics. Although there were "turf" fights among various minorities, there were also many interracial programs that also involved middle-income board members and volunteers with low-income participants. A number of specific innovations of the War on Poverty programs have since been adopted by other agencies. These include neigborhood-based service centers, new types of entry-level jobs for paraprofessionals in a variety of fields, and greater participation of program users on the boards of many public and voluntary agencies.[7]

Program Operation

A number of relatively simple self-help programs grow in scope to become programs organized on a more formal basis with some source of regular financial support, staff, and a governing board of directors. Frequently the board of directors is composed of the people who originally ran the self-help project. Staff also often are former volunteers.

The West Harlem Community Organization in New York City provides an example. It began in the 1960s working primarily on tenants' rights issues. Most of the work was done by the board of directors assisting one to three staff members. By 1982 the organization had a staff of forty-five and a budget of over $1.5 million. Its activities included property management for more than 300 apartments and rehabilitation projects.[8] Funding for the development of such locally operated projects, which came originally from the War on Poverty programs, continued through the remnants of those programs, as well as new programs created in the 1970s. The Model Cities program, created during the 1960s, explicitly targeted resources to poor neighborhoods and created neighborhood plans for self-development programs. In the 1970s it was merged with Urban Renewal and other programs to form the Community Development Block Grant Program (CDBG). The CDBG program did not require that funds be targeted to a specific neighborhood and created city-wide advisory boards. Nevertheless, cities could, and did, use the CDBG funds for a variety of social services and supports, often developed in cooperation with local neighborhood groups and sometimes administered by them.[9] The Office of Neighborhoods, Voluntary Associations and Consumer Protection of the Department of Housing and Urban Development (HUD) created in 1977 began a new program specifically designed to assist the expansion of neighborhood organizations that had successfully conducted small projects by providing funding and technical assistance for more expensive and complex projects. Some of these organizations that had begun by assisting neighborhood residents in minor home repair efforts several years earlier eventually became involved in million-dollar rehabilitation programs.[10]

In addition, community groups have obtained program funds from other federal, state, and local sources, as well as from a variety of foundations and private-sector sources. One study identified over 500 neighborhood development organizations undertaking housing, economic development, and energy projects. Some had hundreds of staff members and budgets in the millions.[11]

These efforts have been severely hurt by cutbacks made during the Reagan administration. The neighborhood office and funds for neighborhood groups at HUD have been eliminated, Community Action agencies have been shut down, and numerous other local efforts have received reduced or no support. Many groups had depended heavily on the now-defunct CETA program (workers paid by Comprehensive Employment Training Act funds) to provide a variety of community programs, including housing rehabilitation, staffing cooperatives, child care, and weatherization. More than one-half of 143 groups responding to one survey in 1981 used CETA workers, and more than 60 percent of these expected their loss would have a strong impact on their activities.[12]

Citizen Participation

Citizen participation is usually defined as formal, structured resident participation in a government program. Its purpose is to make government bureaucracies more responsive by giving citizens a voice in policy discussions or in the design and implementation of specific programs.[13]

The major emphasis on this type of resident involvement began during the 1960s when the federal government made an immense effort to involve the poor in the decision making in the operation of the War on Poverty. Much of the rhetoric of early participants talked of empowerment and citizen control. Shortly after the programs began, local politicians and bureaucrats reacted against the more militant and forceful forms of citizen participation. Congress then made a clear statement that citizen participation was advisory, and some concluded that the heyday of citizen involvement was over. Others claimed that the citizen participation efforts that continued were mostly illusory or manipulative.[14]

The extent of involvement of the poor was criticized. For example, there was a low turnout for Community Action Agency board elections, and low-income board members often deferred to those with more education and experience as board members. Such critics ignored the normally low turnout in off-year city elections and the fact that, over time, many low-income board members would learn participation skills from their more experienced middle-income colleagues. One analyst concluded that although the community participants' influence on the Community Action boards was not great, the boards did represent their constituencies.[15]

The Community Action Agency's citizen participation efforts had positive spillover effects. In 1968, for example, HUD developed citizen participation regulations for urban renewal. Although the regulations had no congressional mandate and were widely criticized by advocates of citizen groups as being weak, during the first Nixon administration some citizen groups were receiving $1 million a year to finance their participation in urban renewal programs.[16]

The amount of actual influence that any neighborhood had in the urban renewal program varied according to the interpretation of the regulations by HUD field offices and local administrators and according to the different organizational and political skills of the neighborhood groups. Citizen participation ranged from perfunctory attendance at city-run briefing sessions to de facto control over government actions in the neighborhood. Citizen groups discussed proposed neighborhood development activities with residents and city officials, monitored relocation and other city activities, conducted social surveys of the neighborhood, operated homemaker programs and child care centers, and (under contract to city government) created plans for neighborhood physical and social development. A similar range of activities continued under citizen participation funded in the 1970s through the CDBG program.

The number of federal programs requiring citizen involvement increased most not during the liberal days of the 1960s but during the Nixon years. In

1969 only sixteen federal programs had citizen participation requirements, but sixty-nine additional programs adopted them before 1975.

The requirements varied widely in objectives, definition of desired participants, and amount of agency financial and administrative support.[17] Most were not addressed to the neighborhood-specific types of participation that are relevant here. In addition, mere adoption of requirements does not guarantee good participation. Good participation is promoted by the following general conditions:

1. Provision of information on an ongoing basis and early in the decision-making process.
2. Availability of trusted technical assistance as an aid to understanding complicated or technical programs.
3. Regular meetings with decision makers during their deliberations rather than afterward.
4. An organization that is perceived by both city officials and neighborhood residents as being representative of the area.
5. An acknowledged right to participate and a clear commitment by bureaucrats to the process of citizen participation.
6. Ability to achieve at least some goals on a fairly consistent basis.
7. Sufficient ongoing stable financial support to relieve a group from spending most of its energies fund raising, often on a crisis basis.[18]

In the almost twenty years of federal support for the process of citizen participation, considerable literature has developed, but there has been little systematic quantitative research that defines clearly what purposes are served by which types and techniques of participation and in what situations.[19] An analysis by the Rand Corporation of fifty-one cases of citizen participation in seventeen states concluded that the more influential groups had four characteristics: they elected their own members, had their own staffs, had the power to investigate grievances, and had power to influence the budgets of organizations providing area services. A study of a variety of municipal services by the National Science Foundation found that supervision of staff was the most important element in establishing client control of services.[20]

Part of the problem of evaluation is related to the multiple goals of citizen participation and to the fact that different participants have different aims. In his study of community organizations, Abraham Wandersman lists possible effects of citizen participation on the individual, the organization, and the community.[21] Difficulties arise when citizens who are determined to change specific government actions and the attitudes of government officials toward them must deal with government officials who wish to co-opt citizens to support their programs and to reduce citizen alienation. The few systematic studies that do exist do not indicate that citizen participation has been tremendously effective either in making major changes in government programs or in reducing citizen alienation toward government in general, although alienation has been reduced toward particular programs.[22]

Why then do many citizens and officials continue to call for increased participation? First, many citizens want only to tailor a program so that it fits the local situation. They believe that the accomplishment of even minor changes justifies their involvement. Second, many are committed to the concept of citizen participation as a means of promoting and maintaining democracy. Third, there have been enough successes to encourage citizens to remain involved. Although evaluations of the services of citizen participation in the CDBG program vary, an analysis of sixty-two cities and counties conducted by the Brookings Institution concluded that citizen participation had a major influence in 42 percent of the cases and some influence in an additional 29 percent. Model Cities organizations, which often were closely tied to neighborhood organizations, neighborhood groups, and senior citizens were the most influential types of group.[23]

William Rohe and Lauren Gates found that in a number of cases communities that have established a neighborhood-based participation program to comply with CDBG requirements have expanded their role and now comment on all aspects of local planning.[24] Approximately 44 cities have neighborhood councils that are officially recognized as a formal means of regular participation in city government. The system of neighborhood councils covers the entire city and permits comments on a variety of issues. Approximately 120 additional cities have a system of neighborhood councils, but input is limited to certain city functions or programs. Other cities encourage participation from neighborhood organizations but do not formally authorise or structure it.[25]

Another way neighborhood efforts have gained broader success is through forming coalitions and initiating reforms at the city, state, and national levels.[26] For example, many banks in older neighborhoods accepted the savings of area residents but made loans only in newer areas. A coalition of neighborhood groups successfully lobbied Congress to pass legislation requiring banks to be more responsive to the neighborhoods from which they received deposits.[27]

Many of the benefits of citizen participation, especially at the neighborhood level, are indirect, spillover effects: increased relationships in the neighborhood, increased knowledge and use of available community resources and institutions, and increased feeling of belonging. None of these is necessarily directly related to achievement of a specific goal, although perception of organizational effectiveness may encourage otherwise reluctant citizens to participate.[28]

The potential value of neighborhood involvement has been documented by many researchers. In his study of northern California communities, Fischer found that 10 percent of those named as part of respondents' networks were fellow organization members. That was approximately the same percentage as those named as neighbors or coworkers. In fact, fellow organization members were more likely to be considered friends than were neighbors, coworkers, or kin.[29]

Hunter's study of seventy-five Chicago neighborhoods found that persons having most of their friends in the area were more likely to feel attached to their area than those whose friends were outside, although they were no more likely to evaluate their area positively. Residents who belonged to a local organization, however, evaluated their area more positively and expressed more feelings of attachment to it. More than half of those who belonged to two or more local organizations expressed attachment to their area, while only a little over a third of those who belonged to no local organizations did so. Belonging to local organizations also affected a resident's ability to name the area and to locate its boundaries.[30] Ahlbrandt and Cunningham's study of six neighborhoods in Pittsburgh found that commitment to the neighborhood was not correlated with satisfaction with local conditions but with a number of other factors more related to social fabric and perception and sense of community. Ahlbrandt recommends that city governments attempting to preserve neighborhoods and their housing stocks provide support for neighborhood organizations. He feels that these organizations should make strengthening of social fabric a major explicit goal.[31]

Another spillover effect of citizen participation is leadership training, especially that given to women and minorities who often have limited opportunities for leadership development in their jobs. In studying neighborhood planning programs in Raleigh and Wilmington, North Carolina, and Atlanta, Georgia, Rohe and Gates found that in each case some leaders of neighborhood groups had ended up on the city council and in one case had been elected mayor.[32]

The increase in activities in the neighborhood directed not so much toward influencing a particular government program but toward a broader concept of community development can also be included among the spillover effects. Active citizen participation encourages people to believe that their efforts to improve their community will be successful and that their struggles are worthwhile. It also generates a flow of information both within and about the community.

Supports That Are Also Spillover Effects

Information Flow

Two types of information flow are important for support of households and community involvement. One provides information to individuals, groups, and institutions about potential resources. The other provides information about events that may affect the neighborhood. Communities vary in their ability to keep members informed, just as residents vary in their ability and willingness to use different channels of information. Thus the techniques useful for one situation may not be useful for another; a variety of information channels may be needed.

Morris Janowitz and others have pointed out the importance of a community newspaper to community integration.[33] Newsletters and handbills mailed to members of the community organization or physically distributed to every household or apartment complex also inform a community. The municipal government in one new suburb of Kyoto, Japan, produces a weekly newspaper listing dates of neighborhood events and the schedule of health checkups for children. These newspapers are given to the leaders of the local organizations who are responsible for distributing them to each household.[34] A formal mechanism with tremendous potential for facilitating community information flow is cable television. This potential, however, will be realized only if community groups are able to use the channels without a fee or at very low rates and receive training on production methods.[35] Less formal methods of information flow include distribution of notices to such public places as churches, community bulletin boards, barber shops, grocery stores, community gardens, and laundromats.

Another approach to information dissemination is to identify local informal leaders or regular gatherings of the people who need to be informed about helpful resources and community affairs. In many neighborhoods certain storekeepers or service providers are known as sources of neighborhood information. The National Institute of Mental Health has funded a project that provides information on resources to bartenders. In Indonesia, a successful program to promote birth control is being carried out by forming groups of the women who have agreed to practice birth control. Regular group meetings are used to educate these women, to distribute necessary supplies, and to encourage them to inform others. The Indonesian government is now planning to provide information on nutrition through the same groups. In Sweden, government-sponsored prenatal classes for parents are now being extended to include the first year of the child's life. In addition to discussing health matters, group leaders provide general information about rearing children and morale support for parents. Such groups become a formal substitute for the informal education and reassurance that used to be given new parents by their own parents or older relatives in the community. Employers are required by law to give paid leave to parents to attend such sessions approximately once a month.[36]

The benefits of increased community identification and a wider flow of information about the community are not restricted to members of a community organization. Hunter found that all residents who knew of community organizations were more likely to have a clear intellectual image of their community and to evaluate it positively than those who did not know about local organizations. Approximately one-third of the community residents studied belonged to such organizations, and another one-third knew about them but were not members.[37]

Special circumstances can make a flow of information especially important. One of these arises when an outside change, such as a redevelopment program, is imposed on a community. Low-income communities in particular are often not aware of the potential negative impact of such proposals until too late. Individuals who suddenly change family status also need a flow of reliable information. Recent divorcees and widows often must act on important matters with little prior knowledge or reliable sources of information. A new term, *displaced homemakers,* has been developed to describe women who served as traditional housewives and mothers for most of their adult lives and were then widowed or divorced. Many have never dealt with the complexities of insurance or financial management. Some have never even written a check. Special programs have been developed for displaced homemakers to provide them information, job skills, and confidence.[38]

Another situation in which information flow is needed develops when people move. Newcomers need to know where to find services and facilities, how to meet neighbors and potential friends, how to become involved in community affairs, and what community norms they will be expected to uphold. Newcomers of a different race or ethnic background or refugees need to know that they are welcome, and existing residents sometimes need to be reassured that the new neighbors will maintain community standards.

Various techniques have been used to provide information to newcomers. In one block in Chicago, the leader called on all new residents, chatted for a while, told them about the block club, and casually informed them about the maintenance standards expected on the block. In Columbia, Maryland, the community association staff initially called on new residents, left a package of information about the community, and invited them to a newcomers' meeting in the community center. A new town developing outside Rochester, New York, provided drop-in child care facilities. Members of the staff called on all new residents, ostensibly to tell them about the child care facilities. The staff also knew of other resources and were able to make social service referrals for a number of family problems. People would have resented anyone calling to ask if they had problems, but they welcomed information about child care, and staff could provide other information as appropriate.[39]

On the whole, however, few neighborhoods have plans for welcoming newcomers and ensuring that they are at least invited to community activities. Because so many people move each year, potential participants are constantly lost. In the six neighborhoods in Ahlbrandt's study of Pittsburgh, the most important factor affecting participation in the neighborhood organization seems to have been mere knowledge of its existence. Only 49 percent of the residents were aware that there was a neighborhood organization. Of those who knew, approximately 30 percent were members or had members in their household. Of those, 70 percent spent some time on organization matters every month. Thus, approximately one in five persons informed about the neighborhood organization might be expected to become active. Another interesting aspect of Ahlbrandt's findings is that participation did not vary by whether the respondent was a home owner or renter if he or she knew about the organization. An analysis by Rich and Wandersman, however, found that participation at the block level might not be significantly affected by increased information. Those who lacked knowledge of the block club had characteristics of community noninvolvement, such as less neighboring, similar to those who knew about the block club but decided not to join. They found, however, that 62 percent of the residents contacted personally by a community organizer did join the block club compared to the 10 percent participation rate of those not personally contacted.[40]

Delay in learning about participation opportunities or waiting to be encouraged to join may increase the time of adjustment for the newcomer. The type of casual contacts or intimate secondary relations often involved in community activities can make newcomers feel at home and give them a chance to have human contact without making long-term commitments.

In terms of democratic government, the fact that residents obtain information about possible effects of a government action is important even if they decide to take no action. A thorough analysis of citizen participation by the Advisory Commission on Intergovernmental Relations points out that people who receive information but decide not to take any action are nevertheless involved. Their decision not to act may reflect informed consent rather than apathy. Although studies of participation classify them as nonparticipants, they may become involved when an issue affects them directly.[41]

Accurate information is essential in situations where racial or other changes may be perceived as threatening neighborhood stability. The same principle applies to situations that began to concern many neighborhood groups in the 1970s when higher-income white professionals started to move into some inner-city neighborhoods, which led to real estate speculation, rising property values and taxes, and a displacement of existing residents. In *Understanding Neighborhood Change,* Rolf Goetze emphasizes the role of expectations in urban revitalization, suggesting that whether people move into or out of a neighborhood or invest their money and energy in home repairs is determined by their perceptions about changes occurring in the neighborhood. He found that these are based on information acquired from the media as much as on realities of the magnitude of the changes: "As life becomes more complex . . . more and more people take their cues from the media instead of trusting their own senses." Residents often overlook the constant change that normally occurs as people move in and out of neighborhoods. Once they notice change, they often distort its extent or abnormality. This is particularly likely when there are racial differences between current residents and newcomers. If current residents lose confidence in the area's stability, they may cease investing in their homes and neighborhood, thus creating the very deterioration that they fear. Goetze recommended that governments increase reliable data and support programs that work cooperatively with neighborhood residents in a method that shares power. One such effort is the Neighborhood Reinvestment Corporation's neighborhood services program, which assists rehabilitation in 134 cities. Local boards are created consisting of representatives from local government, lending institutions, and residents. The residents have a majority vote.[42]

Accurate information flow in the neighborhood is important in still other ways. Donald Warren's study of helping networks found that people's score on a well-being measure and their use of neighborhood helpers was more dependent on their perception of a strong pattern of neighborhood helpers than on the actual pattern. In some neighborhoods with strong social network patterns, residents thought the resources for help were weak and did not use them. In other cases, residents believed their neighborhood had more interaction and resources than it did and overburdened the few helpful people. Access to information about resources can help people become more aware of the existing resources and also enable others to fill existing gaps by becoming helpers themselves.

Warren also emphasized the importance of links to resources in and outside the neighborhood. "Just listening" was an ineffective means of help. What was important was a neighbor's ability to ask questions, provide a new way of looking at the problem, give direct help, or make referrals. Increased knowledge of community and external networks and resources would be likely to increase these abilities.[43]

Active, participating citizens backed by an accurate flow of information will have confidence that their efforts toward neighborhood improvement will be successful and are worth the effort.

Coproduction

Coproduction is a term used to convey the idea that the quality of services and physical maintenance of an area are affected by the efforts of both the government and the residents.[44] The amount of trash on the street, for instance, is a result both of the litter habits of the residents or those passing through and of the quality of the city street sweeping and garbage collection.

Neighborhood participation in coproduction can be passive or active, positive or negative, individual or collective. Passive negative actions include failure to take normal precautions against criminals, such as locking a house door. Passive positive actions include not littering or not parking a car on the street on the day scheduled for street cleaning. Littering is an active individual negative action. Helping a neighborhood recreation center as a basketball coach or burglar-proofing a house is an active positive action. Negative collective actions include breaking school windows by youth gangs. Positive collective actions include establishing a crime watch program.

In his discussion of coproduction, Richard Rich suggests that one reason people do not take positive action on tasks affecting their neighborhood is that often these tasks produce benefits that are collective. Two conditions are needed to motivate many people to expend energy or money for a collective good. First, people must believe that their efforts will result in obtaining the good. That is, if I put my garbage neatly in trash cans or bags but my neighbor does not, the alley will still be a mess, so why bother? Second, people are more likely to make efforts if they believe that is the only way they can obtain the collective good. If through massive neighborhood effort the city provides some additional service to the neighborhood, all residents benefit whether or not they contributed time or money to the campaign for the service. One advantage of strong neighborhood organizations is that they can mobilize and encourage people to participate in coproductive activities. They can provide residents with some confidence that their individual efforts will be worthwhile because they will be matched by those of others.

Rich suggests that organizations with the ability to enforce rules and require financial contributions are more likely to be able to obtain collective goods, partly because they can spend less time raising funds and recruiting members and support. He recommends that governments wishing to increase neighborhood service delivery provide support for formal neighborhood organizations that have a recognized right to participate in the decision-making process.[45]

Neighborhood organizations often are active in establishing neighborhood norms. Sandra Schoenberg and Patricia Rosenbaum consider the establishment of mechanisms "to define and enforce shared agreements about public behavior" one of four criteria for evaluating neighborhood viability. Neighborhood norms cover such things as proper maintenance, garbage disposal, child behavior, and the type of activities permitted on streets, including patterns of visiting.[46] Effective neighborhood groups convey their norms to city officials, explaining that they expect a certain level of city services and respect for their norms from city employees operating in their neighborhood. The ability to establish public norms is especially important in neighborhoods undergoing racial, ethnic, or income changes. Indeed, at least part of the fear caused by such changes comes from concern that the new neighbors will not abide by these accepted norms. One possible reason for the widespread use of strict design review controls over maintenance and changes to private property in new communities may be the belief that written restrictions can convince buyers that all property is subject to the same restrictions regardless of the amount of heterogeneity in the new community.

Neighborhoods concerned with positive resident actions also must address themselves to their public images. Numerous observers have commented on the problem of negative identification of neighborhoods by residents, realtors, city agencies, and financial institutions.[47] Goetze, for instance, stresses the importance of confidence in a neighborhood to people making investment decisions, as well as the need for residents to be able to control the norms of behavior in their area and the need to deliver government programs in ways considered fair and predictable.[48] A neighborhood organization can take active steps toward correcting rumors and promoting positive images of itself through the media and such activities as annual house tours and festivals. Neighborhood organizations also can be helpful in creating positive interaction between old and new neighbors.

Coproduction (and the other participation efforts considered in this chapter) also helps reduce neighborhood turnover by providing informal social networks to residents. Ahlbrandt, for example, found statistically significant correlations among participation in neighborhood organizations, having close friends in the neighborhood, frequency of visiting neighborhood friends, and thinking that neighbors were interested in neighborhood problems and knew each other well. Having friends in the neighborhood and positive relations with neighbors were related to commitment and satisfaction. These, in turn, were related to planning to move. Thirty-six percent of those less committed to the neighborhood planned to move within the next two years compared with 10 percent of those committed. Fifty percent of those who ranked the neighborhood as a poor or fair place to live planned to move compared with 24 percent who did not plan to move.[49]

Politics and Power

Many community organizations are actively involved politically, sometimes out of practical necessity and sometimes in accord with philosophical or organizational principles. Saul Alinsky, for example, advocated identifying and attacking an enemy as a means of creating neighborhood involvement. He used confrontation tactics disliked by many, especially those being attacked and those liberals who favored more traditional methods of persuasion and cooperation.[50] The difference in tactics selected by different groups may reflect philosophical positions, but is also related to the socioeconomic position of the group. Middle-class persons who interact regularly with politicians and city officials at business meetings or social gatherings or whose contributions are politically important do not have to resort to sitting in at the mayor's office in order to have their concerns heard. On the other hand, a study of welfare recipients' organizational efforts concluded that direct tactics were the most successful way for the recipients to gain access to the decision-making process.[51] Direct tactics frequently serve primarily as a means to ensure that the group's concerns are taken seriously. Groups have fairly regularly tried to obtain change through cooperation, found themselves forced to resort to more confrontational tactics and later developed close working relationships with city officials.[52]

Many groups that claim to be nonpolitical nevertheless maintain a variety of formal and informal contacts with their local elected representatives. The Hyde Park-Kenwood Community Conference in Chicago, for example, carefully nurtured its relationships with the two aldermen from the area. One was a middle-income liberal whose style corresponded to that of many of the conference leaders. His wife chaired a number of conference activities. Many volunteers were active both in the conference and in the alderman's local office. The other alderman was a more traditional Chicago ward politician with whom many of the conference leaders lacked personal rapport. Nevertheless, conference staff sought to maintain good relationships with him and to avoid threatening his organization. In addition, conference leaders and volunteers cultivated and maintained working relations with local police, urban renewal officials and staff, building code inspectors, park planners, officials of the University of Chicago, local youth organizations, and local merchants.[53]

Many groups have neither the resources nor inclination to maintain such elaborate formal and informal contacts. Often such groups rely on membership in a larger federation with local block clubs to represent their interests. Hunter found that more than half of the 250 local organizations in Chicago were affiliated with larger federations. The local organizations were primarily small welfare or service organizations and home owner or property owner organizations with budgets of several hundred dollars. The federated organizations had budgets ranging from $30,000 to $100,000. They frequently employed full-time staff who represented the interests of the smaller members in lobbying and negotiating with city politicians and bureaucrats.[54]

Many of the efforts of coalition groups formed across cities, states, and nationally during the 1970s revolved around obtaining power. Training programs were established to give organizers knowledge and skills. National organizations were formed to share ideas and act as lobbying groups. During the Carter administration, these groups achieved policy recognition in the presidential statements on urban policy, the creation of the National Commission on Neighborhoods, which issued a lengthy report on the status of neighborhoods with recommendations for supporting them, and creation of special financial support for neighborhood efforts in a number of federal agencies. Some of the rhetoric remained in the Reagan administration, but the specific funding and policy directives providing support for neighborhood efforts were mostly withdrawn.[55] The emphasis instead is to suggest that the private and voluntary sectors create local solutions.

A number of neighborhood groups and theorists would agree that federal programs have often resulted in waste, poor administration, and development of a "neighborhood-priority-setting-by-what-is-fundable-this-year" outlook. They have sought an alternative to government funding through creation of neighborhood economic development programs and cooperative ventures with private industry. Many of the successful neighborhood economic development efforts of the 1970s, however, were financed directly or indirectly by federal funds. Some commentators have questioned the willingness or ability of private industry to undertake extensive commitments or to provide support for the participatory democracy aspects of neighborhood development because in some cases the neighborhood efforts threaten both corporate profits and philosophy.[56] Businesses have opposed, for example, efforts to alter those operations of the real estate market that may increase profits but decrease community stability.

Other neighborhood theorists and groups have sought to provide increased power to neighborhoods through a variety of neighborhood government or neighborhood-controlled service delivery efforts with varying degrees of autonomy. Some are successfully operating. Their proponents have suggested that many city neighborhoods could provide the same type of internal service delivery as do small suburbs. The difficulty, even beyond getting political acceptance of such efforts, is that they may inadvertently create or reinforce racially and ethnic homogeneous enclaves that will compete with each other for limited city resources, exacerbating problems of racial, ethnic, and class conflict and raising questions of service equity, since the poorer areas are the least likely to have political clout.[57]

Groups without political power often find their neighborhoods ignored when city services are distributed or subject to disruptive actions such as inappropriate redevelopment. Some types of appropriate program delivery threaten local institutional modes of operation and power arrangements. Funding for such programs tends to be politically vulnerable. Many of the arrangements suggested in later chapters involve decisions such as zoning changes, which require political power. It would be naive to believe that the changes needed to provide neighborhood support for families and community institutions will occur without conflict or without gaining access to institutional political power.

Conclusions

A number of types of resident involvement are possible and have positive effects on residents, their feelings about the neighborhood, and their willingness to support it and its organizations. Positive benefits also occur through increasing networks and providing specific programs and services.

Resident involvement can be difficult, time-consuming, expensive, and frustrating. Evaluation is hard, partly due to multiple and sometimes even conflicting goals. Maintaining ongoing efforts can be difficult and requires attention and resources, especially persons, whether volunteers or staff, with considerable time and skill.

Government support for such efforts has varied. Many of the successes, much of the growth of the citizen involvement movement, and many of its leaders date from the 1960s and 1970s. There were limitations and problems with those efforts. Many groups became overdependent on one source of funds, the federal government, and established programs to obtain funds rather than defining their own needs and then designing appropriate programs. Most federal funds have been withdrawn, and to date few groups have successfully replaced those resources, although some sources of funds continue to be available. Many local governments welcome and support resident efforts. Both financial resources and government receptiveness to resident activities are necessary for neighborhood efforts to have maximum success. Otherwise resident energies go toward fund raising and fighting city hall rather than problem solving.

Notes

1. Many of the observations in this chapter are based on my work and volunteer experience.

2. For example, see Peggy Wireman, "Citizen Participation," in *Encyclopedia of Social Work,* 17th issue, ed. John B. Turner et al. (Washington, D.C.: National Association of Social Workers, 1977), pp. 175-180; Peggy Wireman, "Community Development and Citizen Participation— Friend or Foe?" *Journal of the Community Development Society* 1 (Fall 1970):54-62; Robert K. Yin et al., *Citizen Organizations: Increasing Client*

Control over Services (Santa Monica, Calif.: Rand, 1973); Hans B.C. Spiegel, *Decentralization: Citizen Participation and Community Development* (Fairfax, Va.: Learning Resources Corporation/NTL, 1974), vol. 3; Mary L. Pike, comp., *Citizen Participation and Community Development,* Publication 571 (Washington, D.C.: National Association of Housing and Redevelopment Officials, 1975); Edgar S. Cahn and Barry A. Passett, eds., *Citizen Participation: Effecting Community Change* (New York: Praeger, 1971); Stuart Langton, *Citizen Participation in America* (Lexington, Mass.: Lexington Books, D.C. Heath and Company, 1978); *Journal of Applied Behavioral Science* 17, no. 1 (1981); James A. Christenson and Jerry W. Robinson, Jr., eds., *Community Development in America* (Ames: Iowa State University Press, 1980); T.R. Batten, *Communities and Their Development* (London: Oxford University Press, 1957); W.W. Biddle, *The Community Development Process: The Rediscovery of Local Initiative* (New York: Holt, Rinehart and Winston, 1968); Lee J. Cary, ed., *Community Development as a Process* (Columbia: University of Missouri Press, 1970); Murray Ross, *Community Organization: Theory and Principles* (New York: Harper and Row, 1955); Advisory Commission on Intergovernmental Relations, *Citizen Participation in the American Federal System* (Washington, D.C.: Government Printing Office, 1979); *Citizen Participation* 3, no. 3 (January–February 1982); Robert Fisher and Peter Romanofsky, eds., *Community Organization for Urban Social Change: A Historical Perspective* (Westport, Conn.: Greenwood Press, 1981); Eva Schindler-Rainman and Ronald Lippitt, *Building the Collaborative Community* (Riverside: University of California Extension, 1980).

3. Christenson and Robinson, *Community Development,* pp. 18–37.

4. Biddle, *Community Development Process;* Christenson and Robinson, *Community Development,* pp. 3–17.

5. Statutes at Large, vol. 78, Economic Opportunity Act of 1964, Section 202(a)(3), 88th Cong., 1st sess., 1964, p. 516.

6. Sar A. Levitan, *The Great Society's Poor Law: A New Approach to Poverty* (Baltimore: Johns Hopkins Press, 1969), pp. 109–130; Joseph A. Kershaw, *Government against Poverty* (Washington, D.C.: Brookings Institution, 1970), pp. 44–71.

7. Sar A. Levitan and Robert Taggert, *The Promise of Greatness* (Cambridge: Harvard University Press, 1976).

8. Office of Policy Development and Research, "Partnerships for Community Self-Reliance," mimeographed (Washington, D.C.: Department of Housing and Urban Development, 1982).

9. Rick Cohen and Miriam Kohler, "Neighborhood Development Organizations after the Federal Cutbacks: Current Conditions and Future Directions," mimeographed (Jersey City, N.J.: Rick Cohen and Associates, 1983).

10. U.S. Department of Housing and Urban Development, Alice Shabecoff, ed., *Neighborhoods: A Self-Help Sampler* (Washington, D.C.: Government Printing Office, 1979).

11. Neil S. Mayer with Jennifer L. Blake, *Keys to the Growth of Neighborhood Development Organizations* (Washington, D.C.: Urban Institute Press, 1981).

12. Harry C. Boyte, "Ronald Reagan and America's Neighborhoods: Undermining Community Initiative," in *What Reagan Is Doing to Us*, ed. Alan Gartner, Colin Greer, and Frank Riessman (New York: Harper and Row, 1982), pp. 109–124.

13. Wireman, "Citizen Participation;" Yin, *Citizen Organizations*.

14. Sherry R. Arnstein, "A Ladder of Citizen Participation," *Journal of American Institute of Planners* (July 1969):216–224; Daniel P. Moynihan, *Maximum Feasible Misunderstanding* (New York: Free Press, 1969).

15. Levitan and Taggert, *The Promise of Greatness*, p. 187.

16. Experience of the author at the U.S. Department of Housing and Urban Development, 1968–1971.

17. Advisory Commission, *Citizen Participation*, p. 4.

18. Wireman, "Citizen Participation;" The sixth and seventh points are suggestions from Robert A. Aldrich and Janet Gutkin.

19. Advisory Commission, *Citizen Participation*, pp. 165, 166.

20. Ibid.

21. Abraham Wandersman, "Framework of Participation in Community Organizations," *Journal of Applied Behavioral Science* 171, no. 1 (1981):27–58.

22. Advisory Commission, *Citizen Participation;* Roland L. Warren, *The Structure of Urban Reform* (Lexington, Mass.: Lexington Books, D.C. Heath and Company, 1974).

23. Advisory Commission, *Citizen Participation*.

24. William M. Rohe and Lauren B. Gates, "Neighborhood Planning: Promise and Product," *Urban and Social Change Review* 14 (1981):27.

25. Richard C. Rich, letter to Peggy Wireman, July 20, 1983; Advisory Commission, *Citizen Participation*, p. 4; Richard C. Rich, "Neighborhood Governance Programs of the 1970s," *NORG News Bulletin* 2, no. 3 (1979):8–11; Howard W. Hallman, *The Organization and Operation of Neighborhood Councils: A Practical Guide* (New York: Praeger, 1977); Richard C. Rich, "A Role for Neighborhoods in Urban Governance?" in *Neighborhoods: Changing Perspectives and Policies*, ed. Timothy K. Barneko and Mary Helen Callahan (Newark: University of Delaware, 1980), pp. 103–114.

26. Janice E. Perlman, "Grassroots Participation from Neighborhood to Nation," in Langton, *Citizen Participation*, pp. 165–179.

27. Karen Kollias with Arthur Naparstek and Chester Haskell, *Neigh-*

borhood Reinvestment (Washington, D.C.: National Center for Urban Ethnic Affairs, 1977).

28. For a theoretical discussion of the different rewards for participation, see Richard C. Rich, "A Political Economy Approach to the Study of Neighborhood Organizations," *American Journal of Political Science* 24 (November 1980):559-593.

29. Claude S. Fischer, *To Dwell among Friends: Personal Network in Town and City* (Chicago: University of Chicago Press, 1982).

30. Albert Hunter, *Symbolic Communities: The Persistence and Change of Chicago's Local Communities* (Chicago: University of Chicago Press, 1974).

31. Roger S. Ahlbrandt, Jr., and James V. Cunningham, *A New Public Policy for Neighborhood Preservation* (New York: Praeger, 1979).

32. Rohe, "Neighborhood Planning."

33. Morris Janowitz, *The Community Press in an Urban Setting: The Social Elements of Urbanism* (Chicago: Phoenix Books, University of Chicago Press, 1967).

34. Conversation with Yukiko Kada, Kyoto, Japan, April 1981.

35. For a discussion of some of the problems, see Lee Perlman, "Neighborhoods Gain Cable TV Access in Portland, Oregon," *Neighborhood Ideas* (the bulletin of Civic Action, Washington, D.C.) 7, no. 5 (1983):61 and 70-72.

36. Donald Warren, *Helping Networks: How People Cope with Problems in the Urban Community* (Notre Dame, Ind.: University of Notre Dame Press, 1981), p. 230; interviews with staff of the U.S. Agency for International Development, Jakarta, Indonesia, May 1981; Lillian Gottfarb V. Bornsdarff, "Preventive Mental Health Work in Mother-Child Care Centers in Sweden and a Model of Parent Education," *The Child and the City,* ed. National Institute for Research Advancement (Tokyo: National Institute for Research Advancement, 1982), pp. 81, 82.

37. Hunter, *Symbolic Communities.*

38. Herbert J. Gans, *The Urban Village: Group and Class in the Life of Italian-Americans* (New York: Free Press, 1962); Helena Znaniecka Lopata, *Women as Widows: Support Systems* (New York: Elsevier, 1979); Displaced Homemaker Network, *Program Directory* (Washington, D.C.: Displaced Homemaker Network, 1982).

39. Author's experience while block director, Hyde Park-Kenwood Community Conference, Chicago, 1962; author's conversations with Columbia residents, 1975; conversations with staff of Riverton new town, 1972.

40. Ahlbrandt, *Policy for Neighborhood Preservation,* pp. 168, 173; Richard C. Rich and Abraham Wandersman, "Participation and Nonparticipation in Block Organizations," *Social Policy* (October 1983).

41. Advisory Commission, *Citizen Participation.*

42. Rolf Goetze, *Understanding Neighborhood Change: The Role of*

Expectations in Urban Revitalization (Cambridge, Mass.: Ballinger, 1979), p. 61; Howard W. Hallman, *Neighborhoods: Their Place in Urban Life* (Beverly Hills: Sage Publications, 1984), pp. 217-218.

43. Warren, *Helping Networks,* pp. 52, 85.

44. Richard C. Rich, "Interaction of the Voluntary and Governmental Sectors," *Administration and Society* 13 (May 1981):59-76.

45. Richard C. Rich, "The Dynamics of Leadership in Neighborhood Organizations," *Social Science Quarterly* 60 (March 1980):570-587; Rich, "A Political Economy."

46. Sandra Perlman Schoenberg and Patricia Rosenbaum, *Neighborhoods That Work: Sources for Viability in the Inner City* (New Brunswick, N.J.: Rutgers University Press, 1980), p. 32.

47. Musa Bish, Jean Bullock, and Jean Milgram, *Racial Steering: The Dual Housing Market and Multiracial Neighborhoods* (Philadelphia: National Neighbors, 1973); Mark Beach and Oralee S. Beach, "Interracial Neighborhoods in the Urban Community," unpublished manuscript, 1978.

48. Goetze, *Understanding Neighborhood Change.*

49. Ahlbrandt, *Policy for Neighborhood Preservation.*

50. Saul Alinsky, *Reveille for Radicals* (Chicago: University of Chicago Press, 1946); Walter Kloetzli, "Roman Catholicism and Community Organization," in *The Church and the Urban Challenge,* ed. Walter Kloetzli (Philadelphia: Muhlenberg Press, 1961), pp. 47-65.

51. Barry Checkoway and Jon Van Til, "What Do We Know about Citizen Participation? A Selected Review of Research," in Langton, *Citizen Participation,* p. 30.

52. Author's conversations with Department of Housing and Urban Development field personnel responsible for citizen participation, city officials, and with citizen groups, 1968 through 1972.

53. Experience of author when block director and acting assistant director, Hyde Park-Kenwood Community Conference, Chicago, 1962-1964.

54. Hunter, *Symbolic Communities.*

55. Perlman, "Grassroots Participation"; Harry C. Boyte, *The Backyard Revolution: Understanding the New Citizen Movement* (Philadelphia: Temple University Press, 1980); National Commission on Neighborhoods, *People Building Neighborhoods: Final Report to the President and the Congress of the United States,* and *Case Study Appendixes,* vols. 1 and 2 (Washington, D.C.: Government Printing Office, 1979); Boyte, "Ronald Reagan."

56. Boyte, *The Backyard,* pp. 126-147; Rita Mae Kelly, "Neighborhoods, Public Policy, and the Community Development Corporation," in Barnekov and Callahan, *Neighborhoods,* pp. 183-198.

57. Gordon P. Whitaker, "Neighborhood Organization and the Delivery of Human Services," in Barnekov and Callahan, *Neighborhoods,* pp. 117-124; Henig, "Neighborhood Governance."

5 Spillover Benefits: The Federal Urban Gardening Program

Neighborhood programs or services designed and delivered for a specific purpose can have important spillover benefits such as network formation and community development. This chapter examines the Urban Gardening Program, administered by the Department of Agriculture's Cooperative Extension Service, as a means of showing what factors in a program's operation encourage such spillover effects.[1]

The Urban Gardening Program was created by Congress in 1977 in six cities and has since expanded to sixteen of the nation's largest cities. The cities are: Atlanta, Baltimore, Boston, Chicago, Cleveland, Detroit, Houston, Jacksonville, Los Angeles, Memphis, Milwaukee, Newark, New Orleans, New York, Philadelphia, and St. Louis. The program's goals were quite clear: to provide training and technical assistance to enable low-income people to grow food, to encourage youth activities, and to help improve nutrition through canning, other preservation, and educational activities. Funds were not to be used to buy seeds, fertilizers, or plants for program participants.

The Department of Agriculture reported that in 1981 there were 175,000 gardeners in the program, of whom 42,000 were youth. They raised over $14 million worth of food. Almost 90,000 of the gardeners participated in activities such as canning to preserve their food.[2]

The Program

The program is operated as part of the U.S. Department of Agriculture's Cooperative Extension Service, which for over fifty years has provided agricultural technical assistance through a decentralized structure of state and county units. The extent of the spillover benefits from the Urban Gardening Program depended on the structure of the local Extension Service operation, how the new program was structured, and the philosophy and skills of the coordinator. Coordinators varied in career goals, philosophies, attitudes toward the program and the Extension Service, and the skill with which they obtained both needed support and the freedom to define their own programs. Some found funds from other sources to expand on activities that could not be funded from the Urban Gardening Program. Some felt their chief role was to develop people's organizational skills and their communities. Others defined it strictly in terms of telling people how to grow vegetables, considering themselves as technical consultants rather than community organizers.

Coordinators established the criteria used for the selection and training of staff and for program evaluation. They also decided whether programs would emphasize individual or community gardens. According to data from the Department of Agriculture, there was considerable variation in the ratio of backyard to community gardens, ranging from 5 percent community gardens in four cities to 75 percent in three others.[3]

The amount of staff involvement with the nontechnical aspects of gardening differed widely. One coordinator allowed staff to provide only education and technical assistance. Staff in other cities gave direct gardening assistance in the form of plowing, assigning garden plots, and providing seeds and tools. Assistance in organizing the garden varied from "we expect the person who calls us to act as coordinator" to "very heavy and direct involvement . . . initially we physically pulled people out of their homes and put them in the garden."[4]

Some cities already had active gardening programs before the Urban Gardening Program began. In these cases, coordinators of the new program had to work out questions of turf and role. Some concentrated on providing technical assistance on horticulture to gardeners, letting other groups organize the gardens. In other cities the staff began by actively organizing gardens but found, after several years, they had time only to provide technical help to existing gardens. The Los Angeles program provided technical assistance on organizing gardens to a variety of government agencies in several government jurisdictions.

The different orientations of the coordinators and the programs were reflected in staff selection. One coordinator said that he preferred someone with gardening experience, a high school education, experience with people and "some understanding of Extension and our philosophy." His staff did not necessarily live in the area in which they worked. Another coordinator always hired people from the area and made a conscious effort not to consider horticulture as a prime factor in hiring. He stressed that prospective workers should "know their community and have organizational skills."

Coordinators used a range of techniques to attract participants and to convey information about gardening. These included newsletters, special information sheets, floats and parades, radio and television announcements and programs on gardening, attendance at community meetings, ads on buses and billboards, and booths at supermarkets, fairs, and churches. Some programs operated special projects, often using other funds, such as a fish farm in Philadelphia and assistance to neighborhood farm markets in Houston.

Clearly the sixteen programs varied in overall organization and orientation. They also varied in the extent to which they strengthened social networks, supported individual households, and various population groups, and encouraged community development.

Spillover Effects

Support for Households and Individuals

In all cases the program was seen as a means of fulfilling its congressional mandate to provide low-income persons with skills to produce and use food, both to help them financially and to enable them to have better diets. In ten of the sixteen cities, the coordinators also saw the gardening experience as a way to promote better family relations. One community aide from Detroit pointed out that gardening provided families without enough money an opportunity to do something with their children. The Boston coordinator advised that this was particularly true if the family had teenagers, who often pull away from family involvement. The Houston coordinator said the gardens promoted family pride, unity, and self-confidence: "It's a garden we grew as a family." Another said that "many fathers would get involved helping their kids in the community garden." The Los Angeles coordinator felt that the experience promoted better understanding between teenagers and adults because "kids respect people with competence."

Some coordinators encouraged family gardening through a variety of techniques. New Orleans promoted gardening through science classes in schools. The children started growing parsley in containers and then wanted a garden in the yard. Parents often started helping their child and then became involved themselves. One New Orleans parent commented: "You-all showed them how to grow that parsley in the cup, and now I've got the whole backyard dug up." Another program developed activity sheets telling gardeners how to include their children in gardening. Los Angeles published a book on gardening with children. Some recommended setting aside part of a garden as a separate plot for the child or a whole section of a community garden for teenagers.

One coordinator cited many cases of three-generation families working together. Another commented that she did not see nuclear families in her gardens, "but I do see extended families, cousins and sisters-in-law and brothers-in-law and people who have managed to live in the same neighborhood." She told of wondering why one man who lived alone was caring for a very large garden. She found out that he was "feeding seven sisters and their children." A number of coordinators cited cases of grandparents and grandchildren gardening together. On the other hand, many gardeners did not involve their families, and not all coordinators were concerned with promoting better family relationships. One coordinator responded to a question about whether the gardens promoted family unity by indicating that he was sure they did but was "not looking at it from this viewpoint."

The coordinators said that a large proportion of participants were single-parent families, but with one exception they did not give them any special attention. When asked about how location and organization of the gardens could affect single-parent households, the Boston coordinator commented that single parents who are employed have very limited free time and having a garden on their block gave them greater opportunity to garden themselves or to show interest in their children's work by stopping by on their way home. Another coordinator said that the program's encouragement of container gardens helped single parents. One city is planning to provide some sandboxes to keep very young children occupied while their mothers garden. That city specifically recruited single-parent families by working through another extension program that provided one-on-one contacts with low-income homemakers.

Most of the programs actively involved senior citizens. Some provided gardens at public housing projects for the elderly. Others invited the elderly to join gardens at day care centers and schools. The Atlanta coordinator commented that one of their gardens at a county-owned senior citizens convalescent home "gets them out of a room . . . gets them out of a bed," and gives them an opportunity for exercise and recreation. Some programs had staff trained in horticulture therapy. The Philadelphia coordinator believed that the garden was especially helpful to recently retired persons. It put them in contact with people who had been retired longer and it "defuses the trauma of getting put on a shelf."

Twelve programs attempted to use the gardening experience to promote goodwill between younger persons and older ones. A number of the programs deliberately teamed teenagers with the elderly. In some cases, the teenagers performed heavy work—such as tilling the soil—for the older persons. In other cases, the elderly taught workshops for teenagers interested in gardening or assisted them on an individual basis. In some cities teenagers were treated as a separate group. Special programs were arranged, often as part of or in cooperation with the Extension Service's 4-H program.

A few cities provided gardens for various special groups, including the handicapped, delinquent youths, mentally retarded persons, and those in prisons, halfway houses, and psychiatric institutions. Some programs also provided gardens in cooperation with elementary schools or day care centers.

Support for Communities

The gardens were perceived by all the coordinators as a place where people could socialize and meet neighbors. Staff held workshops and clinics at the gardens and in many cases had a demonstration plot there. The garden was also seen as neutral turf, especially important in areas where people were afraid of their neighbors or their neighbors were of a different racial or ethnic background. Although there are no specific data on the extent to which gardens promoted friendships, weak ties, or intimate secondary relationships, they did provide people with a common interest in a public setting and in some cases provided them experience working with their neighbors on organizational matters. When asked whether the garden experience helped people to make friends, one coordinator sensibly responded, "How could it not?" Ten coordinators tried to promote the creation of friendships through the gardening experience. "We try to make our clinics a social affair and furnish refreshments," said one. Philadelphia arranged a number of city-wide competitions to reduce competition within the neighborhood gardens by encouraging them to compete as a group with other areas.

The coordinators thought the gardens helped people get to know each other, even if only casually. The Cleveland coordinator remarked that in "a lot of areas people are afraid. . . . [The garden] gives them an excuse [to talk to their neighbors]." Another coordinator commented that it created a community atmosphere: "Even people just passing felt like stopping and talking to the gardeners." Even recognizing that someone walking on the street is a neighbor rather than an outsider can help reduce fear and tension, especially in interracial or multiethnic areas.

A number of the coordinators fostered relationships between gardens in one area of the city and those in other areas by sponsoring festivals and workshops, bus tours, and permanent city-wide advisory groups. These gave groups a chance to display their work and develop relationships throughout the city.

The gardens created community pride and gave people a "great feeling of efficacy. There is something you can win . . . it's not like fighting city hall." Community skepticism about whether anything would grow or whether the children would destroy it turned to feelings of accomplishment as lots covered with litter were turned into attractive areas. One coordinator commented that even if the neighborhoods never grew anything on the lot but just got the junk off, they would have accomplished a lot. In a few cases, lots used as places to hang out by teenagers and winos were turned into gardens. Some of the teenagers and a few of the winos were even recruited as gardeners.

Fourteen of the programs used the gardens to promote community pride. The gardens created "some sense that the neighborhood is viable." People's perceptions about their neighborhoods are a strong motivator in their actual decisions about investing in home maintenance. The St. Louis coordinator said, "We're trying to get people to know they're not alone and that the people in their neighborhood care about each other. They may [then] call the police for each other if they see something unusual." Considering Fischer's findings that fear of crime was highly related to distrust of neighbors, gardeners' feeling that people would assist them if they were victimized could be very important.[5] The Detroit coordinator commented that in areas of rapid turnover, "People move into an area with very little [thought] that they're going to stay so [they] never bother to join a block club." But they do start to cut the weeds, then garden, and then gradually become involved. He said the garden "gets them out of the house and off the porch and onto a neutral setting where they can start to talk and get to know each other."

Leadership Development

Although fifteen of the coordinators used the garden experience for leadership development, the approaches and extent of involvement varied greatly. In some cities, gardens were started at the request of an existing group or an individual who was expected to serve as organizer. Some cities left all questions of management to the requesting group or individual. Other cities provided some or all of the organizational effort needed to start the garden and took a very active role in ongoing organizational problems. Many provided ad hoc advice to groups having difficulties. One coordinator told a group not to have a chairperson "because they always killed them off." She recommended instead that they generate a committee of the whole so no gardener would become envious of the person with authority.

Staff sometimes promoted functions such as harvest festivals and community-wide garden tours so gardeners gained recognition and status. One coordinator established a number of city-wide advisory committees to give gardeners with leadership potential status and a chance to further their skills. Several programs promoted youth leadership development through working closely with the Extension's 4-H program.

Some coordinators saw the identification and informal training of potential garden leaders as an important part of the staff's job, although most programs did not give formal workshops in leadership training for volunteers, garden coordinators, or staff. Los Angeles, however, devotes two of its five staff persons to volunteer training. Every several months they provide approximately thirty hours of training in gardening or food preservation to people who agree to provide thirty-five hours of volunteer time in exchange. These courses include training in leadership and community organization. They also provide additional in-service training for volunteers, seminars on fund raising, and organization. The coordinator said that "more and more our staff facilitates contacts between volunteers and new gardeners" rather than developing new gardens themselves. In the nationwide program in 1981, there were more than 2,600 volunteers.[6]

The Los Angeles coordinator commented that the "skills they [gardeners] develop in organizing a garden can be applied to any other issue they consider important," They learn to contact their councilmember, to organize, and to set goals and priorities. Several programs encouraged the garden groups to take on more complicated tasks, such as cleaning up other lots, planting flowers or trees, or starting another garden in the community. Only a few groups became involved in cooperative buying, marketing, or fund raising. Some groups successfully pressured the city for new curbs and street trees. Some sponsored activities for children. In Baltimore, "some people started with a very small community garden. They now have six where [before there were] abandoned houses [and] have plans for a green house and a community cannery." Philadelphia groups are combining garden and energy projects and installing solar panels on roofs and greenhouses. In New York a group that started working together on a thirty-by-fifty-foot plot moved onto a program of "sweat equity" (where people do part of the work themselves) rehabilitation for abandoned buildings and now has nine apartments.

Linkages

The extent to which the gardening experience provided people with linkages outside their neighborhoods depended partly on the orientation and efforts of the individual city program. Some involved various other Extension Service workers in their efforts, providing links with nutrition aides, the 4-H program, and classes in canning and food preservation. Links to city agencies were generally with those whose cooperation was necessary for the gardens. Ownership of property needed to be traced through city records and permission and insurance arranged. City parks and recreation departments could loan tools used in their own landscaping efforts. Police and park departments with horses supplied manure. In some cities, staff provided those linkages; in others any linkages were left to the efforts of the gardeners. In still other cities, staff helped gardeners obtain the assistance needed from city agencies as a means of teaching residents how to deal with city bureaucracies. One program involved some fifty-five businesses and city agencies in their program.

Referrals to resources other than the Extension Service or those agencies immediately concerned with the gardening were absent or limited in many programs. Some referrals were made to social service agencies and agencies responsible for food stamps, health, trash collection, and control of rats. The range of agencies used included the local human resources development agency, department of community services, department of housing and urban development, the Area Agency on Aging, and the Urban League. One program helped with social needs. Gardeners called with such problems as, "I'm having this problem about drug addicts, and I'm afraid to call the police." The staff has the confidential police number and will call for the gardener. Although they were not specifically trained to provide information and referral services, they spent a lot of time at it. Also, when conducting workshops on gardening, they frequently invited other agencies to share information on their programs. Another city held workshops on forming food and energy cooperatives and making money by recycling trash. Their newsletter includes data on home weatherization or "anything that comes up of interest to [the] neighborhood."

In New York the coordinator saw "getting people to talk . . . getting people together to deal with priority things" as one of his program's purposes. The gardeners there have become involved in tenant-landlord problems, better housing, and police protection. Philadelphia gardeners now are taking part in overall planning for the neighborhoods and obtaining places on neighborhood coordinating teams. Thus, the gardening experience led to increased links with outside resources in some cases.

Pluralism

Some coordinators did not concern themselves with racial and ethnic relations; others stated there were no problems since the garden experience brought people together on common ground. Since the racial and ethnic composition of the gardeners usually reflected that of the surrounding neighborhood, many gardens had participants from only one racial or ethnic group. Others, however, were mixed in combinations reflecting the wide diversity of America. Gardens were reported with blacks and Puerto Ricans; blacks and Southeast Asians; whites and Southeast Asians; blacks, Puerto Ricans and Philippinos; blacks and whites; Poles, Irish, and blacks; whites and Chinese.

Problems seem to have been rare. One coordinator picturesquely pointed out that when a gardener had a bug on his plant, he was concerned about the color of the bug, not about the color of his fellow gardener's skin. An aide who worked in a multiethnic area in Detroit said she told the youngsters, "We're all as God wanted us to be . . . all flowers aren't the same color and neither are people." The New York coordinator commented, "It's just hard not be friendly when you see somebody else struggling with those weeds."

When coordinators were specifically asked about problems, only two cases were cited. Both arose from differences in cultural approaches to gardening. In one case white middle-class residents objected to the Chinese practice of using urine in their gardening and tying rags in their garden. In a garden shared by blue-collar whites and recent Vietnamese immigrants, the Vietnamese used traditional methods of flooding their plots without realizing that the garden was not constructed to keep the water from overflowing onto the plots of their neighbors using different techniques. More commonly gardeners with different cultural backgrounds found themselves exchanging recipes and learning to grow vegetables they had never grown before.

In one city the coordinator deliberately chose garden plots in areas with representatives of different ethnic, age, and income groups. Another coordinator, in responding to a question about promoting intergroup goodwill, said, "We do, but we don't do it consciously." In his area the Mexicans and Puerto Ricans were "not real friendly [toward each other, but] with gardening [they] have something very much in common." Another coordinator mentioned having a mixed staff whom he assigned to obtain a cross-ethnic mix. Nine of the sixteen coordinators indicated consciously trying to use the gardening experience to promote interracial, interethnic goodwill.

Although the congressional mandate of the program was to serve low-income people, most cities provided some services to higher-income groups because the coordinators felt that the Extension Service should not refuse to assist anyone. In several areas gardens served neighborhoods with mixed-income residents. One was "one-half young professionals and residents of [public housing] projects. [It] works fine." In Philadelphia there is an old Polish and Irish neighborhood with some low-income blacks, new professionals, and housing project residents: "The garden is one of the few places where all of these elements interact both in gardening and in garden management."

Many coordinators concentrated staff effort in low-income areas, responding only to requests for information in other areas. Some directors provided more extensive services to higher-income areas because they felt it was politically expedient to do so, especially if services were requested by a political official. Several coordinators commented that the higher-income areas provided political support for the program and contributed money, supplies, and volunteer assistance.

A few coordinators used the opportunity to increase relationships between members of higher- and lower-income groups. One provided assistance to high-income areas but steered the gardeners into workshops held in an adjacent low-income area. Another said that their end-of-the-year tour took people into neighborhoods they would not otherwise have visited.

Conclusions

The evidence from the Urban Gardening Program indicates that service programs designed for one purpose—in this case, food production and utilization—can have long-lasting spillover benefits. Some programs promoted joint family activities and intergenerational contacts. Some actively undertook identification of potential community leaders and encouraged development of their leadership skills. The gardens promoted neighborly relations and community pride. One program conducted a survey in which 90 percent of the respondents said they felt better about themselves, 45 percent felt better about their neighbors, and 47 percent felt better about their families.[7]

In some cases, the gardens created positive relations among gardeners of different ages, races, ethnic groups, and incomes. A few groups organized to manage the gardens began undertaking more ambitious community projects. One group is attempting to incorporate and use the gardening as a profit-making venture to support other community projects. In all cases the amount of spillover benefits depended partly on the local structure of the program and partly on the philosophy and skills of the coordinator.

Because the original congressional mandate did not direct garden coordinators to consider household support, neighborhood relations, or community development as part of their effort, the achievement of these spillover benefits was difficult and haphazard. Although coordinators were allowed enough flexibility to work toward these goals if they wished, some did not attempt to achieve them or consider them in staff selection. Opportunities were lost to train both staff and garden leaders in community development, an effort that might have brought long-term benefits to many neighborhoods. More garden programs also could have been used as means for dissemination of information about various resources available to the community with some conscious effort and increased funds for longer newsletters and more postage.

The Urban Gardening Program was justified to national officials and politicians primarily in terms of dollar value of food grown and number of persons involved, an approach that can discourage coordinators from working with difficult, time-consuming situations—such as a garden in a tense racially integrated area or with mentally retarded children—and from spending energies on community leadership development.

Because coordinators were not asked to obtain data on the social benefits of their programs, questions on social benefits were included in only a few of the questionnaires sent by coordinators to gardeners. In most cases, however, social benefits were not quantified at all. When asked whether anything about the physical location or organizational arrangements of his program helped single-parent families, one director answered that he did not know: "[It's a question of] accountability. We gear our internal reports to get data for [the Department of] Agriculture. If that document asked other questions we would [have] gotten data." Another commented, "We do report and calculate the value of food [produced]. The thing we don't do is look at the part we play in the betterment of the community."

Despite these limitations as a vehicle for strengthening social fabric, the Urban Gardening Program illustrates several types of resident involvement. It shows how such programs can operate to assist potentially at-risk groups, such as the elderly, to help communities handle pluralism, to create a variety of social networks, and to develop stronger community leadership to deal with other community issues.

Notes

1. The information in this chapter is based on interviews in 1981 and 1982 with the sixteen coordinators; an interview with the national program leader, Ricardo E. Gomez; written materials from the Cooperative Extension Service; newsletters and reports from the sixteen cities; and conversations with Allison Brown, a horticulturist who had studied the program, and draft reports on her visits to the sixteen cities. Coordinators interviewed were: Jerry East, Atlanta; Steven Altman, Cleveland; Steve Brachman, Milwaukee; Gregory R. Stack, Chicago; Jacqueline Keller, Baltimore; Stuart Jacobson, Boston; William Mills, Detroit; Arnold Brown, Houston; Marcie Kelt Oehler, Jacksonville; William Vasser, Memphis; Robert Brown, Newark; Juanita Franklin, New Orleans; Albert Harris, New York; Brenda Funches, Los Angeles; Libby Goldstein, Philadelphia; and Ann Rackers, St. Louis. I also talked informally with Ron Baker when he was coordinator of the Los Angeles program, and Eleanor Downs, an Extension 4-H Program Assistant in Detroit, and drew on Allison Ann Brown, "Extension Urban Gardening: A Survey of Techniques Drawn from the 16 Cities Urban Gardening Program," draft (1981), and "Extension Urban Gardening: The 16 Cities Experience: Intern Report," draft (n.d.).

2. "Urban Garden Program Data, 1981," mimeographed (Washington, D.C.: Urban Gardening Program, Cooperative Extension Service, U.S. Department of Agriculture, 1982).

3. Ibid.

4. All of the quotations in the remainder of this chapter are from interviews conducted by the author during 1981 and 1982.

5. Claude S. Fischer, *To Dwell among Friends: Personal Networks in Town and City* (Chicago: University of Chicago Press, 1982), p. 246.

6. Interview with Ricardo E. Gomez, program leader, Horticulture Program, Urban Gardening Cooperative Extension Service, 1983.

7. Gregory R. Stack, "Chicago Urban Gardening Program," *Illinois Research* 22 (Summer 1980):4.

6 Columbia: Accomplishments and Limitations of a Private Community Association

The founder of the new town of Columbia, Maryland, James Rouse, believed that people in cities lacked the community relationships and the democratic involvement he had experienced in small towns. He also believed that large numbers of households are needed to provide a community with the variety that makes life interesting, as well as the market and tax base necessary for good services, and he thought that people should be exposed to a cross-section of ages, races, and economic status. He wanted to build a new town that would include a mixture of housing, shopping, and amenities and be both racially and economically integrated.[1] In the mid-1960s Rouse acquired more than 13,000 acres in a rural section of Maryland halfway between Baltimore and Washington, D.C. Columbia was built as an unincorporated town consisting of a series of villages of approximately 12,000 persons, each with its own shopping and community center, and a projected total population of 110,000.

Columbia Association

Owners of each dwelling unit in Columbia pay an annual assessment to a town-wide organization, the Columbia Park and Recreation Association (CA). This money is used to repay the developer for such community amenities as swimming pools and community centers or for loans used by the CA to build facilities, to maintain the extensive community open space, and to pay the operating expenses of the various facilities. Separate fees are charged to residents who use the pools, golf courses, and other facilities.[2]

In addition to maintaining the open space, the CA owns and operates a number of recreational, cultural, and social facilities. At the time of my research, its facilities included neighborhood pools and a swim center, two golf courses, lakes and boat docks, a horse center, an ice rink, an athletic club, neighborhood and village center buildings, and over twenty-five miles of pathways.[3]

Columbia was designed to be a good place to rear children. Many houses in Columbia are located on cul-de-sacs adjacent to community-maintained open space. An extensive pathway system provides safe access to shopping and schools, as well as a protected place for bicyclers. The neighborhood centers provide convenience shopping; a larger choice of goods is available at the village centers.

The CA subsidized a town-wide bus system, heavily used by children, the elderly, and those at home without cars. CA staff arranged space for child care in neighborhood and village centers and elsewhere, established standards for provision of quality care, and provided training and technical assistance to child care staff. They also subsidized the care, including providing a sliding-scale fee system, designed to enable residents of all income levels to use the child care.

By 1975 the CA had a large staff and an operating budget originally projected at $2.5 million. It owned $15 million of facilities and equipment. The board was composed of village representatives, one elected from each of the completed villages, and members appointed by the developer. Rouse's plan was to replace developer-appointed members gradually with ones elected by the villages as population, then 35,000, increased. In 1975, there were four developer votes and two and a half village votes. Each village also had an elected board responsible for commenting on matters of concern to the village and operating the community centers.[4]

By 1975 an overall depression in the housing market had slowed the pace of sales and created financial pressures on the developer. In addition, a change in the Maryland property assessment procedures resulted in a 10 percent reduction of CA revenue and a corresponding need for drastic CA budget reductions.

The annual preparation of the CA budget took several months. The CA professional staff first prepared a proposed budget. After the proposed budget was reviewed by the CA board of directors, it was presented to each of the village boards, which held community meetings and commented on it. This was followed by community-wide public hearings before final action by the CA board.[5]

From the point of view of this analysis, three aspects of the 1975 budget controversy are noteworthy: the nature of the cuts and controversies about them, the difficulty of the process for the residents, and the fact that the developer possessed ultimate control.

Although cuts were proposed in all program areas, the most severe were in human services. Cuts in staff included a highly popular coordinator of volunteers and the staff who assisted in the establishment and support of child care centers. Funds were cut for community center operation and eliminated for the Oakland Mills Teen Center. Initially the center had been used exclusively by the white teenagers. Gradually blacks began using it, and the whites left. Frequently blacks who used it were not residents but older low-income youth from elsewhere in the county. Some Columbia residents saw this as a perversion of the original idea of the center and an invasion of Columbia by outsiders. The board of directors of Oakland Mills Village saw it as a realistic method of providing constructive opportunities for teenagers who would be attracted to Columbia regardless of the desires of Columbia's residents.

The Oakland Mills Village board was concerned that the proposed budget cuts would seriously interfere with its ability to operate the community center, and they were incensed that they were expected to operate the teen center out of their village community center budget since the teen center served a population of concern to all of Columbia. They proposed an alternative budget and then performed detailed analyses of the next CA proposal. During the month before the public hearings, the members of the village board worked almost every night.

Analyzing the budgets and making effective comparisons between various proposed budgets and budgets from past years was difficult. The materials were extensive. There were several different proposed budgets, one of which was 137 pages. More important, the accounting system the CA used was unorthodox. One mathematician who was employed by the federal government to analyze cash flows of proposed new towns said it would take him a week to figure out the CA documents.[6]

The public hearings were formal affairs, with rigidly enforced time limits on speakers. The hearings lasted two long evenings and were attended by approximately 500 people the first evening and 300 the second. In addition to requests for more money for community centers and the teen center, residents asked for increased funding for specific sports, for child care, for retention of the coordinator of volunteer services, and for maintaining subsidies for the bus system, the only public transportation in Columbia.

The CA board made some concessions to resident requests. The transportation budget was raised by $40,000, the teen center was given $20,000, and $36,000 was added to community center funding. The basic thrust of the cuts, however, was not changed. The new budget raised fees for child care and for use of a number of recreational facilities and reduced the hours of operation of the bus system, thus lowering support for amenities designed to make Columbia an easy place to rear children or for households on limited budgets to live.

The essence of the budget controversy was highlighted by a long discussion of a proposal by one village representative regarding the tulips in the town center, Columbia's large shopping and office area. She recommended that funds for professional gardening services be dropped and volunteers be used to plant bulbs. She pointed out that the CA was about to entrust human service operation mostly to volunteer effort. The general manager of Columbia, a CA board member, protested that the appearance of the town center was vital to Columbia's public image and therefore to sales and the well-being of the entire community. Paid staff for assisting child care centers was cut; professional tending of the tulips remained.[7]

Support for Social Networks

There is no definitive research on the social patterns and networks of Columbia residents. Certainly the patterns are not those of the close-knit structure of an older inner-city ethnic neighborhood. The residents are primarily nuclear families with young children. Although low-income residents tend to socialize among themselves and black residents have some separate social organizations, individuals in both groups are linked to members of the white middle-class residents by a variety of weak ties and intimate secondary relationships, as well as by individual cases of friendship.

The village centers and CA were designed partly to facilitate community interaction. By 1975 they had succeeded. The CA structure provided opportunities for people to meet as participants in a variety of specialized activities ranging from dance classes to pottery. The CA itself had a number of advisory committees for different activities. In addition, people participated on village boards and the CA board. The neighborhood pool and the village center stores and facilities became places for informal meetings. All of these encounters created an overlapping network of relationships that criss-crossed the community and facilitated racial and economic class integration.

The shifts in priorities observed in 1975 evidently reduced this support for social fabric. In June 1982, I attended a day-long forum held to celebrate Columbia's fifteenth birthday and to assess its past and future as a community. At a session on the function of village boards, most of the discussion revolved around whether village boards should continue to exist. The participants identified the 1975 budget decision to charge rental fees for space for community activities as a major turning point in the loss of involvement in village activities. Someone noted that now people outside the community are renting the space in the village community centers and asked, "Why are our facilities going to the highest bidder?" Someone else commented that there had been a "real shift in CA. [It] moved from human needs and community service to what it [is legally] called, 'Parks and Recreation.'"

One woman said, "They gave up the spirit of Columbia." She commented that she had been a member of an open bridge group held in the village center where anyone could walk in and play for a quarter. For years she had played with women whose ages ranged from forty to seventy-eight:

"If I moved into Columbia today, that opportunity wouldn't exist." That group, and many others, either became more homogeneous private clubs in people's homes or disbanded. Someone else commented that the establishment of fees had "dissipated the sense of community" by eliminating the opportunity to mix naturally in the community building. The people at the 1982 forum seemed surprised by what they viewed as unexpected results of the budget cuts of 1975. In fact the Oakland Mills board had rather explicitly defended their proposed 1975 alternative budget on the grounds that the planned CA cuts in human services would harm Columbia's sense of community.

Support for Community Development

The CA fostered Columbia's community development both directly and indirectly. Its own activities and structure provided numerous opportunities for residents to become involved and to practice and develop leadership skills. Initially it also provided free or subsidized space for meetings of other groups. Staff encouraged residents who were trying to develop a program. The community center programs offered low-key opportunities for residents to participate. In arguing against the cuts in the community center funds, the members of the Oakland Mills Village board complained that the CA board did not understand the developmental aspects of their program. Staff, for example, might spend considerable time helping a woman who had a skill but no teaching experience to organize her class and recruit students. The Oakland Mills board felt the value of their program was in assisting such residents to develop new skills as much as in offering programs. If staff were limited, they could not offer such help.

Much of this informal aid to individual and group development was curtailed after the budget crisis. In addition there were a number of activities that the CA never undertook. Unlike many other grass-roots community organizations, the CA did not offer leadership training. And considering the CA resources available, the support for non-CA-initiated activities was extremely limited. In 1975 the CA had a proposed operating budget of $2.5 million, far more than the usual inner-city community organization even considering the CA's extensive responsibility for maintenance of facilities and open space.[8] Many inner-city programs are far more active in conscious leadership development and in supporting a variety of community development programs than was the CA.[9]

Despite its resources, the CA had far fewer links to external resources than many poorer inner-city community organizations. This was partly because the role of developing the relations between Columbia and the county in which it was located was left to the developer. In a sense, too, the

CA was a private government designed primarily to provide supplemental amenities not available from state and county governments. The services provided by the CA were more extensive and designed for a higher-income and more highly educated group than those provided by government in a traditional rural area. CA staff and residents may well have felt that by operating independently they could more quickly deliver innovative services, closely geared to the needs of their residents. The CA did not attempt to develop foundation or other alternative sources of support for services that were not available from the county or provided through its own programs.

Support for Pluralism

Columbia is a town with a growing industrial and commercial base. As children mature, they may be able to find jobs in Columbia. If not, many will be able to find employment in Baltimore or Washington, D.C., both of which are within relatively easy commuting distance. If the Columbia plan to include a full range of housing types and prices is realized, young adults with low starting salaries will have the option of continuing to live in their home town. The original design called for a range of housing priced to enable anyone who worked in Columbia to live there. That effort, however, has been severely hampered by the rising costs of producing housing, the unavailability of subsidies for low- and moderate-income housing from the federal government, and the escalation in property values in Columbia.[10]

The CA contribution to support for elderly households had always been limited. It consisted primarily of subsidies for the bus and provision of space in one of the community centers for meetings of a county-sponsored senior citizen club. Attention had been given to building the newer village centers in a barrier-free fashion. Also, the developer had been active in establishing a hospital and a prepaid medical plan in Columbia available to anyone who could afford it. The recreational opportunities and medical facilities in Columbia and in nearby Baltimore make it possible that some residents' parents might choose to locate near children in Columbia, especially if lower-priced rental units, housing for the elderly, and nursing homes become available.

CA support for economic diversity was evidenced in its provision of the sliding-fee scales for child care and through informal waiving of fees for recreational activities for children who could not afford them. Support for racial diversity was expressed partly by policies supporting low-income families and through support for the teen center, which was used exclusively by blacks. The CA had been criticized by a group called the Concerned Black Fathers for ignoring the different tastes of blacks. None of the top management staff of CA was black. The CA provided lights for basketball courts only after considerable pressure from the Concerned Black Fathers, although lights were provided regularly for tennis courts, a game traditionally played by whites. Part of the lack of substantial support for sports and programs specifically designed to appeal to blacks was undoubtedly due to complicated dynamics of race relations. In general residents tried to ignore racial differences in tastes or behavior since to acknowledge any differences might be perceived as racial prejudice or as evidence that the much-valued integration was not working.

Accomplishments

The general layout of Columbia and the facilities and services of the CA did provide a number of supports for households. Mostly, however, these were geared to the stereotypical middle-income nuclear family with two parents and children. There was almost no consideration of the needs of the same families during periods of marital stress or divorce. Given the fact that the divorce rate among similar families nationally is high, it would have been logical to expect that many Columbia couples would also experience divorce. The growth of Columbia coincided with the beginning of the women's movement, yet when the women in Columbia formed separate organizations to deal with their concerns, they received only token assistance from CA.[11]

Columbia has, however, the range of facilities and the potential income to provide needed services to a variety of household types in the future. If, as planned, Columbia attracts more industrial and commercial establishments, jobs will be available for people with many interests and skills. If a range of sales and rental housing is available, including small apartments, people at different stages of family formation and income will be able to live in Columbia.

The CA and the design of Columbia have been successful in fostering the development of a variety of social relationships. People do know their neighbors and do use the village facilities. Although at the time of my research, only a limited number of people actually used the community centers, the centers did provide public space for activities and at that time served as a focus for intense involvement by a small number of residents.

Limitations

The CA has played a limited role in community development in Columbia for three reasons: residents had varying perceptions of the purpose of CA, the CA developed into a bureaucracy under developer control, and both developer and residents were determined to maintain high property values.

The legal name of the CA is the Columbia Park and Recreation Association. Many residents considered CA efforts to provide services beyond recreational programs to be outside its legitimate functions. Comments were made at the budget hearings that the CA was not a social service agency. Many assumed that recreation meant only swimming pools, tennis courts, and organized sports. Partly because of the CA accounting system, which did not include repayment of individual facility construction costs as part of the operating expenses of that facility, the high subsidies for child care were easily identified and criticized, while those for golf courses and the athletic club were hidden.

The CA was a large organization with a complicated legal structure and bureaucratic procedures. Its budgets were difficult to understand. During debates within the CA board, the developer's representatives could use their professional backgrounds in business and finance as well as CA staff expertise about Columbia. Building Columbia was their job, and serving on the CA board was part of that job.

Participating in CA activities was only the avocation of the volunteer village representatives and board members, many of whom lacked training in business and budgets. Their volunteer status affected the amount of time they had to participate, their decision-making processes, their schedules, and their resources. At one meeting, the developer's representative decided to postpone consideration of a budget issue for forty-eight hours. This gave him two working days to prepare his position and have his secretary type and photocopy the documents. The village board members, in contrast, had two evenings after work with no personnel or resources for typing and copying.

Thus, ironically, the average Columbia resident dealing with the CA, which was designed to foster democratic participation, had all of the difficulties of a neighborhood resident dealing with a city government. The developer's representatives had access to staff, and they controlled the timetable of events, the flow of information, and the agendas.

In the case of Columbia, as in the case of most neighborhood-city negotiations, everyone knew who had the power. During the voting on the budget, the village representatives sometimes opposed the developer, but generally the wishes of the developer (and indirectly those of the out-of-town bankers financing Columbia) were recognized and supported. This support was not necessarily because of a desire to obtain favor or status, although that may have been present. Most acknowledged the developer's expertise and had a strong desire as property owners not to make any decisions that would interfere with the growth of Columbia and the protection and growth of their property values.

Columbia: A Private Community Association

The question of property values and perceptions of what preserves them underlies much of the dynamics of American communities. This concern is not surprising; buying a house represents most Americans' biggest lifetime investment. Moreover, since Americans are mobile, they need to be able to sell their homes at a price sufficient to enable them to purchase another in their new location. But this concern with property values, legitimate as it may be, limits the flexible use of a privately financed community association for promoting the multiple values of community life.

Community associations in new town developments, as well as home owners' associations in smaller subdivisions and condominiums, are based on concepts from property law rather than from democratic government. Membership is automatic and mandatory based on a property deed covenant. Procedures for mandatory annual or monthly assessments are established as part of the legal documents. Arrangements for modification usually are conservatively structured, requiring high percentages of voter approval. The purpose of these types of arrangements is to protect the investment and management control by the original developer, as well as the investment of the people who purchase property. In this way the availability of funds for ongoing maintenance is assured, and owners are protected against the possibility that their neighbors may be unwilling to vote funds for necessary maintenance.[12]

The problem with the system from the viewpoint of community building is its narrowness and inflexibility. In the case of Columbia, the name, Columbia Park and Recreation Association, created a mind-set among some residents that funds were legitimately to be spent only to maintain recreation facilities, which many residents did not even use. Especially after the fees were raised, some could not afford to do so. When the budget was cut, many services these households needed were curtailed. Nevertheless, they still had to pay the annual assessment of several hundred dollars a year.

Even considering the desirability of maintaining property values, such a narrow approach may be self-defeating. Community appearance is not only a matter of the number of maintenance workers but also a result of the amount of trash dropped by residents or visitors. Expenditures for staff for the teen center might have been more useful for the long-range maintenance of property than direct maintenance expenditures if the activities of the staff created good relationships with local teenagers. Enjoyment of neighborhood recreational facilities depends not only on the quality of the facilities and programs but also on the ease of access in a safe environment. In evaluating urban neighborhoods, Schoenberg used safe passage through the streets and using shared public spaces as indicators of neighborhood viability.[13] Frequently the funds of community associations are used for direct property maintenance but not for indirect purposes that might actually be more effective in achieving the desired results.

In addition, many community associations have architectural review standards and committees, established to ensure the visual quality of the area. The standards often are specific, forbidding residents to change such details of their property as fences, plantings, and paint colors without approval of the review committee. Usually the actions of the committees are accepted, although residents in a few communities have sued. The emphasis is on home as investment rather than home as a focus for living. A man in one neighborhood in Columbia reportedly complained because a neighbor's child was growing corn, which he considered unsightly. His major concern, however, was not aesthetic but economic. He feared the potential effect on the resale value of his house if he wanted to move.

The accomplishments and limitations of the CA illustrate one approach to conscious community building. Although such associations serve to reassure owners that their property interests will be protected, they represent a different approach to community building from that of normal local democratic government. The amount of involvement in community building possible under this private government approach depends partly on internal structural arrangements and partly on the dynamics of the interactions among residents and between residents and the developer.

Notes

1. Gurney Breckenfeld, *Columbia and the New Cities* (New York: Ives Washburn, 1971); Richard O. Brooks, *New Towns and Communal Values: A Case Study of Columbia, Maryland* (New York: Praeger, 1974).

2. Peggy Wireman, "Meanings of Community in Modern America: Some Implications from New Towns" (Ph.D. diss., American University, 1977). Except where noted otherwise, all information in this chapter is drawn from that work.

3. Community Association, "The Briefing Book: Background Materials on the Columbia Association" (Columbia, Md.: Columbia Association, 1974).

4. Columbia Association, "Annual Report" (Columbia, Md.: Columbia Association, 1975).

5. Wireman, "Community"; Columbia Association, "Annual Report" (Columbia, Md.: Columbia Association, 1975); "The Briefing Book: Background Materials on the Columbia Association" (Columbia, Md.: Columbia Association, 1974); "FY 76 Budget Process: Executive Committee Work Session, October 22, 1974 (Columbia, Md.: Columbia Association, 1974); "FY 76 Budget Process: Executive Committee Work Session, Dec. 3, 1974" (Columbia, Md.: Columbia Association, 1974); "Option Document," Jan. 21, 1975 [original misdated 1974] (Columbia,

Md.: Columbia Association, 1975); "Executive Committee FY 76 Recommended Budget" (Columbia, Md.: Columbia Association, 1975); "The Columbia Park and Recreation Association, Inc. FY 1976 Staff Recommended Budget" (Columbia, Md.: Columbia Association, 1975).

6. Wireman, "Community"; Oakland Mills Village Board, "Oakland Mills Village Budget Recommendations for Fiscal Year 1976" (Columbia, Md.: Oakland Mills Village Board Files, 1975); Columbia Association: "Briefing Book"; "FY 76 Budget Process: Work Session, October 22, 1974"; "FY 76 Budget Process: Work Session, Dec. 3, 1974"; "Option Document"; "Executive Committee FY 76 Recommended Budget"; "The Columbia Park and Recreation Association, Inc. FY 1976 Staff Recommended Budget."

7. Wireman, "Community"; Columbia Association, "FY 76 Approved Budget."

8. The Columbia Association, "Budget Summary" (Columbia, Md.: Columbia Association, 1975).

9. Author's personal experience as community organizer, Chicago, 1962-1965, and as program analyst, Office of Neighborhoods, Voluntary Associations, and Consumer Protection, U.S. Department of Housing and Urban Development, 1977. See also such discussions of neighborhood efforts as Alice Shabeoff, ed., *Neighborhoods: A Self-Help Sampler* (Washington, D.C.: Department of Housing and Urban Development, 1979).

10. Roland Warren, "Some Observations on the Columbia Experience," in *Psychology of the Planned Community,* ed. Donald C. Klein (New York: Human Sciences Press, 1978), pp. 158-166.

11. Louise Yolton Eberhardt, "Developing a Support Base for Women," in *Psychology of the Planned Community: The New Town Experience,* ed. Donald C. Klein (New York: Human Sciences Press, 1978), pp. 99-110.

12. Author's experience while employed at the New Communities Administration, U.S. Department of Housing and Urban Development, 1972-1978.

13. Sandra Perlman Schoenberg and Patricia Rosenbaum, *Neighborhoods That Work: Sources for Viability in the Inner City* (New Brunswick, N.J.: Rutgers University Press, 1980).

7 The Dynamics of Integration

The American melting pot dilemma is whether members of different ethnic groups can become "American" without losing their cultural heritage. Integration is defined in several ways in academic literature and general use. Some use the term to describe an assimilation process whereby the non-majority group gradually loses any traits of distinctiveness. Others use it to mean pluralism, either structural or cultural, or both. In structural pluralism, minority and majority groups have equal access to power and status. Cultural pluralism implies a positive recognition of the different values of the groups in question. The question of race is linked to that of class. Not only have blacks as a whole had lower incomes and education than whites, but whites historically often have labeled anything done by blacks as inferior and "lower class."[1] Part of the nuances of integration in the communities considered here was the difference in the definition of integration used by different participants.[2]

Columbia, Maryland

Racial Integration

Columbia's developer, James Rouse, pursued racial integration by refusing to permit realtors to practice techniques of racial discrimination commonly used at that time and by providing some financial and moral support for the building of low- and moderate-income housing in Columbia. Although Columbia has been criticized as having only token amounts of integration or low-income housing, both were higher than in nearby areas. In 1975, the population of Columbia was approximately 20 percent black. In Howard County as a whole, where Columbia is located, the black population then stood at 9 percent, and in nearby Montgomery County, where residents had levels of income and education similar to Columbia, the population was 11 percent black.[3]

Racial and, to a lesser extent, class integration has occurred successfully in Columbia in the sense that both whites and blacks of differing incomes live within the community in housing that is not substantially segregated by race or class. In addition, residents have expressed strong support for integration. Respondents to a survey said that having additional moderate-income whites or blacks would not harm their neighborhood. Responses were practically identical toward prospective whites and prospective blacks. Over 60 percent of the respondents did not think that low-income families making less than $5,000 would harm their neighborhood. In fact, when asked what they would like to see more money spent on, respondents wanted housing for low-income families more than anything else.[4]

The success of racial and class integration cannot be judged only by the support it receives from whites and those of both races of higher incomes. Its success must also be measured by the experience of black and lower-income residents. One black questioned about integration in Columbia cited a number of instances of behavior she considered racist; nevertheless, she said she liked living there. When asked why, her response was that in other cities living sections are segregated, and "the street sweeper doesn't come down the black streets" whereas in Columbia that type of discrimination could never occur. One study has found that black residents were more satisfied with Columbia than were the white residents. Perhaps because many blacks have had to struggle to obtain decent community services, they are more appreciative of Columbia than are their white neighbors. Blacks also liked Columbia more than blacks living in a nearby black middle-income suburb liked their community.[5] The mere fact of physical integration in Columbia gives blacks access to community assets they otherwise might not enjoy.

The limited data available on Columbia's lower-income residents indicates that integration has been successful for them. In her study of five communities with subsidized housing, including Columbia, Helene Smookler concludes that a move to a new community improved the overall quality of life of low-income families. The prediction that such residents might be isolated and unhappy within the more affluent community was not realized; Columbia's low-income residents did not feel their neighbors to be hostile. They interacted more with their relatives and friends than their high-income neighbors did and more than low-income residents in a non-new community studied as a comparison. The residents of subsidized housing ranked facilities and services better than in their previous communities and were more positive about job opportunities, cost of living, and their neighbors than were residents in subsidized housing in control communities.[6]

Integration in Columbia has not meant a complete amalgamation of people. In most cases white respondents indicated that although they were friendly with black neighbors or acquaintances, they did not have close personal friends who were black, although their young children did. This correlates with the observation made by one resident that the preteenage children got along well because they largely lacked prejudice and the adults made a conscious effort to be friendly to each other. Also the adults knew that the Columbia ideology fostered racial equality. One respondent explained that the white person looks at a black neighbor and says, "Now, I'm going to be friendly to this person." And the black neighbor looks at a white neighbor and says, "Now we're going to be friends, and I'm not going to say that I don't like them or that they don't like me."

If this approach does not necessarily create intimate friendships or solve all problems, it does create a generally receptive and neighborly atmosphere. One of the white respondents, who stated, "I'm not an affirmative-action person, mainly because I'm not prejudiced. I don't see anyone out there affirmatively acting for me," nevertheless summed up the situation by stating that "integration is an accepted way of life" in Columbia. Blacks confirmed this view. One commented that in Columbia she expected to be accepted, whereas in some areas of the county she was not sure she was welcome. Overt expressions of racism were rare and not condoned.

Subtle expressions of racism did occur, however, as well as some friction and misunderstandings. One white observer commented to me that many of the whites moving to Columbia had liberal views but no personal experience with black subcultures. The result was that they did not know how to relate to the blacks they met and frequently insulted them without even being aware of it. They did not know black expressions or how to interpret them, and they used words that were offensive. Frequently whites did not recognize or acknowledge a black in a situation where such recognition would have been made for a white.

Black adult respondents volunteered comments to me about a "very subtle kind of racism; on the surface everything seems to be all right." One black respondent suggested that whites and blacks come from different cultural backgrounds and "things have different meanings for both groups." There were reports, for example, of high school teachers addressing teenage black youth as "boy," seemingly unaware of the historic use of the term to deny the manhood of black men.

One respondent suggested that whites did not look blacks in the eye. He stated that blacks in Columbia are suspicious of whites and frequently test them in subtle ways, tests that the whites too often fail, thus reinforcing the mutual distance. This testing was particularly marked among youth, which may account for some of the difficulties that were experienced in maintaining integrated teen facilities, as well as some of the difficulties between adults and teens hanging around the village centers. The respondent further suggested that the black teenagers resent the fact that the whites fear them. At one point a black youth from a family with a $40,000 annual income would dress in blue jeans, hang around the teen center, and either by minor verbal comments or merely facial expressions test white adults to see whether they would respond with fear. The whites usually did, although the actual threat was no greater than in interchanges they had with their children's white friends. The effect of the incident was to reinforce the stereotypes and suspicions of both participants.

The problem for the teenagers was heightened by several factors. Unlike their parents, they did not consciously choose to live in an integrated situation although they were old enough to have well-established prejudices. In school they were forced into constant interracial contact and sometimes subject to peer pressure to be loyal to their own race. Some blacks in Columbia and others who visited Columbia from nearby areas came from lower socioeconomic backgrounds with more aggressive attitudes toward fighting. In addition, blacks and whites often have different tastes in music and styles of dancing, which are far more important to teenagers than to adults.

The teenagers therefore tended to segregate themselves racially. In her study of Columbia, Lynne C. Burkhart concluded that black middle-class youth chose segregation because they could gain more power by identifying themselves as blacks than as members of the middle class.[7] Whatever the reasons for the self-segregation of youth by race, it made Columbia adults uncomfortable since it countered the Columbia ideology. Burkhart noted that it was rarely discussed openly. Certain terms began to acquire special meanings that enabled people to discuss questions of race and class in relation to teens publicly without really facing the issue of race. That is, when the word *teens* was used in a context referring to problems other than lack of participation in programs, it meant black teens. The term *black teens* meant lower-income black teens. Reference to "problems with teens" meant young black adults of high school age or older who congregated in public places. On the other hand, if people asked, "What else can be done for teens?" they generally meant whites between ages thirteen and high school graduation.[8]

This lack of candor in addressing questions of race illustrates one way in which integration in Columbia works. Many residents seem to assume that integration is equivalent to total assimilation. Those who subscribe to this ideology hold that since we are all human beings, color must be viewed as irrelevant, and to connect any behavioral patterns with color would be an admission of unconscious racism. Many whites who have never known many blacks are also afraid of inadvertently using the wrong words or displaying conscious or unconscious racism. Therefore since people are uncomfortable about noticing any differences between themselves and their acquaintances of a different race, they ignore the fact of racial differences and do not confront problems directly, an approach that can create further mutual misunderstandings. For example, reluctance to expect appropriate behavior from black children can be insulting to their parents. One black cited a teacher's permitting her daughter to play in school rather than work as an expression of racism; that is, the white teacher did not expect the performance from the black child that she would have demanded from a white one. The point is that even given goodwill on both sides, racial misunderstandings occur. The fact that they generally are not addressed openly in Columbia probably does not mean that fewer incidents occur. It does mean that opportunities for communication between races are lost. Whites can lack knowledge about black culture or even be inconsiderate or insensitive without necessarily being racist. If no one tells them to stop using expressions with racist connotations, they will continue the offensive behavior.

While whites in integrated communities may be uncomfortable for fear of offending and because they have not known many blacks previously, blacks also may be uncomfortable since many must have come from segregated neighborhoods and have known whites mainly as teachers, bosses, or in other formal situations. For them the problem is not just being a minority in a situation in which their special experience or language may be misunderstood. They also must constantly judge when frictions or minor disagreements are due to prejudice.

One black board member indicated that for a year he was never sure whether his comments were being ignored because he was the new member of a previously close board or whether he was a victim of subtle racism. He also objected to being considered an instant authority on all matters relating to blacks. When a problem occurred involving blacks, other board members would look at him. Sometimes he would look away. His attitude was "don't look at me as if I'm the savior. I didn't want them to think that I was there to deal with the black problem. I was there elected to the board just like they were." In addition, he felt it "crippled the white people on the board for them not to have the opportunity to deal [with the problem]."

The reluctance of Columbia residents to speak of racial differences was also evident in discussions of social relations. Many residents were uncomfortable about stating that there was little socializing between the races. Differences in styles of socializing were reported. One black woman asked why she should socialize with whites when she liked different types of dancing, different types of entertaining, and a different style of social life.

Traditionally much of black middle-class social life has revolved around clubs that combine social activities with fund raising for charitable purposes. Blacks in Columbia have established chapters of a number of these organizations and have created new ones. Several chapters of national fraternities and sororities exist, as well as a black singles club and a chapter of Jack and Jill, which sponsors activities for children and social events for families. Membership is limited and by invitation only. Two organizations of black men have been created for a combination of political, civic, and social purposes. One is the Black Fathers, with a core group of approximately ten members and perhaps fifty others who assist in certain activities such as fund-raising events and sponsoring a highly successful basketball league. Unlike village boards, the Black Fathers meet in each other's homes. There is a Baptist church that is predominantly black. Memberships in these black organizations overlap and involve entire families. The fraternities tend to have women's auxiliaries. A favorite fund-raising activity of sororities is sponsoring dances to which couples are invited to buy tickets. The total structure is quite different from that of the village boards, which involved intimate secondary relationships, or from completely unstructured exchanges of dinner invitations among couples.

Although the existence of these black organizations was not mentioned as a reason for limited black-white socializing or limited black participation in the community association and other activities, it may have been influential, if only because of the conflicting time demands. In addition, several blacks volunteered that much of their social life revolved around family and friends in Baltimore or Washington, D.C.

Here again, the degree of communication between the races seems limited. Many whites did not even know of the existence of an all-black social structure. Indeed one white respondent seemed indignant when asked about it, indicating that he had been active in Columbia affairs for two years before he had learned of it.

The fact that the existence of these differences between the races was only half-acknowledged reflects the general ideology of nondifference that exists in Columbia. Because the differences in accepted social patterns were not discussed, there was a great potential for minor misunderstandings and hurt feelings on the part of whites who were friendly with individual blacks but were not included in their club-oriented social events. On the other hand, blacks may have felt excluded when not invited to participate in white social events because they did not fully realize that their interactions with whites were primarily in situations that generally did not lead to further socializing among whites. That is, blacks know whites in Columbia mainly because they are neighbors or members of the village boards or other organizations. Neighbors frequently deliberately avoid becoming personally intimate with other neighbors. White members of boards of directors of community groups are not necessarily personal friends in the same manner as members of black civic organizations, whose memberships tended to involve whole families and overlap with friendship circles.

The fact that social relations among blacks and whites are limited and that members of each race may have experienced occasional bewilderment or even hurt feelings does not deny the substantial success of integration in Columbia. First, members of both races have the opportunity to know each other and to further their mutual social interaction at whatever pace they prefer. Burkhart concludes that "the combination of mutual respect, assertiveness, and friendliness that characterizes casual contacts between blacks and whites in Columbia is unusual enough that it ought never to be minimized."[9]

Class Integration

The question of the success of class integration is even more complex. The data are limited but those that exist indicate that the differences among inhabitants based on class are limited. Burkhart indicates that in many ways the residents of the subsidized projects were similar to other Columbians. About the same percentage of project residents and townhouse residents were active in their respective self-management plans. About the same number planted flowers and participated in picnics and other social events in their housing development. There were similar variations in numbers of children, child-rearing habits, and social network density in the two development types.[10]

Another study indicated differences between residents in subsidized and nonsubsidized units in income, race, two-parent households, and employment outside Columbia. Nevertheless, the similarities were striking, and residents of both groups were satisfied with Columbia, believed race relations were better there than elsewhere, thought that there were about the right number of people of the same social background in the neighborhood, participated equally in community affairs, and rated equally the amount of their own influence in Columbia decision making.[11]

Some of the misunderstandings occurred because of the middle-income residents' lack of understanding of the practical implications of a limited income. For example, residents living near some of the subsidized housing were critical of the abundance of possessions left outdoors but not sensitive to the fact that this was a response to limited storage facilities in small homes.[12]

The question of acceptance of class differences, whether those based on real differences in habits and tastes or those necessitated by lack of money, is complicated by the fact that public discussion of class in Columbia was frequently a subterfuge for discussion of race. Burkhart examines the various euphemisms used to discuss race in some detail and concludes that much racial prejudice was masked behind class prejudice, always expressed in terms of realistic problems with residents of subsidized housing. She points out, for example, that white Columbians consistently perceived the subsidized units as being "80 or 90 percent black," although the actual figure was less than 40 percent. She concludes that this vagueness of discussion and unwillingness of anyone to be branded as racist actually granted blacks, or advocates of programs for low- and moderate-income residents, considerable power since anyone opposing them risked being considered opposed to the Columbia integration ideology.[13] Burkhart also emphasizes that all blacks benefited by the wide range of incomes of Columbia's black families. The low-income black was assured of being treated with respect during ordinary daily interactions such as shopping, since the store clerk never knew whether the person he or she was serving was a janitor or a famous Washington lawyer. Since one aspect of being black in our society has been the need to adopt white middle-class values and styles in order to gain acceptance, the middle-class black also gained freedom from being part of a community whose ideology stated that lower-income blacks were to be accepted. Therefore in Columbia the power to decide what is proper behavior does not automatically belong to the whites. The black lawyer does not have to base standards of dress and behavior on the unspoken model of middle-class whites.[14]

One black woman told me about being at a meeting where a white man related a conversation that contained vulgar expressions frequently used by black youth. He immediately apologized for using the words in front of her. She pointed out that whites at the meeting had also used expressions of religious profanity. Since these were swear words generally considered acceptable in white society, no one had thought of apologizing. Yet the profane swear words were as offensive to her as the vulgar ones since she had grown up with a strict religious background. She was asserting that whether a swear word is appropriate needs to be determined by its offensiveness to the cultural backgrounds of both the black and of the white persons present, not just to that of the whites.

Burkhart concludes that the simultaneous existence of both class and racial integration has strengthened each. The black middle-class person would not permit demeaning remarks about the lower class since such remarks often are a euphemism for racial prejudice. Concern with appearing racially prejudiced can also motivate whites to support programs for low-income persons of both races. In addition, the presence of low-income residents in the community, recognized by all as a legitimate part of the community, has provided middle-income black residents with more opportunity to express aspects of black culture that do not conform to middle-income white tastes. Burkhart emphasizes that the type of subtle negotiations for good relations, status, and power that are occurring continually in Columbia are not an indication of the failure of integration but rather of the political power of blacks to determine their own standards. The conflict was "not over *what* is an appropriate life-style, but over *who has the right* to determine how an individual, or collectivity of individuals, shall conduct their lives."[15]

Reston, Virginia

Reston is another new town located within commuting distance of Washington, D.C., similar to Columbia in design and socioeconomic composition. As in Columbia, its developer, Robert E. Simon, exercised strong leadership in order to achieve his goals of racial and economic integration. In fact, Simon was forced to market housing himself since no local realtors in the late 1960s would sell homes on an integrated basis. Although Simon later sold his interest to the community, his beliefs created expectations that have continued to influence the development of the community.

In 1975 Reston had a population of 25,500, of which 11 percent were black. Eleven percent of the families had incomes below the poverty level. This was substantially more racial and economic integration than had occurred elsewhere in Fairfax County, in which Reston is located, or in a suburb used for comparison in a national study of new towns. As in Columbia, black residents live scattered throughout the community. There are low-income families in several locations, although there is a marked concentration of low-income housing in one area.[16]

A black respondent to a query I made in 1976 said that not only was Reston successfully integrated in the sense of a lack of concentration of blacks (other than some in the subsidized projects) but also that he knew of no instances of realtors steering blacks to locate in certain sections. This statement is significant when compared to Simon's initial difficulties.

The dynamics of race and class in Reston seem to have been similar to those in Columbia: somewhat limited social interaction between races and an extensive system of all-black social organizations. There are alumni branches of fraternities and sororities and a number of all-black couples' clubs, women's clubs, and men's clubs, as well as a local chapter of Jack and Jill.

Blacks in Reston were more vocal than in Columbia at an early point in the town's development about their desire to obtain community recognition of their black identity and to deal with racial issues. Shortly after Reston began in the mid-1960s, a number of blacks formed an organization called Black Focus, which sponsored an annual Black Arts Festival and other events emphasizing black culture. The group also protested instances of subtle racism. For example, a local youth group had a fund-raising event in which the youth were auctioned as slaves for the day. Members of the Black Focus talked to the leaders of the group, explaining that blacks found the event offensive since it treated an unhappy part of their history in a nonchalant manner.

Black Focus was formed to give black families black support—a kind of an extended family. Although the core group consisted of twenty to thirty couples, the organization was loosely structured and supported any volunteer who wanted to run a project within the basic goals. A black resident estimated that probably 80 percent of the black families in Reston had participated in some Black Focus activity. Black Focus also attempted to make sure that blacks were represented on city and county governmental bodies.

Black Focus members addressed the issue of race by sponsoring a series of discussion groups and urging attention to black issues in the schools. Initially the group faced resistance to addressing racial matters openly. "Blacks who came to Reston were concerned that there was a black organization . . . wasn't that a racist thing to do?" Blacks were also afraid that the first Black Arts Festival might not succeed; nevertheless the leaders felt it was important to establish that blacks, as well as whites, "had a right to make a mess." The festival was successful in both its goal of attracting potential black residents to Reston and reminding black people that "they could maintain their own life-style and still be part of an integrated community . . . that [they] did not have to act 'white.' [They] could contribute their special things and have them appreciated by the white community."

Integration in Reston generally resembled that in Columbia, and the fact that it existed at all represented a significant achievement for the community and its residents. It provided blacks with access to a community in which they could move freely without fear of overt discriminaton and with total access for themselves and their children to the cultural, educational, and other advantages of the community. Both blacks and whites had the opportunity to meet each other in a nonthreatening environment in which mutual respect generally was the accepted norm. Social relations could be formed according to the personal inclination of each individual, but the lack of widespread, close interracial friendships did not exclude blacks from enjoying the other advantages of the community.

Subtle, and occasionally not so subtle, instances of racism did occur; sometimes they were ignored because of the overall ideology and a concern that identifying issues as having racial overtones would be considered racist. On the other hand, once such issues were openly acknowledged, they sometimes became magnified out of proportion to their numbers or seriousness. A problem that arose in an integrated moderate income housing unit, which will be referred to as Green Lake, illustrates both of these reactions. The project was located in a high-density area with a large number of subsidized units and a large number of nonsubsidized units occupied by persons who had income lower than that of other Reston residents. There seems to have been general agreement that the area had an overconcentration of low- and moderate-income housing. In addition, Reston respondents unanimously stated that the management of the Green Lake project had been poor. The project is located across from a swimming pool but, unlike every other apartment complex in Reston, the management did not purchase pool privileges for its residents. After considerable community pressure, the privileges were purchased, but by then the residents had been publicly stigmatized as being different from other residents using the same pool. This may have accounted for subsequent vandalism at the pool, although some vandalism occurred at all of the pools in Reston.

The original residents of the complex had attempted to form a tenants' organization and to organize recreational activities for their children, but management had not supported the effort. A series of incidents then took place involving exchange of racial insults among teenagers and persons using the nearby shopping center. Elementary school children were shaken down for lunch money by other elementary school children, although this stopped when women of both races started jointly patrolling the pathways to the school. Teenagers from the project playing basketball at the nearest court were perceived as a threat by the surrounding townhouse cluster, which then issued buttons to its members to ensure that only those entitled would use the court.

Many of the original Green Lake residents disliked the management and the general atmosphere. They left, creating a situation of high vacancies. The management responded by filling the units without properly screening the tenants, a responsibility of any apartment manager. A number of the new tenants were families with long histories of difficulties, including eviction from other subsidized housing projects in the county. Several of the families reportedly had been feuding for a number of years. Tensions increased, culminating during the summer of 1976 when teenagers shot at a patroling police car. Shortly before the incident, the developer and the Homeowner's Association had jointly contracted with the Fairfax Community Action Agency to place a community worker in the project. Soon after the incident, the manager was replaced, and assistance of different types began coming from various groups.

The dynamics of the situation reflect some of the same complexities and reluctance to deal with questions of race and class that were observed in Columbia. First, the problem had been developing over several years with little serious attempt by any community group to address it. A representative of a community group indicated that he had realized there were deficiencies in the initial planning for the project but had not taken the effort to mobilize community concern. It was also his view that the community would not have been willing to address any potential problems at that time. Although the community association had strongly objected to the project from the beginning on the grounds that it created an overconcentration of low- and moderate-income housing in one area, the Homeowner's Association Architectural Review Committee had reviewed the plans and found them architecturally acceptable, without raising any related questions about needed recreational or other facilities. A new elementary school was opened, and although an attempt was made to recruit teachers with inner-city experience, some teachers evidently were not sufficiently prepared to handle children who did not have the same educational advantages usually enjoyed by other Reston children. An attempt to have meetings with area parents whose children would be attending the new elementary school met no response. The Homeowner's Association provided only minimal special programming or other assistance.

The 1976 Homeowner's Association budget indicates the extent of the reluctance to address the issue openly. The funds for the Fairfax Community Action Agency staff are not mentioned. The reference to "a broader liaison and cooperation system both with agencies in and outside of Reston" actually refers to efforts to obtain more county social services for residents of this project. Nowhere in the ninety-two-page document are the words *race, low income, middle income* or *subsidized housing* used. There are references to free swimming lessons for "disadvantaged persons" and to arranging the hours of the swimming pools in a manner that permits meeting "the time constraints of most residents and to provide a positive program to counteract the spillover of urban social problems into the . . . community pools program area." A proposed "urban problem spillover redirection program" was aimed primarily at youth, including white youth, most of whom had moved to Reston not from nearby Washington, D.C., but from rural parts of the county.

This reluctance to address the issue clearly makes finding solutions to problems more difficult. After the shooting, Reston's developer arranged for a meeting with the management firm and asked what it intended to do. When the firm replied that it had replaced the former white female resident manager with a black man, the developer did not pursue the matter further to ask what specific actions would be taken to control the behavior of the several individuals and families who were actually causing the trouble. The implicit assumption was that the selection of a black manager would somehow eliminate the problem.

Although respondents were concerned that Reston might have increased racial violence, they assured me that their problem was not racial but class or economic. Yet it is difficult to determine whether an individual's reaction is based on attitudes toward class, toward race, or merely toward the specific event. It is noteworthy that national publicity about racial problems in Reston that appeared after the Green Lake incident did not clearly state that the actual problems seemed to have been caused by fewer than 10 families out of more than 700 units of integrated low- and moderate-income housing. The statements probably reflect more about idealized views of the desirability of homogeneity as a means of ensuring an ideal community with no conflict than they do about the actual experience in Reston or the value choices of the residents who live there. In fact, the attention devoted to the incident both within and outside the community seems to have been disproportionate. The Green Lake incident in which no one was hurt, for example, received far more attention than the shooting death of a white storekeeper by a white man in a store several miles outside Reston or a fairly widespread use of drugs by white teenagers.

Other Integrated Communities

Mark Beach and Oralee S. Beach spent one year living in three integrated neighborhoods in Baltimore, Maryland; Cleveland Heights, Ohio; and Portland, Oregon, and visiting additional ones in fifteen other cities. Their findings are similar to those of the Reston and Columbia research and are in accord with my earlier experiences in the integrated neighborhood of Hyde Park-Kenwood. Positive efforts are needed to counter the racist practices of real estate companies, banking interests, and government administrators. Beach and Beach recognize that residents of interracial communities generally are reluctant to address racial differences and issues forthrightly but stress that the complex dynamics of living in an interracial situation can be rewarding for both races and for the growth of community spirit, pride, and involvement.[17]

The Beaches' sensitive discussion covers a range of issues relevant to communities in which residents are not ethnically homogeneous. In addition to treating the functioning of the real estate market, they consider such issues as fear, schools, neighborhood organizations, and the racism of language. Beach and Beach suggest that the use of euphemisms or code words enables whites to convey racist thoughts without seeming to be racist. For example, in an interracial neighborhood, a white discussing "trouble" in a school conveys to the white listener that racial conflict has occurred since otherwise the speaker would provide specifics about the nature of the trouble. *Teenager* and *outsider* are used by whites to stand for *black,* thus allowing objectionable behavior to be discussed without admitting to any racial differences. The term *outsider* is frequently used by whites in interracial neighborhoods to brand black delinquents whom they do not want to believe could be from their own neighborhood. They do not, however, label obnoxious real estate agents, uncooperative loan officers or zoning officials, apathetic mayors, or hostile superintendents of schools as "outsiders."[18] The Beaches comment on the inability of whites to observe the correct percentages of blacks involved in a situation. This was also evidenced in the furor over Green Lake in Reston and in the estimates by Columbians of the percentage of blacks in the subsidized housing projects. The

Beaches note the inability of some adults to witness two ten year olds fighting without assuming that the cause is racial.

Finally, they emphasize the importance of community organizations and suggest that one means of evaluating the success of a community effort to maintain an integrated neighborhood is the quality of the experience of interracial contact during whatever length of time the integration lasts. A neighborhood that becomes all black may still be a successful neighborhood in terms of this understanding of integration. The success of the integration looked at in this way is not measured solely by the length of time the neighborhood maintains a certain numerical count of persons of different races but by the effect on those individuals who have had an experience in interracial living not frequently found in the United States.[19] That there may be certain difficulties, unpleasantness, or uncomfortableness about the experience should not invalidate its success. Many residents of interracial communities might not welcome living next to a person of another race, but many of them would not enjoy living next door to their own adult children.

Conclusion

The experience in these integrated communities suggests that successful integration is possible but complex. An understanding of the dynamics will help avoid unrealistic expectations and discounting successful experiences because they do not match an idealized *Gemeinschaft*. The view that integration should be problem free may not be helpful. It is important to be sensitive to the nuances of integration, its problems as well as its richness. The definition of success developed here includes unafraid physical proximity, unhampered access by all to services and facilities, lack of tension among neighborhood residents around each other, an opportunity to make friends with unlike neighbors, and no more friction or conflict than occurs in nonintegrated communities.

A community that is integrated successfully will be characterized by the following: integrated housing; access for both races to facilities and services; opportunities for members of different racial groups and economic status to associate in civic affairs and voluntary associations and to form friendships; some recognition by all residents of the unique experiences and contributions of all groups; and no more interracial or class conflict or discomfort than exist elsewhere in the society.[20] This definition does not require that blacks and white become friends, merely that they have the opportunity to do so. Nor does it require that all conflicts cease. Some Columbians do not get along with members of other races, but some Columbians do not get along with members of their own race.

The conceptual framework used to consider interactions in neighborhoods needs to be broad enough to include a range of real relationships. Not all neighbors are friends, yet in their role as neighbors they can provide a supportive community. Bender suggested that judging communities only by their communal aspects, the *Gemeinschaft* relations, is less appropriate today than an emphasis on the quality of civic life.[21] The many Americans who now have or will have neighbors of different races, ethnic backgrounds, and incomes need to know how to maintain appropriate public behavior and promote desired networks. The creation of a community-wide institution, such as Columbia's community association, is one method. Another is delivery of whatever programs are introduced in a community in a manner that promotes community spirit and networks.

Notes

1. Ray C. Rist, *The Invisible Children: School Integration in American Society* (Cambridge: Harvard University Press, 1978).

2. The observations in this chapter were made during research on my study, "Meanings of Community in Modern America: Some Implications from New Towns" (Ph.D. diss., American University, 1977). I had made similar observations while working as a community organizer in an integrated neighborhood in Chicago. The material presented here about racial integration in these multi-income communities is pertinent to planning in other heterogeneous situations. The exact dynamics, however, may vary in communities consisting of different combinations of minorities or ethnic groups: Mexican-Americans and Anglos, for example, or Italians, blacks, and Puerto Ricans. The dynamics also vary in single income situations. These are not treated here. Unless otherwise noted the material in this chapter comes from my dissertation. See also Mark Beach and Oralee S. Beach, "Interracial Neighborhoods in the Urban Community," manuscript (Rochester, N.Y., 1978).

3. Peggy Wireman, "Some Nuances of Integration" (paper presented at conference, Fair Housing: An American Right, Rosslyn, Va., June 1977).

4. Raymond J. Burby III and Shirley F. Weiss, *New Communities: USA* (Lexington, Mass.: Lexington Books, D.C. Heath and Company, 1976); Center for Urban and Regional Studies, "Community Profile—Spring 1973: Columbia, Maryland" (Chapel Hill: University of North Carolina, 1974).

5. Burby and Weiss, *New Communities*.

6. Helene V. Smookler, "Deconcentration of the Poor: Class Integration in New Communities" (Ph.D. diss., University of California, 1975), pp. 139, 140, 144.

7. Lynne C. Burkhart, *Old Values in a New Town: The Politics of*

Race and Class in Columbia, Maryland (New York: Praeger, 1981), pp. 82-83.

8. Ibid., pp. 72, 75.

9. Ibid., p. xiv.

10. Ibid., pp. 93-94.

11. Columbia Association, "A Profile of Columbia Residents Living in Subsidized Housing," mimeographed (Columbia, Md.: Office of Planning and Evaluation, 1974).

12. Burkhart, *Old Values,* pp. 119-120.

13. Ibid., p. xv.

14. Ibid., pp. 141-142.

15. Ibid., p. 145.

16. Wireman, "Community" p. 267; Burby and Weiss, *New Communities.*

17. Beach and Beach, "Interracial Neighborhoods."

18. Ibid., p. 56.

19. Ibid.

20. Wireman, "Some Nuances," pp. 2-3.

21. Thomas Bender, *Community and Social Change in America* (New Brunswick, N.J.: Rutgers University Press, 1978), p. 148.

8 Community Design for Families with Children

The number of children living in families with two employed parents or living with only one parent is increasing. One analysis predicts that 59 percent of the children born in the early 1980s will spend at least part of their childhood living with only one parent.[1] Since this parent is usually the mother and the incomes of women are significantly lower than those of men, this chapter includes a description of one successful program developed for the group most likely to need community assistance: families headed by a single mother with low income.

Physical Environment

A community's environmental health conditions affect everyone who lives in an area regardless of whether they participate in other aspects of community life. Children in urban areas are particularly affected by air pollution, noise pollution, lead poisoning, traffic safety, crime, and the availability of safe areas for play.

Although there is no definite research on the subject, it is possible that the effects of air pollution on children are more serious than those on adults. Children probably are more exposed to pollutants than adults because they breathe more frequently, play in dirt that contains fallen pollutants, are more likely to breathe through their mouths and therefore not filter the pollutants out, and are more physically active than adults. They also spend more time out of doors while playing, and because they are smaller they breathe the air closer to the level at which it is expelled from the automobile exhausts in concentrated form. Indeed Los Angeles authorities have warned against allowing children to play out of doors during high pollutant periods. Air pollution can cause or aggravate a number of health problems, including asthma and chronic bronchitis, and is considered to lead to difficulties in growth, development, and mental health. The pollution not only screens out the beneficial sunshine but also has been found to discourage children's tendencies to play outdoors.[2]

Data are beginning to indicate that children also may be particularly susceptible to noise pollution. Children living in noisy environments may

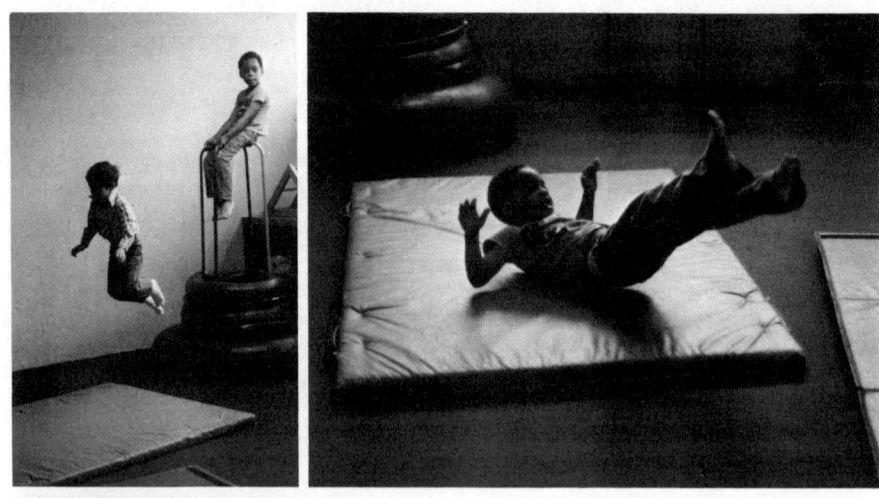

The indoor playground at the child care center in the Warren Village apartment for single-parent families.
Photos: Peggy Wireman

learn to screen out sounds—including the voice of their teachers. There is some evidence that noise can lead to mental and emotional stress and difficulties in language development. One study found that noise in the home was detrimental to children's ability to learn to read. Noise was more important than several other factors, including parents' educational background.[3]

The data on lead poisoning are clear: lead poisoning causes mental retardation and damage to the central nervous system and is associated with learning disabilities. A report of the surgeon general indicated that 6,000 children are damaged each year and another 300 to 400 die from lead poisoning. In some inner-city neighborhoods, as many as one-fourth of the children between one and six years old have elevated levels of lead in their bodies from eating paint from dilapidated buildings, as well as from exposure to automobile exhaust.[4] Neighborhood groups can take action by educating all residents about the dangers of chipping paint in old buildings, sponsoring health screening events, and working to reroute traffic away from play areas.

The data on traffic safety are also disturbing: traffic accidents are the leading cause of death among children over one year old. Although many of the fatalities are children who are passengers in cars, especially those being held by their parents or sitting by themselves without a seat belt, pedestrian accidents to children crossing the street or playing are also frequent. In 1978 almost 75,000 children under fourteen were killed or injured when walking or riding bicycles in the street. Some research indicates that until age eleven or twelve, many children do not have the ability to deal safely with traffic. Their hearing and sight and ability to distinguish right from left, fast and slow, near and far may not be fully developed.[5]

Children themselves are aware of their limitations and suffer psychologically when forced to contend with dangerous traffic, as evidenced from poignant comments from Norwegian first graders, 70 percent of whom expressed fear of the traffic. Many described physical symptoms of anxiety: headaches, pains in the stomach, sweating, and fast heart beat. They said that they were afraid of being killed and reported such dysfunctional behavior as closing their eyes at the crossing and running so they would not see the cars.[6]

Children like to play near home. One scholar has commented that children play near home whether or not it is safe or bothers adults. Very small children are not allowed to go beyond calling distance—about the length of a football field. Even elementary school children play in their own neighborhoods, most of the time within several blocks of home. This is partly because they play in short snatches of time—before dinner, between school and a piano lesson, or while waiting for their parents to take them someplace. And these older children, who theoretically know how to handle traffic, are often careless or forget. They may run after a ball or a friend or be dared into taking risks.[7]

Planners are aware of the problem of traffic dangers for children. In many new areas, houses are clustered around cul-de-sacs, and through traffic is routed away from residences. Some communities have paths for walking and biking that connect homes to schools, shopping, and recreation. In older neighborhoods, parents sometimes have been successful in routing heavy traffic outside their areas, obtaining traffic lights, and even closing streets to automobiles during certain hours.[8] Other approaches include widening sidewalks and placing physical barriers between sidewalks and streets.

Children need active physical play to develop their large and small muscles, strength, coordination, and balance. Through play they learn to relate to other children and have a chance to practice leadership skills and teamwork. They develop their intellectual and creative abilities. They invent things, build playhouses, act out dreams; they discover how to manipulate the physical environment and how to do things independently.[9] Thus, play areas should offer children a variety of activities, as well as a chance to observe and interact with children of other ages and adults.

In the past large yards, little-used streets, or vacant lots provided such opportunities. Today's street traffic is likely to be heavy and yards smaller or nonexistent. Vacant lots have been converted to housing or other uses. Too frequently playgrounds in townhouse areas are designed for preschool children only. They quickly become boring to older children, who ignore them or abuse them. Often planners provide structures that are visually interesting to adults but do not provide creative play opportunities.

Many neighborhood groups have worked together to turn vacant lots into play areas. One neighborhood in San Francisco worked for several years to transform an asphalt school area into a yard full of trees, dirt, and water. The children, their parents, and teachers grew plants, studied ecology, and continually created and evolved new play opportunities.[10] The desirability of appropriate nearby play areas raises the broader question of the range of services and facilities needed in neighborhoods by children and their parents.

Basic Services

The burden of all families is eased when basic services are located within a neighborhood. A number of studies in different countries have indicated that when women are employed outside the home, they continue to perform almost as many household chores as if they were not employed. Although increasing numbers of men do assist, their contribution is generally still quite limited.[11] Employed women with children have two jobs: one paid and one unpaid. As mothers and employees they have a dual role and double burden. The employed mother who is rearing children by herself has an even harder task, especially since her income is generally limited.

If public transportation is available and streets are safe, older children can travel to the doctor, to friends, and to places of entertainment by themselves. Women who do not have the use of a car also need transportation to commute to jobs outside their neighborhoods.

Neighborhood location of child care facilities, shopping, and household services is also a great advantage for employed women who usually cannot attend to family obligations during normal work hours. One reason why many hospital emergency rooms are overburdened with non-emergency cases or cases that should have been treated earlier is that most doctors are not available during the hours when women can take their children to them without losing a day's pay or annual leave. Increasingly grocery stores, banks, and other services are open early and late. Organized community groups might be able to persuade government offices and schools to keep more flexible hours.

Some neighborhood groups have been active in pressuring city agencies to be more responsive to the needs of children. This has included efforts to gain control of institutions such as schools or to make them more responsive. In some cities schools operate in partnerships with the community, using its resources as part of the curriculum and welcoming a variety of volunteer assistance. Efforts at neighborhood economic development have sought revitalization of neighborhood commercial areas partly as a means of providing jobs to local youth. Many neighborhoods build play areas or sponsor day care or recreation activities. Some even operate neighborhood dispute settlement programs, including mediation between teenagers and neighborhood adults. Others have started programs for youth offenders.[12]

Community Atmosphere

Relationships among neighbors and in the neighborhood create a pleasant or unpleasant atmosphere for children as they play and travel about. One type of relationship, which might be called friendly recognition, describes the nodding recognition among people who ride the same elevator in an apartment building. It is an acknowledgment that the other person is not a stranger and has a legitimate right to be present.[13] Even this level of relationship can be very important for children, especially in a pluralistic neighborhood. It creates a friendly atmosphere, which in turn helps to reduce fear of street crime. When people recognize who belongs to a community, they can watch strangers carefully, thus reducing chances of crime. The real and perceived safety of streets and play areas is of vital concern to the well-being of children and reduces the difficulties of parenting. In some cases parents will not allow their children to play outside because of fear for their safety.

In some neighborhoods, residents have pushed for greater mixed use in neighborhood design to provide the natural surveillance by storekeepers and others coming and going at different times. They have also encouraged better street lighting and improved police protection. They have started neighborhood crime watch programs: residents learn safety precautions, such as installing appropriate locks and putting identification on property such as cameras, and agree to call the police for their neighbors. Some participate in whistle-blowing programs in which residents carry whistles and neighbors respond to such calls for help.

In interracial neighborhoods, it is particularly important that adults recognize and acknowledge the legitimate presence of teenagers of another race. Children and youth need to have their right to be on the streets acknowledged. Fear of children of another race can prevent establishment of adult control over outdoor neighborhood activity. If people are afraid or suspicious of neighbors, they will not make requests for appropriate behavior. In cases of racial, ethnic, or class differences, they also may be afraid of appearing prejudiced. The manner in which local agency representatives and storekeepers treat children and youth, and vice-versa, is also part of the community atmosphere. In addition to creating a supportive atmosphere for children throughout the neighborhood, neighbors and other adults working in the area can provide supportive relationships for individual parents and access by children to adult role models beyond those offered by their own parents.

Community Relationships

Many Americans do not rely on relationships with people in their neighborhood for friendship or other types of personal support other than those related to neighborhood as place. Nevertheless, appropriate planning and public policies can help to create neighborhoods that will offer residents supportive social relationships.

Neighborhoods in which close-knit relationships exist provide considerable support for parents raising children. Probably the most important public policy directive regarding such areas is not to destroy them by locating highways through them, gradually withdrawing mortgage money or city services, clearing land for urban revitalization projects, or sponsoring rehabilitation or code enforcement that forces inhabitants to move because of rising taxes or rents. Policies that can help preserve such areas include provision of housing and facilities for young families so that the young are less likely to leave, location of nursing homes in the neighborhoods, and tax abatement for older persons.

In addition to preserving communities where close-knit relations already exist, planners might consider ways to encourage contacts among children and relatives and to provide children with contacts with adults other than their parents and teachers. The sense of history and continuity of life that grandparents can provide are particularly rewarding for children. If planners include a mix of housing in residential areas and contract for barrier-free construction, older people could locate in an apartment near children if they wished. Frequently neighborhood zoning prohibits construction of apartments, low-income housing, or nursing homes. Many children do not know their grandparents well or have much contact with any older persons. Indeed some research has found that children have negative attitudes toward the elderly and about being old.[14] Attempts to promote relationships between older persons and children should be encouraged. One example is the Foster Grandparents program in which low-income persons spend time with retarded or emotionally disturbed children. The Urban Gardening Program also has teamed the elderly with teenagers and children in schools and day care centers.

Several churches have created programs to provide some cross-generational contacts by creating artificial extended families. One woman who belonged to such a program in Hartford, Connecticut, started another one when she moved to New Jersey. Her entire Hartford "family" came to her New Jersey church and presented a service on extended families. She now belongs to a church-created extended family in Virginia. She spoke warmly of her families, especially of the opportunity it gave her children to play with children of different ages: "When I was little we went to the corner and played . . . [today it's] age structured [you only play with them] if they're in your school class." The ages in her first family ranged from one to eighty-six. The family experienced a wedding, a death, and an eighty-sixth birthday. In addition to couples with their children, there were older couples whose children had left home and single parents with their children. The group, which met regularly for a potluck supper, provided a variety of adult role models for the children, as well as continuing relationships with adults who were neither parents nor teachers.[15]

Participation in community activities can give residents a chance to form friendships, weak ties, and intimate secondary relations, which are partial substitutes for close-knit relationships. Several churches in Washington, D.C., run structured discussion groups followed by dancing for single people. Some sponsor support groups for widows or divorcees. These groups often serve as a source of information about community resources for participants. Finally, neighbor relationships, including intimate secondary relations, are important in establishing community norms and also in mobilizing residents to obtain needed services from city officials and private organizations to create neighborhoods suitable for children.

A few single parents are trying another approach to the problem of the double burden by sharing households. This eases problems of adult companionship, babysitting, household maintenance, and finances. In some cases, zoning prohibits such arrangements. Since the adults in a shared household are not related by blood or marriage, they do not conform to local legal definitions of family. In other cases, organizations have attempted even more complicated arrangements that combine housing and social services. So far such innovative approaches have received little support from public agencies or private foundations.

Alternate Housing for One-Parent Families

One attempt to provide coordinated services is Warren Village, Denver, Colorado, which provides alternate housing for one-parent families, mostly headed by women.[16] Women who are single parents often have a combination of difficulties that reinforce each other: low income, limited education, no job or a job that pays poorly and has no advancement opportunities, low self-esteem, limited ability to deal effectively with bureaucracies that provide services, and difficulty in personal relationships. Many emerge from a crisis such as death, divorce, or separation to find themselves single parents.

Warren Village is a nonprofit, nonsectarian organization that built and now operates an apartment building for ninety-one single-parent families with young children. The purpose is to create a setting in which single parents with young children can develop independence and self-sufficiency. The idea and initial organizational efforts came from members of the Warren Methodist Church. Some of the rents are subsidized by the U.S. Department of Housing and Urban Development. The board of trustees raises funds from churches, businesses, individuals, foundations, and civic groups to provide supportive services to the families. Warren Village has a staff of about thirty-five, some of whom are part-time employees who provide apartment management, child care, family services, and administration. During 1982, volunteers contributed between 600 to 900 hours of service each month.

The housing itself gives residents important security and access to resources. Decent, inexpensive housing not located in high crime areas is extremely difficult for a single parent to find. Warren Village is located in a downtown Denver neighborhood near a park, shopping, public transportation, colleges, employment, and various social service agencies. The Learning Center provides day care for preschool children and after-school and summer care for older ones.

Part of the purpose of Warren Village is to create a sense of community for residents, many of whom arrive in a state of emotional and financial crisis. It is assumed that residents can support each other by babysitting, trading special skills in cooking or typing, and offering emotional support during times of crisis. Women who have enrolled in school, learned how to interview for a job, know how to cook nourishing meals quickly, or settle arguments among their children serve as role models for new residents.

The founders of Warren Village were influenced by some of the approaches used by businesses in their management development efforts. Residents are expected to learn how to look at alternatives, how to see what information is needed, and how to find people who have information. All residents are expected to set goals for themselves that will help them become independent and self-sufficient. These goals may deal with social relationships, housekeeping, rearing their children, school, or employment. The expectation that each resident will establish personal six-month goals and work toward them is discussed during a lengthy interview at the time of application. A Family Services counselor works with each resident to help her obtain the resources to meet those goals and to reexamine the goals and perhaps set new ones every six months. This timetable is set not merely to assist the woman to achieve a specific goal but also to help her learn problem-solving techniques. The Family Services staff also arranges for various programs, provides referrals to other agencies, and offers informal counseling about the minor emergencies of daily life, which can become overwhelming to women who lack money, time, and skill in dealing with bureaucracies.

Many women who come to Warren Village are used to crisis as a way of life. Warren Village helps them to see that they do not have to live that way; they can learn to manage their own affairs. Some women initially might see the Family Services staff as often as every other day, then once a week for several months, and finally cease consultations altogether. Counseling is given on educational opportunities, filling out application forms and resumes, scheduling studying and child care, and handling questions in a job interview. Workshops and classes are arranged on such practical matters as tax preparation, child rearing, and dating. Some minor, but often crucial, tangible support is provided, such as emergency loans or use of a typewriter for resumes and class papers. Women who cannot afford a telephone can use the office telephone for job hunting or message referral.

Women try out new skills by serving on committees and task forces. One former resident realized that "I really do have the ability to carry a leadership role, to express my needs. I learned that I could have an effect, I could be in control of *something* even if it was only a bake sale."

Finally, support is also provided by other residents. Everyone is encouraged to learn how to create support systems for herself so that she will have them when she moves into a less supportive environment. Women are not expected to stay in Warren Village indefinitely; they are to use it as a place to learn how to care for themselves and their children successfully.

The program tries to serve women who are most in need of its services. Women who have clear personal goals and are already established in school or a good job will be referred to other housing. Women are not allowed to remain in residence once their oldest child becomes twelve years old because neither the physical building nor the services are designed for teenagers. Women are not allowed to permit another adult to live with them because a woman who has established such a relationship has some financial or emotional support and does not need Warren Village. One former resident said, "It's designed for you to grow out of it. It's sort of like living in a college dormitory. You [suddenly realize] you don't need all that support anymore."

In eight years of operation, Warren Village housed more than 650 families. The average length of family residency was eighteen months, suggesting that the women do not develop an undesirable dependence on the services.

The residents clearly like Warren Village; 60 percent of the new residents are referred by a current or past resident. Only 20 percent are referred by social service agencies.

An evaluation of the program was completed by Abt Associates in 1980. At that time the average resident was a female between twenty-seven and thirty years old who had one child living with her and had lived there for fifteen months. Slightly more than half of the residents were white, 38 percent were black, and 3 percent were of Hispanic origin. Few received alimony or child support.[17]

Most were high school graduates. Only 15 percent had not completed high school; only 1 percent had more than twelve years of education. About 36 percent were enrolled in educational programs, of whom only 20 percent had been enrolled at the time of application to Warren Village. Only one-third of the residents, many of whom had very young children, were neither enrolled in school nor employed.[18]

At the time of application, 47 percent were employed. The success of the program is evident in the results of a survey conducted by Abt consultants, which indicates that 94 percent of former residents were employed and that the number receiving Aid to Dependent Children had dropped from 61 percent to 6 percent.[19]

Over 60 percent of the respondents considered that their housing situation had improved by moving to Warren Village. Nearly two-thirds use the child care facility. Most considered this service an improvement over their previous child care service. Nevertheless, at that time, a number of residents could not use the service because their children were under one year old or were handicapped, because they needed night-time or weekend care, or because the facility lacked space for additional children.[20]

Most respondents indicated that they had more interactions with their fellow Warren Village residents than with neighbors near their previous place of residence. They did not, however, generally report feeling close to their neighbors.[21] This may not be too surprising considering Warren Village's transitory nature. Also, an important element of network systems is that intimacy is not a prerequisite for support. Since one of the purposes of Warren Village is to assist women to develop supportive networks so they can function without its special services, a more relevant measure of success than feelings of closeness with other residents may be the fact that over half of the residents who have left continue to maintain relationships with former residents.

Abt found participation by residents in community projects and resident advisory committees limited, probably because single parents enrolled in school or working have little free time. Committees were mostly composed of nonresident volunteers. Residents tended to become involved for a short time to resolve a specific problem and then to withdraw to concentrate on their own self-development.[22]

Most residents fulfill Warren Village's expectation of becoming sufficiently self-reliant to move elsewhere after an average stay of eighteen months. Often they move when they find a job, marry, or begin living with someone. In 1983 approximately six families had lived there for over four years but were not actively involved in self-development. Warren Village now requires goal setting as part of their lease and takes eviction actions against families when necessary.[23]

Warren Village is adding another building in Denver. The program is only one of a number of possible approaches, however. It is expensive. The capital costs of an apartment building are high, and rents, child care, and social services are all subsidized. Without these, Warren Village would be a concentration of families with potential problems. Since the current building is occupied by young mothers primarily with one young child, the community is a limited one. Children lack male role models, as well as the opportunity to see two-parent families. Nevertheless, it illustrates one model and the extent of community resources needed for success.

Conclusions

A number of areas are important when providing supportive environments for households with children in cities. The following questions may be useful to planners and community groups in assessing a neighborhood as an environment for children:

1. Are there pollutants dangerous to children: air pollution from traffic or factories, noise pollution from traffic or other sources, buildings with

peeling lead-based paint, vacant lots which are or have been used for dumping chemical wastes?
2. Does the environment enable children to play and travel alone safely and to learn about the adult world? Are there safe play areas for children under five within sight of home? Is heavy traffic routed away from homes or slowed down by traffic lights, signs, or bumps in the road? Are overpasses provided that enable children to cross areas of heavy traffic? Can they take bicycles across? Is there convenient public transportation safe for children to use? Are children safe from criminals and from bullying by gangs of other children? Do residents feel a responsibility to keep an eye on children in the area and protect them if necessary? Are there recognized places where children in trouble can go for help when their parents are not at home? Are police and storekeepers polite and friendly to neighborhood children? Is good day care available, including preschool, after-school, and summer programs? Can children walk to activities? Are there opportunities for them to observe the work world and learn skills and work attitudes through part-time employment? Are there opportunities for them to know older people?
3. Are the resources necessary for household maintenance available, convenient to use, and appropriate for tastes and incomes of residents? Can grocery and other regular shopping be accomplished quickly in the evenings and on Sunday, as well as during the daytime? Is child care available, including that needed for emergencies, for short-term periods, and by women who are employed on weekends or in the evenings? Is public transportation available to places of employment and services that are not available in the neighborhood?
4. Are there opportunities for childrens' parents to form varied social relationships that provide information and support? Is the community a close-knit one? Are there any public or private programs or processes that would destroy this? Is there a varied housing stock that permits people in different stages of family formation to live in the community? Are there apartments suitable for the elderly? Does zoning permit such residences? Are there a variety of organizational opportunities in which people can meet and form friendships, weak ties, or intimate secondary relationships?
5. Are there institutional means for parents to negotiate with institutions for services and facilities appropriate for their children? Does the area have an effective community organization that can negotiate with city and private institutions? Are there public places for holding community meetings, self-help activities, and operating programs? Do community newspapers, bulletin boards, or other means for exchanging information about community programs and activities exist? Are their mechanisms for community dispute settlement?

Some of these questions also are relevant for another population group likely to be at risk: the elderly, who are considered in the next chapter.

Notes

1. Paul C. Glick, "Marriage, Divorce and Living Arrangements, Prospective Changes," *Journal of Family Issues* 5, no. 1 (1984):24.
2. William Michelson and Ellis Roberts, "Children and the Urban Physical Environment," in *The Child in the City: Changes and Challenges,* ed. William Michelson et al. (Toronto: University of Toronto Press, 1979), pp. 430–431.
3. Ibid., pp. 432–433; U.S. Environmental Protection Agency Office of Noise Abatement and Control, *Noise: A Health Problem* (Washington, D.C.: Environmental Protection Agency, 1978).
4. U.S. Department of Health, Education and Welfare, *Healthy People: The Surgeon General's Report on Health Promotion and Disease Prevention* (Washington, D.C.: Government Printing Office, 1979).
5. Michelson and Roberts, "Children"; National Safety Council *Accident Facts, 1979 Edition* (Chicago: National Safety Council, 1979), p. 61; Anne-Marie Pollowy, *The Urban Nest* (Stroudsburg, Pa.: Dowden, Hutchinson and Ross, 1977), p. 97.
6. Magne Raundalen and Tora Synøve Raundalen, "Interviews with Four Thousand Norwegian Girls and Boys about Their Daily Life and the Future" (Paper presented at the International Congress on "The Child in the World of Tomorrow," Athens, Greece, July 1978), p. 12.
7. Arza Churchman, "Children in Urban Environments: The Israeli Experience" (Paper delivered at the MAB International Symposium on Managing Urban Space in the Interest of Children, Toronto, Canada, June 1979), p. 11; Central Mortgage and Housing Corporation, "Design Guidelines: Play Opportunities for School Age Children, 6 to 14 Years" (Ottowa, Canada: Central Mortgage and Housing Corporation, 1977).
8. Donald Appleyard with M. Sue Gerson and Mark Lintell, *Liveable Urban Streets: Managing Auto Traffic in Neighborhoods,* Final Report dot-fh-11-8026 (Washington, D.C.: Federal Highway Administration, 1976).
9. Central Mortgage, "Design Guidelines."
10. Randolph T. Hester, Jr., *Neighborhood Space* (Stroudsburg, Pa.: Dowden, Hutchinson and Ross, 1975), pp. 192–200.
11. Mary Jo Bane, *Here to Stay: American Families in the Twentieth Century* (New York: Basic Books, 1976), p. 80; Office of the U.S. Secretariat for the World Conference of the UN Decade for Women, 1980, *Report of the United States Delegation to the World Conference on the UN Decade*

for Women: Equality, Development and Peace (Washington, D.C.: Department of State, 1981), pp. 28–32.

12. Citizens Planning and Housing Association, *CPHA's Baltimore Neighborhood Self Help Handbook* (Baltimore, Md.: Citizens Planning and Housing Association, 1982), pp. 88, 93.

13. Peggy Wireman, "How Can a Home for the Elderly Be More Like a Home?" (Paper delivered at the Thirty-second Annual Scientific Meeting of the Gerontological Society, Washington, D.C., November 1979).

14. K. Ferock and C. Seefeldt, "As Children See Old Folks," *Today's Education* 66, no. 2 (1977):70–74.

15. Interview with Carolyn Grafton, November 4, 1982.

16. The material for this case illustration is based on interviews with the executive director, Charles Mowry, members of his staff, in April 1979, an evaluation of the program performed by Abt Associates, a reinterview of Charles Mowry in April 1983, and the Warren Village 1982–1983 Annual Plan.

17. Ruth H. Chapman, John F. Doucette, and Gini Egan-McKenna, *Warren Village Program Evaluation: Task Two Report* (Englewood, Colo.: Abt Associates, 1980), pp. 43–46.

18. Ibid., pp. 83–87.

19. "Warren Village: A Community for One-Parent Families," brochure (Denver, Colo.: Warren Village, n.d.).

20. Chapman, Doucette, and Egan-McKenna, *Warren Village,* pp. 62–68.

21. Ibid., pp. 88–92.

22. Ibid., pp. 69–78; interview with Mowry, 1983.

23. Interview with Mowry, 1983.

9 Community Supports for the Elderly

Physical Environment

Some of the physical changes that occur during the aging process make the elderly particularly susceptible to certain environmental conditions. Specific changes likely to occur include increased hearing and vision difficulties, decrease in flexibility and strength of limbs, and decreased ability to absorb oxygen. In addition, many elderly suffer chronic conditions or diseases that affect their reactions to their environment. Some of these factors make the elderly particularly susceptible to air pollution. Where there is excessive noise, elderly persons with hearing impairments may have difficulty catching the low tones of normal conversations. Twenty percent of the elderly have mobility problems. These, along with hearing and visual difficulties, especially reduction in night vision, make them particularly vulnerable to pedestrian accidents. In fact, the elderly suffer three times the rate of traffic fatalities of younger adults. Mobility problems also affect the elderly's ability to flee from dangers, including street crime, fires, and such natural disasters as flash floods.[1]

These physical factors must be considered in the location and design of homes or communities expected to have elderly residents, in development projects intended for them, and in modifications of existing communities where elderly reside. Community groups can attack particularly hazardous conditions. For instance, they can persuade city governments to make curbs barrier free and set traffic lights to provide enough time for slow-moving persons to walk across the street before the light changes.

The elderly need access to transportation. Many elderly, like other Americans, drive automobiles. Since reaction time slows with age, easy access onto and from busy traffic arteries is especially desirable for them. Well-lighted parking near homes open to surveillance by neighbors for crime protection is needed. But, as people age, they frequently stop or limit their driving because of physical impairments, inability to renew their license, and costs of gasoline and car maintenance. Many of today's elderly women never drove and lose mobility when their husbands die. Almost 50 percent of the central city elderly and almost 30 percent of suburban elderly lack access to a private car on a regular basis, including cars driven by a

Like millions of other widows, this 84-year-old woman lives alone in her own home. Like many others, she has a child living nearby, trusted neighbors, and old friends in her neighborhood. Yet she is concerned about possible illness and the chores of keeping up a large house.
Photo: Peggy Wireman

spouse or a friend. In fact, over 80 percent of central city renters over seventy-five years old do not have access to a private automobile.[2]

For many elderly, therefore, transportation means walking, taking buses, or using special transportation provided through community programs. Few use taxis because of expense. If the elderly are to walk safely, streets must have sidewalks free from cracks, uneven places, ice, snow, high curbs, dark unlit areas, excessive slopes, street crimes, and dangerous pedestrian crossings. Rest benches are helpful. Experts suggest that many elderly can use services within one-quarter of a mile walk.[3]

The services and facilities most crucial to elderly well-being obviously vary according to the individual. One work indicates that in four Los Angeles communities, thirty-two services accounted for two-thirds of the trips taken. Eighty-four percent of those trips were to only fifteen of the services.[4] Even if planners know how frequently different services are used, they still may not know the relative importance of each service to the user or the economic ability of users to support the desired service. For example, an individual may use the emergency services of a hospital only once in five years, yet the availability of that service presumably is considered more important than a club luncheon attended twice a month. The problem of determining sufficient economic demand for a service is difficult, but a reliable estimate is needed if the service is to be provided by the free market or even by agencies on a partially subsidized basis. Of the thirty-two services mentioned in the study, only one, shopping for food, was used by as many as 50 percent of the elderly in all four communities as often as once a week.[5]

The same problem of determining demand applies to recreation facilities. Experts do not know what facilities will be used by a particular elderly population. Although some reasonable projections can be made, the percentage likely to use any one type of specialized recreational facility is so low that planning or providing such facilities becomes difficult. If, for example, some of the elderly population can be expected to bowl, while others swim and still others square dance, what should be done? Is there any functional equivalency among the various types of facilities? That is, can the bowlers be persuaded to square dance if no bowling lanes are available, or will they simply stay home?

This discussion is relevant to community planning in several ways. First, it indicates the need to determine as exactly as possible the characteristics, tastes, needs, habits, and preferences of the elderly living or likely to live in the community. This includes the needs of those over age 75, sometimes referred to as the frail elderly. Second, it indicates the need to think creatively about alternatives. For example, almost everyone in a modern society needs to cash checks. This can be done by a bank, but in some cases it also can be accomplished at a grocery store. Third, there is a need to encourage people to use the services that are available and, if necessary, to provide special transportation to them.

Social Environment

The social environment of the elderly includes actual and perceived crime rate, racial or ethnic tensions, attitudes and behavior of children and teenagers toward the elderly, attitudes and behavior of commercial establishments and institutions toward them, amount of friendly recognition among residents, and the extent of their own relationships. Programs and community organization efforts that promote recognition of the elderly as a desired part of the community affect these factors. Programs that involve the elderly with people of different ages, such as the Urban Gardening Program, affect friendly recognition, as well as closer relationships. Older people who are involved in community projects that interest them will develop friendships, weak ties, and intimate secondary relationships from which they can gain emotional and practical support.

Many elderly currently live in close-knit communities where they own homes and have friends and relationships of many years standing. Their support systems are well established but are often threatened by factors beyond their control: general decline of the neighborhood as young prosperous families move to the suburbs, rising taxes, rising utility and maintenance costs, displacement of elderly renters or their friends from buildings being converted to condominiums, and rising rents due to general inflation and gentrification (purchase and rehabilitation of properties by middle-class families with a resulting rise in area taxes and prices). Well-established areas of central cities containing many elderly are also often selected as sites for major roads or urban development projects. Thus, governments concerned with support systems of elderly residents should adopt development policies that discourage the destruction of supports that already exist. They should also consider creative ways to provide additional supports and to modify existing supports to take into account the increased dependence of an aging population. For example, the towns of Beulah, Hazen, and Glenullin, North Dakota, used Department of Transportation funds to purchase fourteen-passenger vans with chair lifts in an attempt to help older citizens to be self-reliant. The county pays for the gasoline and maintenance, and volunteers drive the elderly to local events and to medical facilities and shopping eighty miles away.

Litwak has indicated that services for the elderly can be most appropriately provided by several different groups. Functions best performed by family are those that require intimate knowledge about the entire person and his or her long-term concerns. Litwak suggests that only family members who have an intimate concern with their relative's long-term welfare should handle an elderly person's finances.[6] Adult children are the most likely to be able to cater to their mother's special food desires or know how she wants to celebrate her birthday. Some services can be provided by mail, telephone, or purchase of hired assistance accountable to the family. On the other hand, only a nursing attendant or a neighbor will realize that the elderly person has not been seen all day and may be sick in bed. Neither family nor neighbors alone are equipped to provide twenty-four-hour care for a seriously ill person in need of constant monitoring with expensive equipment. Only an institution can perform that role. Institutions also are needed to perform tasks requiring high degrees of specialized training.

Questions for community planners are: what kinds of changes in community design, institutional regulations, or services will help to encourage family involvement with the elderly who are in institutions, permit the elderly to remain longer in their own homes and neighborhoods, assist families who are caring for an elderly person in their home, and assist the elderly to maintain contact with their family and community networks. A variety of programs and experiments currently are being attempted to permit the elderly to maintain themselves in their existing homes. The federal Senior Companion Program provides support services for elderly in their homes, as well as liaison and advocacy with community agencies. The low-income companions serve twenty hours a week, providing care and companionship to three or four clients. They receive a two dollar an hour stipend. After forty hours of preservice training, the companions are assigned to an organization that provides supervision and additional in-service training. In many cases, an individual care plan is developed to meet the needs of each client. As of September 1981, over 5,000 senior citizens were working in eighty different projects throughout the country.[7]

Other programs address the financial problems of maintaining a home on a fixed retirement or social security income during a period of rapid inflation, rising taxes, and increased utility costs. Some communities offer tax rebates to elderly property owners. Others provide subsidies for utilities. Some experiments are being conducted that would defer taxes until such time as a house is sold, possibly shifting the tax burden from the elderly person's current living expense to the children's inheritance taxes. Since repair of older structures can become a burden for the elderly, a number of communities have devised programs whereby community youth assist in repairs. Many localities used federal funds to hire unemployed youth to repair and weatherize homes of the elderly. Such projects provide training and job experience for the youth, practical benefits for the elderly, and improved community relationships between the two groups.

Another type of program is aimed at daily assistance in the home. Meals on Wheels uses volunteers to take prepared meals to the homes of the elderly. The volunteers provide a source of regular human contact and sometimes other services for house-bound elderly. Home nursing services offer care to the elderly during periods of temporary illness. Some communities have arranged for telephone reassurance programs. One senior citizen center director who helps confused elderly remain in their homes rather than be institutionalized described her relationship with one person as follows: "I call her on the phone every day, and remind her to cash her social security check, things like that." The woman might respond, "I'm okay, I did all my errands."[8] In some cases, the checkers are themselves elderly volunteers. This not only encourages contact among age peers but also gives the checkers a useful role.

Although many elderly do need assistance with daily tasks, most are self-sufficient and generally in good health. Many enjoy volunteer activities; others would volunteer more or take jobs if given the opportunity. One study of New Jersey older persons concluded that an estimated 44 percent of those aged sixty to eighty were potential volunteers or employees.[9] In addition to providing services, community groups can create opportunities for the elderly to volunteer. Often their participation is restricted for minor reasons: lack of transportation, lack of funds for expenses connected with volunteering such as lunches, supplies, and postage, and reluctance to travel at night, especially alone. Small payments for volunteer expenses, escort or transportation services, slight rearranging of the organization's normal work schedules, or matching the job to the capabilities of the volunteer could overcome these difficulties.

Communities can provide multipurpose senior centers, which offer a variety of supports, including transportation, legal aid, recreation, and meals. In 1982, group meals were provided at 13,000 places to 2.8 million elderly, with another 517,000 elderly receiving meals delivered to their homes.[10] These kinds of community services help the elderly remain independent.

A different aspect of support for independent living by the elderly is assistance to their families if they are living with them. Two types of problems exist and are expected to increase. First, the woman who in previous times might have provided extensive care for an elderly parent today is often employed full time outside the home. Many women with elderly parents are themselves divorced, widowed, or single and cannot quit work to provide extensive care for their parents without forgoing their own livelihood, including retirement benefits needed for their own old age.[11] Such women must add care of elderly parents to their present double jobs as workers and housewives. In addition, many are still providing financial and other support to their own children, even those who are young adults. The second problem is that with increased longevity, the caretakers themselves are older. The person available to care for an eighty-five-year-old mother may well be sixty-five years old and not capable of the strenuous physical work often involved.[12] Many women caring for the elderly are struggling with an almost impossible burden. Many do perform it, but with extreme difficulty and risk to their own health.

A number of programs are being developed to assist families involved in long-term elderly care. One of these is respite care—places where the family can leave the elderly person for a day or weekend and have a rest from the physical and emotional demands of twenty-four-hour-a-day care.[13] Another type of service is offered by a mental health outreach program in central Oklahoma, Project SENIOR (Serving Emotional Needs in Older Recipients). It operates a monthly discussion group designed to allow family members caring for elderly relatives to express their frustrations, learn more about normal changes to be expected with aging or with specific diseases, exchange ideas about how to cope, and offer emotional support to each other.[14]

The need for such support services for families was noted in a report on abuse of the elderly. Although accurate data are difficult to obtain, studies have identified serious problems of physical and psychological abuse, as well as negligence and financial exploitation. An estimated 4 percent of the elderly, generally elderly women living with relatives, are victims. The psychological strains on an individual and family caring for an elderly person can contribute to abuse problems. Interestingly, one study found that the type of assistance people said they needed in caring for their elderly changed if an elderly person was living with them. That is, those whose parents were living separately wanted money, but those whose parents were living in the same household wanted services.[15]

In addition to providing services, communities could encourage more visits between younger family members and the elderly, including those in nursing homes, by making facilities for visits convenient, safe, and pleasant. This would mean barrier-free hotels or homes, motels near neighborhoods with many elderly residents, places for grandchildren to stay, and something for them to do. Such contact is important. Grandchildren are not only a source of pride and enjoyment for the elderly but also promote feelings of self-worth.[16] A national study of recreation patterns showed that museums, aquariums, and carnivals were among those facilities used most frequently by persons over sixty-five.[17] This high rate of use may well have been because these are places to take visiting grandchildren. Children's play facilities near housing for the elderly might be desirable, as well as places in the housing to store grandchildren's toys and even a guest room where they could sleep.

A final way to maintain family relationships is to increase telephone use. Lower long-distance rates undoubtedly have enabled the elderly to keep in closer contact with kin. Any rise in rates will cause many to limit those contacts. In areas where there are high concentrations of elderly, it might be possible to develop some forms of shared low-cost rates, even video exchanges. One report suggests that advances in technology could provide better communication with distant relatives and also offer client-controlled access to bureaucratic services. That is, two-way computer-controlled cable television could join the home with a range of service providers on a face-to-face basis. The elderly person and his or her family could use the computer to locate and communicate with the proper services. The service provider would have computer access to information about the patient, such as medication currently being taken, and would discuss appropriate action with client and family. Access to such a system would also enable the family of an elderly person to act as an advocate in dealings with the bureaucracy.[18]

Thus, a variety of measures exist that could be taken by national and local officials, private agencies, community organizations, families, and the elderly themselves to help older persons remain an integral part of their social networks and families as long as possible. Strict single-family residential zoning can prohibit a number of potentially creative approaches. If present trends continue over the next twenty years, millions of suburban homes could be inhabited by single, older females whose husbands have died.[19] As these women age, the costs and work needed in home maintenance will become increasingly difficult. Perhaps, however, they could manage by renting a room to a student in exchange for household maintenance and errands. Shared living could also be considered.

Case Studies

Mutual Help Program: Benton, Illinois

Benton, Illinois, is a town of approximately 7,000 persons of whom almost 30 percent were elderly in the mid-1970s.[20] The town's economic base is primarily coal mining, with some jobs in business, education, and county government. Many of its younger people are leaving.

Phyllis Ehrlich, a social worker with a community organization orientation, chose Benton as a site for a demonstration project funded by the Administration on Aging. She had noted that many elderly face loss of their social roles when they retire or a spouse dies. Few communities have organized means of assisting them, and often any assistance provided by social agencies creates dependency rather than developing the elderly's own resources. Ehrlich developed a mutual help model, which relied heavily on the theoretical model of Litwak. The model was designed to provide new roles for the elderly and to strengthen their capacities to help themselves and each other.

Ehrlich established the project over a period of months through a methodical and sensitive community development approach designed to gain entry and cooperation. She visited the mayor and was introduced by him to a councilwoman, who arranged for a meeting with a number of the elderly in the area. She talked to the clergy and community agencies. She relied on the advice of local people as she began establishing her project and, except for a researcher, hired only local people.

The staff consisted of a director and twelve half-time community workers who were residents with a history of community involvement. Neither prior training nor education was a selection requirement, and workers represented a cross-section of ages. Workers were given a two-week orientation program, regular supervision, and ongoing in-service training. Since part of the aim of the project was to affect the service delivery of the formal agencies, agencies providing services for the elderly were invited to join the orientation. Community members, including clergy and nursing home

Community Supports for the Elderly

workers, were also included. After the orientation, workers functioned as community organizers, case workers, and case managers, coordinating assistance from formal and informal sources. Over time they encouraged the elderly themselves to use these sources to solve problems.

The project organized small groups of approximately thirty elderly residents in ten neighborhoods. Members of these groups were encouraged to identify their own needs, assist each other in a number of traditionally neighborly ways, and/or request additional services from agencies responsible for elderly services. The groups met weekly or biweekly for such activities as socializing, discussion of what was happening in the neighborhood, educational programs, potlucks, or playing games. The worker brought news about problems they had learned about while talking to other people in the neighborhood. By identifying problems and encouraging neighbors to help each other and homebound residents, the community worker served as a catalyst for the elderly to expand their neighborly role. These informal peer groups called homebound neighbors on a regular basis, assisted neighbors with chores or transportation, shared garden produce and meals, visited the sick, and gave surprise birthday parties. The homebound assisted group efforts by serving as a telephone committee.

The neighborhood groups also undertook more ambitious projects for the entire community—sponsoring a fall picnic and shopping trips, developing a senior chorus and a bowling program, obtaining information on fuel rebates and weatherization eligibility, and organizing a health screening-blood pressure program. Retired nurses performed the health screening, thus giving them an opportunity to perform their professional role again. Blood pressure checks were held once a month. Some neighbors who did not otherwise participate in the groups would attend for this purpose only, thus giving them a chance to meet their neighbors.

The neighborhood groups also identified problems of neighbors that could be appropriately referred to existing services of agencies and asked agencies to provide additional services. Their most successful effort was obtaining a nutrition center.

The formation of the neighborhood groups and their gradual assumption of neighborly support actions was not a spontaneous activity. It resulted from a carefully designed, deliberate intervention in neighborhood life using substantial staff assistance, based on a theoretical model. The approach stressed the importance of building informal support networks among neighbors that enabled them to assist each other rather than depend on agencies. This mutual peer support was considered important by the program's designers partly because it provided assistance to some needy elderly but even more because it created role opportunities for the helper. Initially the elderly saw the program as a traditional social program where a professional helper provided assistance to someone who needed help. They did not see that someone who needed help was also capable of providing help to themselves and others. At first participants relied on staff to solve problems or call an agency. The workers gradually and deliberately encouraged people to take more responsibility for solving their own problems and for helping their neighbors to solve theirs.

The project results were assessed in several ways. The community in which the project was operated was matched with a nearby town with similar demographic characteristics. Interviews were held with elderly in both communities before the project began and after the project had been in operation eighteen months. The interviews indicated that participants in the project made more friends and visited people more frequently than did elderly in the same community who did not participate or the elderly in the control community. The participants had more informal relationships, more contacts with institutions, played more of a role in the community, and maintained a higher morale than did the elderly nonparticipants or elderly in the control community.

The program's effectiveness was also measured by asking the children of the participants about the effect of the program on their parents and on family members. Ehrlich notes that caution in interpretation is necessary because of the low number of respondents (thirty-six). The responses, however, were highly favorable, with 78 percent indicating that the program had had psychological and social benefits for their parent and with 90 percent indicating that they themselves had benefited. Presumably the program had relieved them of some of the sense of responsibility and concern about their parent.

The program model was developed not only to increase the ability of the elderly to support themselves and their neighbors but also to enable them to obtain better services from formal organizations. At the beginning of the study, the project interviewed representatives of forty-four organizations with programs or services relevant to the elderly to determine the services offered, numbers served, criteria for eligibility, outreach efforts, home visits, costs, and opinions about needed services. After eighteen months of project operation, 50 percent of the agencies indicated that they had increased their outreach services, 22 percent claimed that they made more home visits, and 83 percent said their services to the elderly had improved. They did not perceive the project as unwelcome competition but rather as complementary to existing services.

The project was successful in providing support for the elderly living in a variety of household arrangements. Some of those participating were married couples, others were widows living alone, and still others lived with their children. Some of the groups even provided assistance to group members who moved to institutions during the time of the project.

The study did not examine the precise types of network relationships discussed previously in this book. It did, however, indicate that participants made new friends and visited friends more. Community development occurred in three ways: new community groups were formed, many elderly persons became leaders for a number of activities, and agency staffs reported that their understanding of the elderly and their needs had increased. Thus the project illustrates how network formation and community development can be used to provide additional support to an at-risk population, to strengthen community institutions, and to improve links between the neighborhood and outside groups.

Shared Housing: Washington, D.C.

Shared housing is a way for nonrelatives to live together, cutting housing costs and increasing social contacts.[21] In 1983 it was being tried in 274 programs around the country.[22] In recent years Washington, D.C., has undergone one of the highest rates of real estate price escalation in the nation. Several large areas have been undergoing gentrification as young professionals buy older homes and rehabilitate them. The disappearance of these homes from the rental market, the ability of single professionals to pay high rents for group housing, and real estate speculation have made low-income rental units increasingly rare. As in other communities, many elderly live on fixed incomes in a time of inflation.

The sponsoring organization for this project was the nonprofit Richmond Fellowship of Metropolitan Washington, which operates community homes for psychiatric patients and group homes for adolescents in a number of cities. Several fellowship members concerned about the problems of single elderly with low incomes decided to develop a model of group housing for senior citizens. They obtained a small grant to hire a staff person.

Even before the grant was approved, the sponsors had invited over one hundred individuals and agencies to a meeting to consider the idea. The goals were to provide autonomy as well as increased financial and physical security to participants through the use of existing housing. The fellowship undertook to rent a home, which they would then sublet to a number of adults. The living arrangements were expected to be semipermanent, but the model was not designed to care for people who became seriously ill or handicapped.

The first resident of the shared home was a seventy-year-old woman who attended that meeting. She lived in public housing but was lonely and depressed. The second resident was a retired man being evicted because his apartment was being turned into a condominium. Joining them were a woman over ninety, a woman in her late seventies whose arthritis made mobility difficult, and a woman in her late fifties who recently had become single. The age range of the group spanned over thirty years, which, along with other differences, created some problems. Staff worked with the members to help them function as a group. Although there has been some turnover of members, the group continues in the shared home. It is, indeed, just that. Birthdays and other holidays are celebrated and members provide caring support for each other. This does not mean, however, that they have lost all their autonomy. One man commented that he liked the companionship and having people around who cared about him, but he also liked the fact that they did not make too many demands. In 1982 the house had continued for over eight years.

David Harre, one of the founders, has published a manual that points out the importance of the role of a credible sponsor. The establishment of the shared housing involved locating a suitable house, recruiting potential participants, assisting them in making a decision about moving in, and helping the occupants to function as a congenial group. In each of these steps, the existence of an established sponsoring organization with respected reputation was important.

Staff needed to locate a house large enough for five or six persons in a location relatively free from crime with adequate transportation and services. Because of housing prices in Washington, D.C., the rentals for such property precluded persons of very low income from participating in the program even though their rent would be subsidized. In addition to finding a suitably priced unit, any such program faces the problem of timing; that is, the unit may be available before a group of residents is committed to move in or a group might be ready at a time when no suitable house can be found. Once the house is leased, the sponsoring organization must pay the full rent even if the group has not recruited all potential residents.

The existence of a respected sponsoring organization was an asset not only in negotiating with realtors and landlords but also in recruitment. Staff and volunteers spoke at church groups, senior citizens' centers, and other organizations that had contact with the elderly.

Once an individual expressed an interest in the program, it might be months before she or he was able to make a decision about participating. Although taking in boarders was a common practice during the nineteenth century, the idea of sharing a home with someone other than family is outside the life experience of many—although by no means all—of the present elderly population.[23] They need time to think through all of the implications. Many are lonely and need the financial benefits that would result. Nevertheless, they lose privacy and some autonomy in a society that places high premiums on both. The program found, for example, that no one who could afford housing of their own with a private bathroom was willing to share a bathroom even if they wanted the companionship, increase in security, and financial benefits.

Staff found that in making the decision, it was helpful for the elderly to see the actual house and actual or potential participants. In cases where the shared home was already established, the potential newcomer would spend a weekend or so there. Staff also assists the potential housemates to work through decisions about who should have which bedroom and how much personal furniture could be placed in the common rooms. After participants move into a house, staff continues to meet with them at a weekly session for scheduling chores of housekeeping and cooking and resolving problems. These sessions are not therapy sessions but assistance in the exercise of group decision making.

Such homes offer an alternative to living alone in an apartment, remaining in a large home after expenses and maintenance have become burdensome, moving into the home of a relative, or going to a nursing home. The extent to which such homes can operate in many cases depends on such factors as zoning laws and whether federal assistance payments are reduced if the person shares a house.[24]

Notes

1. Peggy Wireman and Antoinette Sebastian, "Important Considerations for Environmental Assessments of Housing Sites for the Elderly," in *Housing an Aging Society,* ed. Robert J. Newcomer, M. Powell Lawton, and Thomas O. Byerts (New York: Van Nostrand Reinhold, forthcoming); U.S. Department of Health, Education and Welfare, *Healthy People: The Surgeon General's Report on Health Promotion and Disease Prevention* (Washington, D.C.: Department of Health, Education and Welfare, 1979); U.S. Environmental Protection Agency, Office of Noise Abatement and Control, *Noise: A Health Problem* (Washington, D.C.: Environmental Protection Agency, 1978); Marjorie Bloomberg Tiven, *Older Americans: Special Handling Required* (Washington, D.C.: National Committee on the Aging, 1971); William Haddon, Jr., and Susan P. Baker, "Injury Control," in *Preventive Medicine,* 2d ed. ed. Duncan Clark and Brian MacMahon (Boston: Little, Brown, 1981), pp. 109-140.

2. M. Gutowski and T. Feild, *The Graying of Suburbia* (Washington, D.C.: Urban Institute, 1979).

3. M. Powell Lawton and Thomas O. Byerts, ed., *Community Planning for the Elderly,* (Washington, D.C.: Gerontological Society, 1973), p. 31.

4. Victor A. Regnier, E. Murakami, and S. Gordon, "The Relationship of Goods and Services Retrieval Patterns to the Perceived Neighborhood Context of Four Los Angeles Communities" (Paper presented at the Seventh National Transportation Conference of Elderly-Handicapped, Orlando, Florida, 1979), pp. 14, 16.

5. Ibid.

6. Eugene Litwak and Stephen Kulis, "Changes in Helping Networks with Changes in Health of Older People," in *Evaluating the Welfare State: Social and Political Perspectives,* ed. Shimon E. Spiro and Ephraim Yuchtman-Yaar (New York: Academic Press, 1983); Eugene Litwak, "The Modified Extended Family, Social Networks, and Research Continuities in Aging," in *Proceedings of Seminars 1976-80,* ed. George L. Maddox and Elizabeth Aulds (Durham, N.C.: Center for the Study of Aging and Human Development, Duke University Medical Center, 1981).

7. Elinor Bowles, "Older Persons as Providers of Services: Three Federal Programs," *Social Policy* 7 (1976):81-88; Margaret Pearson conversation with Emily Osmon, program specialist, Senior Companion Program, April 1983.

8. Dwight Frankfather, *The Aged in the Community: Managing Senility and Deviance* (New York: Praeger, 1977), p. 40.

9. George Dannenberg, Gerald Gioglio, and Elizabeth Fuccello, "The Utilization of the Elderly in Child Welfare Services" (Paper presented at the Thirty-second Annual Scientific Meeting of the Gerontological Society, Washington, D.C., November 1979), p. 12.

10. Interview with Eleanor Sneed, program analyst, Administration on Aging, U.S. Department of Health and Human Services, January 1984.

11. Elaine M. Brody, "Women's Changing Roles, and Care of the Aging Family," in *Aging: Agenda for the Eighties* (Washington, D.C.: Government Research Corporation, 1979), pp. 11-16.

12. Ibid.

13. National Retired Teachers Association, American Association of Retired Persons and Wakefield Washington Associates, "Family Support Systems and the Aging: A Policy Report" (Paper prepared for White House Conference on Families, n.d.), p. 9.

14. Jacqueline B. Cook, "Caring for the Caretakers: Elders' Family Circle" (Paper presented at a conference "The American Dream—Assessing the Status of Older America," National Council on the Aging, Washington, D.C., April 1, 1982).

15. Ann Langley, "Abuse of the Elderly," *Project Share Human Services Monograph Series* 27 (Rockville, Md.: Department of Health and Human Services, 1981); National Retired Teachers Association, "Family Support," p. 8.

16. Helena Znaniecka Lopata, *Women as Widows: Support Systems* (New York: Elsevier, 1979).

17. Heritage Conservation and Recreation Service, *The Third Nationwide Outdoor Recreation Plan: Appendix II, Survey Technical Report 3* (Washington, D.C.: Department of the Interior, 1979).

18. Dean K. Black and Vern L. Bengtson, "Implications of Telecom-

munications Technology for Old People, Families, and Bureaucracies," in *Family Bureaucracy and the Elderly,* ed. Ethel Shanas and Marvin B. Sussman (Durham, N.C.: Duke University Press, 1977), pp. 174–195.

19. Sylvia Fava, "Women's Place in Suburbia" (Paper presented at the Seventy-third Annual Meeting of the American Sociological Association, San Francisco, September 1978).

20. The material that follows was based on Phyllis Ehrlich, *Mutual Help for Community Elderly: Mutual Help Model,* vol. 1: *Final Report,* and vol. 2: *Handbook for Developing a Neighborhood Group Program* (Carbondale: Southern Illinois University, 1979). Additional material from author interviews with Ehrlich, April 1982, and telephone conversations and correspondence in 1983.

21. The following material is based on David S. Harre, *Shared Housing for Older People: A New Approach: History and Lessons Learned* (Washington, D.C.: Richmond Fellowship, 1980). Additional material from my interview with Harre, March 1982.

22. *National Directory of Shared Housing Programs for Older People* (Philadelphia: Shared Housing Resource Center, 1983).

23. For information on the extent and variety of sharing, see Tamara K. Hareven, "The Family as Process: The Historical Study of the Family Cycle," *Journal of Social History* 7 (Spring 1974):322–329; Carol A. Schreter, "Room for Rent: Shared Housing with Non-Related Older Americans" (Ph.D. diss., Bryn Mawr College, 1983), p. 120.

24. Lloyd Turner, with Carol Schreter, Bonnie Zetick, Glen Weisbrod, and Henry Pollakowski, *Housing Options for the Community Resident Elderly* (Washington, D.C.: Department of Health and Human Services, Office of Human Development Services, 1982).

10 Conclusions

Policymakers, planners, and citizens must recognize that many common beliefs about the American family and neighborhood are myths in order to make realistic decisions about community programs. Those who realize that there is no typical American family, support system, or neighborhood free themselves to look carefully at the particular community or population being considered before developing programs.

Policymakers, therefore, should start by determining the household composition of any area potentially affected by their decisions. They should ask a series of questions: What will be the effect of the proposed action on extended families, including those members who are not part of the household? On nuclear families? On single-parent and single-person households? How will the proposed action affect the ability of the elderly to live independently? How will it affect the ability of children to move around in the neighborhood without adult supervision? How will it affect the availability of such supervision? How will it affect the ease of household maintenance?

Just as the idea of the typical American family and the typical American community may be useless myths, so the idea that all productive neighborhood relations must develop into friendships may be potentially limiting. The functions fulfilled by good neighbors are quite different from those fulfilled by good friends, although in some cases individuals may play both roles. In addition, the relations that develop among those involved in neighborhood organizations may instead approximate intimate secondary relationships. Policymakers need to ask whether programs encourage a range of productive relationships among residents.

How will the proposed actions affect the ability of informal groups to get together, initially and later? Will it help neighborhood organizations to support themselves financially? Will it help them to find out about proposed government and private policies or programs and to influence them? How will the proposed action affect local self-help efforts, neighborhood-based programs, and informal support groups? What will be the effect on the patterns of information exchange within the neighborhood and between the neighborhood and other areas? How will the proposed action affect racial and/or ethnic relations in the area? How will it affect relationships among those of different ages, incomes, or life-styles?

Although there are some general policies that make sense in most situations, the most productive plans will be tailor-made and based on an objective analysis of the particular population group and the dynamics of the particular community and its organizations and institutions. Attention needs to be paid to how actions affect those organizations and the neighborhood's ability to deal with the outside world. A definition of neighborhood effectiveness must include its ability to provide residents with links to non-neighborhood institutions and to attract resources from government and private sources.

An important directive for policymakers arises out of the discussion in this book. Steps need to be taken to ensure that informal support systems and neighborhood institutions are not overburdened. These systems are vital to the American social fabric and well-being, but they are not the only parts of that fabric. Informal support systems do not have the power or resources to handle many of the basic problems of individuals, families, and neighborhoods, which are caused by national, and even international, economic, political, and social forces. It is naive, if not callous, to expect informal systems to alleviate or solve problems caused by the adverse effects of these forces. Tasks demanding large amounts of technical expertise and funding cannot be performed by small, underfinanced groups. The history of voluntary programs since the days of the settlement houses in the late nineteenth century is the history of the transfer of successful projects performed by voluntary groups to government auspices as the only means of expanding coverage to the extent necessary to serve the population for whom the service was initiated. It is not realistic to expect people to handle major consequences of societal forces in their spare time with funds raised from bake sales or even by more sophisticated methods. This is why, historically, efforts to alleviate spinoff effects of modern industrial and postindustrial life have led concerned groups rapidly to social reform attempts in addition to ameliorative services.[1]

In terms of the themes of this book, what are some changes that could lessen the burdens on the informal and neighborhood support systems? First, more men could support their children. Many men, regardless of their incomes, do not agree to contributing to the support of their children, or do not make payments they have agreed to. In 1981, 40 percent of the women with children whose father was absent did not have an agreement from the father to make payments. Less than half of the women who had agreements, including court orders, received the full payments promised, and 28 percent of them did not receive any payments. Such nonpayment contributes to the fact that about half of the nation's 13 million poor children live in female-headed households.[2] A variety of proposals have been suggested for changing the situation. They include more equitable legal settlements, payment of child support to the court, use of federal resources to track men who avoid payment by fleeing to another state, stricter wage garnishing procedures, automatic withholding of child care payments from wages, and arrangements requiring fathers to post a bond or purchase insurance guaranteeing payments.[3] Social security, pensions, retirement provisions, and health care policies need to be examined to see how they together affect the likelihood of creating a population of older persons who do not have enough money to support themselves. To force persons to retire at sixty-five is often to force them into poverty. Those who are unable to purchase nourishing food and medical care reduce their own strength and hence their ability to care for themselves. Given the projected size of our elderly population and the state of medical technology, it may make sense to shift resources and research from dramatic, expensive organ transplants to questions of chronic and debilitating illness. Our policies permit expenditure of funds to maintain the life of elderly persons in a coma despite the expense but not the payments for special foods and household assistance needed to maintain their health in their own homes.

While efforts to strengthen and build on informal networks in neighborhoods are supportive of the philosophy underlying this book, caution is needed. First, careful analysis must be done to divide responsibilities appropriately among agencies and informal groups and organizations. Release of mental patients from hospitals over the past decade without adequate preparation or programs, for example, has overburdened many neighborhoods. Second, in a computer society, questions of privacy will become increasingly complex and important. Many people left small towns because they did not like their neighbors knowing all their business. What happens when knowledge about residents, which is an accepted part of informal systems, is also available to an agency with computerized files? Who should be allowed access to data on alcoholism or the limitations of a retarded child? Who checks this information for accuracy? Can it be passed to other agencies? Does anyone have to check with the individuals involved? Can it be sold to politicians, researchers, or advertising agencies? What happens to trust in a neighborhood if information shared in one context is passed to another, even for the best of helpful reasons?

Finally, the question of co-option must be carefully considered. Informal networks that become outreach systems for agencies can easily lose their independence and ability to counter that agency's policies when necessary. Many neighborhood organizations that undertook the operation of programs sponsored by the federal government found themselves overwhelmed by paperwork, requirements that did not fit their situation, and by financial incentives to operate programs that did not necessarily match neighborhood priorities. Some became more concerned with management efficiency than encouraging the growth of volunteers trying new tasks. Many nevertheless used the progams to increase their operations and their expertise and ability to serve their neighborhoods. Some bargained for arrangements that gave them considerable autonomy. Sometimes groups protected themselves by diversifying their activities and funding sources so the loss of one contract did not destroy the neighborhood organization. Some, however, decided that the possibility of being co-opted was too great and did not participate. Thus, any efforts to involve neighborhood groups should be structured in a manner that does not divert them from neighborhood priorities or subvert their community organizing and advocacy potential. Representatives of neighborhood organizations should be consulted whenever plans are being developed that have the potential for overburdening these systems.

Numerous actions can be taken to strengthen families, networks, and neighborhoods. For example, the strength of neighborhood organizations is always affected by government and foundation policies toward the nonprofit and voluntary sector of the society. These include subsidized postal rates, provision of free or subsidized space for activities in public buildings, the availability of government or foundation funds especially for basic overhead costs, the availability of free or cheap government publications that explain the laws and regulations in clear, simple English and in other languages, and requirements that voluntary groups must be consulted by local governments or those operating governmental programs. If neighborhood and other voluntary organizations must expend all of their time in struggling for organizational maintenance—fighting increases in postal rates for nonprofit groups, for example—they will not perform those services for residents and society that they are eminently qualified to provide.

Policymakers must consider how to support a variety of volunteer efforts without eliminating their spontaneity, autonomy, or ability to experiment. Related to this is the need to document formally and to acknowledge the value of the spinoff benefits of increased community confidence brought about by citizen community development: increased home owner investments and reduced rates of neighborhood conflict, mental stress, crime, and institutionalization of the elderly.

The chapter dealing with the elderly described a successful example of building informal neighborhood networks to support elderly residents. Naparstek, Biegel and Spiro describe projects in several working-class ethnic neighborhoods designed to provide links between those residents naturally sought out by neighbors for help to professional mental health resources. These projects were designed to strengthen existing community networks and institutions, and they were successful in creating supportive informal networks, developing local leadership, and creating more responsiveness from existing service agencies. Each, however, required a slow, careful development process over several years by skilled organizers. These examples were funded as demonstration projects.[4] The problem is how to pay for such efforts in hundreds of thousands of communities across the nation.

Conclusions

Even when external funding is available, its timing and dependability can be a problem for programs. In the Urban Gardening Program, for example, uncertainty about funding and funding levels affects the coordinators' abilities to provide continuity of staff, careful recruitment, and timely training of new staff and volunteers. Nature controls the time when gardens must be planted; even a few weeks' delay in obtaining funds and starting spring activities can create serious program problems. Since community development is a process, maintenance of continuity becomes a problem if there is excessive staff turnover. Because staff must plan their own budgets and careers, funding uncertainty hurts morale and stability.

In addition to taking direct actions to support neighborhood groups and informal activities, policymakers need to pay more systematic attention to the question of how to develop mechanisms that encourage coproduction. What is the best way to purchase public goods in a society that believes in individual choice through the private market? Although community associations have limitations and problems, they may provide some alternatives. Associations that can enforce behavior and can command individual payment of fees do provide some assurance to residents that others will do their part in property maintenance and hence that their own efforts will not be in vain. In order for neighborhood organizations to play a similar role, they need formal recognition and cooperation from local government and a reliable source of funds.

On a broader scale, recent attempts at public-private partnerships have similar possibilities. First, they may increase recognition by the private sector that their actions may have spillover effects on families and neighborhoods. Corporate policies on flexible hours and part-time work affect employment possibilities for mothers. Consultation with the affected neighborhood can ease its adjustment to the relocation or enlargement of a branch store.

Second, the private sector has significant resources—not only money but also management and other expertise, as well as access to data and credit often lacked by informal groups. Here again, however, the potential problem of co-option does exist. Also, the very bottom line analysis that can help a group in task accomplishment can also destroy the informal, emotionally supportive atmosphere that initially made it a growth experience for the participants.

Another potential problem of private sector involvement is that policymakers may assume it can eliminate the need for public funds. One analysis of private sector involvement with neighborhood preservation efforts concluded that while such partnerships are "important and valuable . . . they are not a substitute for sustained and adequate public commitment."[6]

The true costs to society of private sector contributions must be calculated. One oil company employee participating in a group concerned with the elderly and energy said clearly that the extent to which she could participate depended on the extent to which she could prove it benefited her company. If participating companies join public-private ventures solely to increase their profits or their public image, the activities they can undertake will be limited. The private sector traditionally has been reluctant to lend considerable support to controversial activities dealing with basic inequities in society such as the civil rights or women's movements. Finally, contributions made as tax write-offs indirectly reduce the amount of funds available through the government to solve social problems. This raises serious questions about whether elected government officials or private companies should determine which activities of neighborhoods and which problems of families deserve taxpayer support.

Another question to be considered is what is the best use of corporate resources for societal purposes. Would it be better, for instance, for a company to contribute funds to a local group providing social services to the elderly or to restructure its pension plans so that the wives of employees receive some benefits even if their husbands divorce them?

New thinking also is needed about the spillover effects of business decisions based solely on profit-making factors. What, for instance, is the effect on a neighborhood when its only grocery store is closed because higher profits can be made in more affluent areas? Thus, the whole area of involvement of the private sector in solving societal problems is both an opportunity and a challenge. New forms of participation and partnership are called for.

The need for new conceptualization about possible roles of the private sector leads back to my major theme: the need to rethink concepts about family and community. The concept of family needs to be broadened to include a variety of household types and those kin who provide support to its members. The concept of neighborhood must include not only the neighborhood's resources and relationships but also its ability to draw on external relationships and resources. Within a neighborhood, various forms of relationships from nodding recognition to intimate secondary relationships need to be recognized as valid. Varied informal and voluntary groups should be recognized, supported, and explicitly valued. Governments need to recognize the value of neighborhood organizations, support them, involve them in decision making, and foster coproductive activities. The value of less-than-perfect integration needs stating and affirming. These are part of the current American search for new forms and meanings of family, supportive networks, and community.

Notes

1. Jane Addams, *Twenty Years at Hull House* (New York: Macmillan, 1910); Allen Freeman David, "Spearheads for Reform—The Social Settle-

ments and the Progressive Movement, 1890-1914" (Ph.D. diss., University of Wisconsin, 1959); Clarke Chambers, *Seedtime of Reform: American Social Service and Social Action, 1918-1933* (Westport, Conn.: Greenwood, 1980); Arthur Schlesinger, *Age of Roosevelt: The Crisis of the Old Order* (Boston: Houghton Mifflin, 1957), vol. 1.

2. U.S. Department of Commerce, Bureau of the Census, Current Population Reports, Series P-60, no. 140, *Money, Income and Poverty Status of Families and Persons in the United States: 1982* (Washington, D.C.: Government Printing Office, 1983), table 15, and its Current Population Reports, Series P-23, no. 124, *Child Support and Alimony: 1981* (Washington, D.C.: Government Printing Office, 1983), table 1.

3. Conversation with Paul Smith, director of research, Children's Defense Fund, April 1983; also see Senate Finance Committee hearings on Federal Child Support Enforcement Program.

4. Phyllis Ehrlich, *Mutual Help for Community Elderly: Mutual Help Model,* vol. 1: *Final Report* (Carbondale: Southern Illinois University, 1979); Arthur J. Naparstek, David E. Biegel, and Herzl R. Spiro, *Neighborhood Networks for Humane Mental Health Care* (New York: Plenum Press, 1982).

6. Rachel G. Bratt, Janet M. Byrel, and Robert M. Hollister, *The Private Sector and Neighborhood Preservation* (Cambridge, Mass.: Neighborhood Policy Research, 1983), p. 102.

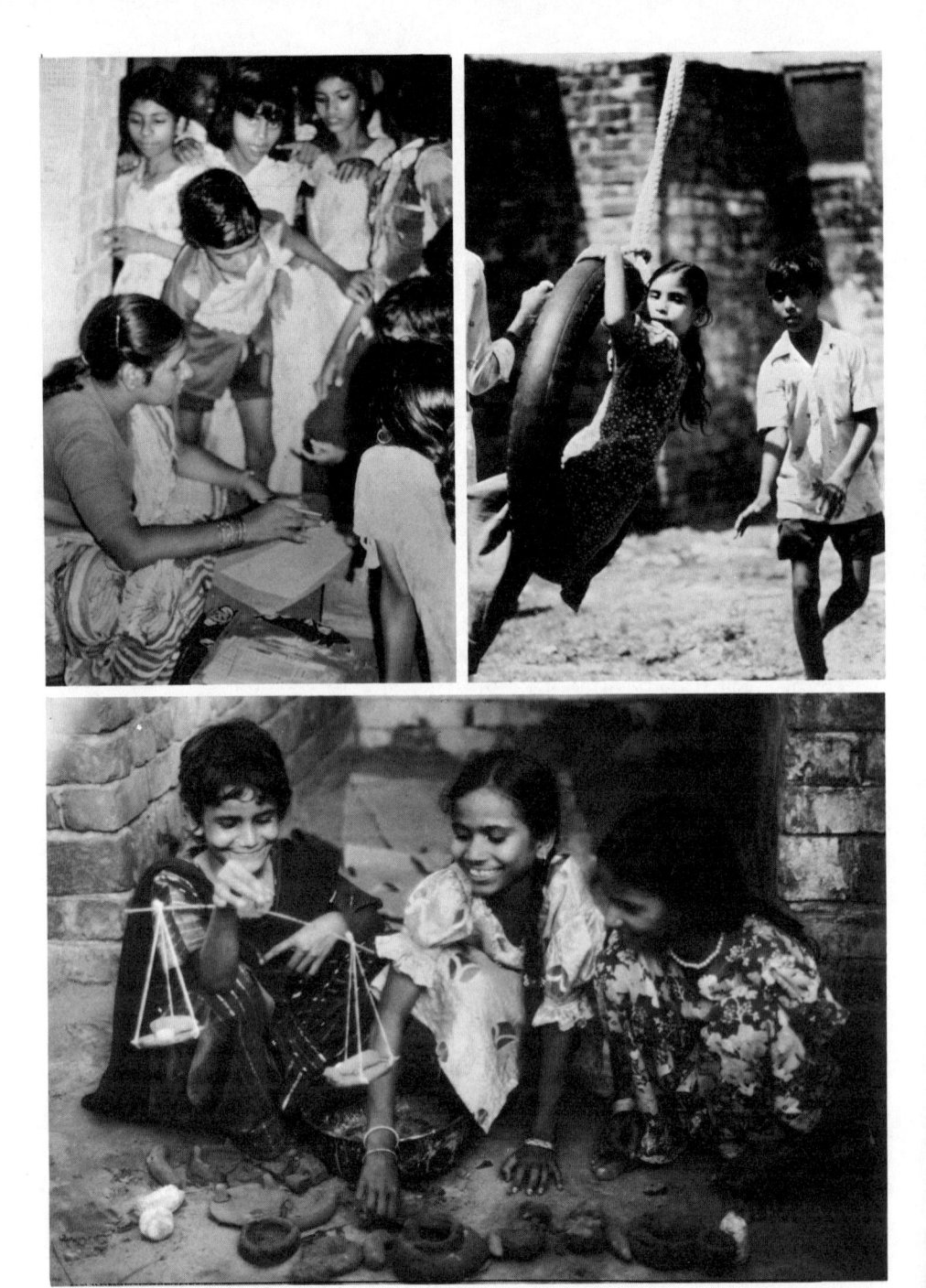

The author helped teachers and children design and build a simple playground in Ahmedabad, India.
Photos: Peggy Wireman

11 Postscript: Relevance of the American Experience for Other Countries

Too frequently American models are implicitly used by other nations in making policy decisions, especially in Third World development. Students, overseas policymakers, and Americans advising them who have read this book will realize that there is no one model of American family or community but a complex variety. It would be inappropriate to assume that support systems developed for the American situation can be simplistically imposed successfully elsewhere. Nevertheless, my observations while touring Asia for almost six months in 1981 indicated that other countries, both highly industrialized and developing, are struggling with some of the same questions of changes in traditional support systems. This chapter presents some of my observations, supplemented by data from scholarly works.[1] Together, these findings indicate that many of the questions raised in this book and some of the approaches to sustaining support systems may have relevance abroad.

Shifts in family composition are taking place throughout the world and, as in the United States, this can result in gaps in support systems. Changes include a shift from a three-generation to a nuclear family structure, shifts in other kin relations, and an increase in single-parent families. All have implications for child rearing and care of the elderly.

Changes in birthrate and life expectancy, which often accompany industrialization, may greatly alter traditional family living patterns. The Japanese bride who historically moved into her mother-in-law's home generally was not subject to domination throughout her adult life, since the older woman often died within five to ten years of her son's marriage. In addition, the years of residence with a mother-in-law were also the years in which a woman was rearing young children and most in need of assistance. These dynamics may change since today's Japanese family has only a few children, who are soon in preschool, and today's mother-in-law can be expected to live some thirty more years.[2]

As in the United States, many mothers in Asia are employed outside their homes. If policymakers desire to increase the numbers of women who are employed after childbirth, encouragement of three-generation families may be desirable since they alleviate the difficulties of child care and household management of the employed wife (unless the mother-in-law is likely to exert a strong influence against her daughter-in-law's employment). As the family ages, however, the employed woman will face a problem now occurring with increased frequency in the United States: how to retain a job and provide nursing care for an elderly parent. Approaches such as those described in this book may be more appropriate both economically and in terms of human relations than either institutionalization or expecting an employed woman to quit her job and devote her full time and energies to care of the elderly.

Several aspects of housing policy discourage or encourage three-generation families. One is the unavailability of housing, which is affected by a number of government policies on such matters as land tenure, zoning, and interest rates. When housing is unavailable, people must live with kin regardless of personal choice. The second relevant aspect of housing policy is design criteria, especially the size and structure of units. Although an apartment in a high-rise building cannot be modified, low-rise housing often allows the flexibility of adding another room for parents or a growing family. Many residents in New Delhi's low-rise units have added an adjacent room or built a unit on the roof. One person in Singapore commented that three-generation living has fewer tensions in villages than in city apartments because in villages people rarely spend much time indoors and thus are not in constant contact. Because village doors are open and people sit in front of their houses, much casual interaction with neighbors occurs. But when people move into high rises, doors shut and people tend not to know their neighbors.[3] The chapter on intimate secondary relations considered the need in the United States for public places where people can have friendly contacts and yet maintain some distance. This concept may also be applicable in other heterogeneous societies.

Housing policy regarding allocation of units is also related to the extent of three-generation living. The Hong Kong Housing Authority, for example, has recognized that many young couples do not wish to share living arrangements with their parents and are providing smaller separate units for nuclear families.[4] In Singapore, however, adult persons living with their parents cannot obtain a unit of public housing by themselves or with another unmarried adult until they reach age forty-five. Since 70 percent of the housing is government controlled, this policy encourages either marriage or living shared among different generations. In 1981 Singapore had recently started two policies that encourage three-generation closeness. One permitted a three-generation family to pool resources for purchase of a unit but not to count the full value of the combined incomes when considering income limits for eligibility. Another policy permitted a three-generation family to request units near each other.[5] Policymakers also control the definition of family used in matters such as permitting long-term visitors or even boarders. Are aunts, sisters, cousins, second, or third cousins considered family or unpermitted outsiders? In some societies, important relationships exist not only with extended kin but also with people who are given fictitious kin designations.

The question of who is treated as family raises the question of reciprocity of services. Kin systems are based not merely on bonds of affection but also, and often more significantly, on bonds of reciprocal rights and obligations. A young couple raises and educates its children and expects these children to care for them in their old age. Since many kin exchanges are complex, not direct equivalents, and often repaid after long periods of time, it is important that government policy not disturb the complicated systems of exchanges that people are using for their present and future support systems. One city is considering rules forbidding nonpermanent residents to use educational and health facilities. Certainly the government has valid reasons for such a position, for example, to prevent overuse of facilities and to use a city's tax revenues for its own citizens. Nevertheless, a couple's cousin may live with them in the city to obtain a high school education, while the cousin's relatives may care for the couple's property in the village where they expect to live in their old age. In many cases, one or more family members migrate to the city temporarily or seasonally. Excluding them from services limits their ability to assist their rural relatives and/or encourages them to move the entire family to the city. This may further overload city services and limit the family's options in emergencies. The policy trade-offs are complex and situation specific. However, policymakers should weigh the implications of proposals that limit benefits in a manner that weakens existing informal support arrangements.

Another major problem for policymakers is the growing number of female-headed households. One analysis of seventy-four developing countries indicated that in each case the percentage of female-headed households was higher than that in the United States. The average was 20 percent. The range was from 18 to 65 percent of all households in a country. Other data indicate that one-third of the households in developing countries are headed by women (this includes situations where the male is away due to employment outside the area or other reasons).[6] Such households are likely to be the most poverty stricken, just as in the United States. The women have less education than men, suffer job discrimination, and have few opportunities to work in the modern, more highly paid sectors of the economy both because of tradition and because they need jobs that permit them to care for a child and perform other home responsibilities.

The traditional family support systems that might be expected to assist such women are changing. In some societies, extended kin are not traditionally obligated to provide significant support to a divorced or single woman or to a widow. In other cases, because of migration, financial pressure, or other reasons, kin are not providing the traditional support due such women.[7]

The rate of female-headed households seems likely to increase because of a variety of trends: easier divorce procedures, increased geographic mobility, increased options for women to support themselves, and the development process, which in many cases undermines traditional support systems and obligations.[8] Policymakers should verify all assumptions about the state of the family and employment of women outside the home by empirical data collection of household composition in a given area. One means of reducing the cost burden of such data collection is to include collection of data about household composition, women's employment, and other factors of special concern to women whenever data are gathered for other projects. The second policy implication is the need to strengthen existing kinship and community support systems that assist female-headed households or employed women. The third implication is the need for special services, such as child care centers and skills training for employment. The fourth, and most important, is careful design of all policies so that they do not inadvertently add to the burdens of such women—for example, by relocating them far from markets. Culturally specific solutions will be needed based on the body of available research and thoughtful analysis.

Many of the suggestions made earlier in this book on designing communities to make them more habitable for children are relevant with appropriate local modification. A number of Asians made this sort of comment: "We need play space but we can't have it." There were, however, some places near the homes in the crowded areas where additional play space might have been created and where children could have played under the supervision of family and neighbors. The open drains along each side of the footpaths in Jakarta, Indonesia, could have been covered with boards, making the path a foot wider, sufficient for much play. Where roads had been kept narrow and bumps provided to slow traffic down, the roads could have been used for play space. Small areas several feet wide squeezed in occasionally along the path system would have provided space for several children to sit and play or even for a single piece of simple play equipment.

The changing family and changing needs for provision of care for children and the aged point up the potential significance of the local neighborhood support system. Many Asian cities in fact consist of merged villages that continue their local traditions. In other cases, people from the same rural region or village come to the same area of the city through a series of network exchanges of information, assistance, and moral support. In still other cases, there are formal or informal systems of neighborhood organization. Japan, for example, has an ancient system developed first in the rural areas. The neighborhood organization, originally a unit for tax collection, consists of approximately ten families. The elected head is responsible for distributing the municipal weekly newspaper and any other government data to each household (a task usually performed by a wife since the leaders generally are men). The newspaper includes much information relevant to that area, including the dates for mothers to bring their children to the clinic for various shots. Such associations also are responsible for maintaining the local shrine, for arranging festivals, and for arranging funerals. The last service leaves the bereaved family free for the important emotional task of grieving. Although membership and contributions to the association are no longer compulsory, refusals are rare. New persons in the area are expected to visit each household with a small gift to indicate their intention to conform to appropriate behavior.

Every association elects one member to a larger organization, which represents the neighborhood on area issues with the city government. It seems, however, to play a role limited primarily to information exchange. Rarely does it become politically active or vigorously oppose the wishes of the elected officials.[9]

Although the system is not as active in the newer apartment areas, it continues to exist with some modifications. The developers of one new town, for example, called resident meetings and asked them to elect representatives to an association organized on the basis of one per building rather than per ten families.

There is a similar system in Jakarta, which was established by the Japanese during their occupation of Indonesia. The Indonesians retained it and are now using it as the lowest city government link with residents in slum improvement projects. Such systems clearly provide the potential for information flow and for mobilization of residents. Singapore currently is attempting to establish a similar system in its high-rise buildings.

A number of anthropologists and development specialists have documented the strengths of neighborhood organizations and the voluntary and informal support systems in urban neighborhoods, including squatter settlements.[10] People from one village or area often settle near each other. Residents provide newcomers with temporary housing and assistance, help in finding work, and adjusting to urban life. In many cases home-place associations are formed. Broader ethnic associations are also common.[11]

Efforts to strengthen informal systems and to use them for development purposes are widespread. Whether a neighborhood association is an effective vehicle for community organization and development depends on control, autonomy, leadership development, and continuity. As in the United States, such efforts are most successful where they have governmental support, good leadership, technical assistance, and the other prerequisites for success. In some cases, government officials, as in the United States, see such organizations as a means of obtaining support for policies but not as a mechanism for significant decision making.[12] In others, local leaders have clear responsibilities and powers, such as obtaining information about neighborhood priorities or obtaining neighborhood agreement about whose land will be taken to widen a footpath. Many of the issues raised in the chapter on resident involvement are relevant abroad. The concept of coproduction has special significance since many governments cannot afford to maintain the facilities they are building in their slum improvement projects. Many projects are not well maintained because of a lack of local leadership or proper involvement of the residents from the beginning of the project. Since creating something new is more exciting than daily maintenance, it might be more realistic to develop a way for residents' labor to lower initial building costs but to hire someone for ongoing maintenance.

Although the concept of intimate secondary relationships has not been explored in Asia, models for appropriate behavior among members of different ethnic, racial, religious, and class groups might be helpful. Racial, ethnic, religious, and class friction are not unique to the United States and are a problem in many rapidly developing heterogeneous cities.

In Singapore a deliberate attempt has been made to disrupt the residential homogeneity of ethnic enclaves and to rehouse people, scattering various groups throughout high-rise public housing areas. Residents of the public housing have complained that they miss the neighborliness of their former residences (although not the poor sanitation and lack of drinkable water). Newspaper commentary expressed great concern about a survey that showed that people did not visit their neighbors. More relevant questions might be: Would you assist your neighbors in an emergency? Would your neighbors assist you? In case of conflicts about noise or use of public places, can you talk to your neighbors comfortably and settle the disputes? Can you work with your neighbors to obtain a needed playground or protest a government action?

Thus some of the same issues discussed in this book regarding American families, households, and communities have potential relevance to other countries, including those in the Third World. Their solutions may be useful for the United States, and vice-versa. In all cases, new support systems and new definitions may have to be developed in response to changing conditions and in terms of specific cultural traditions.

Notes

1. Among the most helpful discussions were those with the following: colleagues at the International Symposium on Children and Cities in Tokyo arranged by Noboru Kobayashi; Hiroko Hara, Ochanomizo University, Tokyo, Japan; Yukiko Kada, Kyoto, Japan; Kirtee Shah, director of the Ahmedabad Study Action Group and his staff, India; Amila R. Dhelakia, chief, Rural Wing, Self-Employed Women's Association (SEWA), Ahmedabad, India; faculty and students at the School of Architecture,

Ahmedabad, India; staff of the housing authority and school of planning in New Delhi, India; Wismu M. Ardjo, of the Jakarta City Planning staff, Indonesia; Nini Kusumaatmadja, program coordinator, Area and Kampung Services, United Nations Children's Fund, Jakarta, Indonesia, members of her staff and participants in the training program for regional planners in Bali, especially M. Dishmar; Winnie Tang of the Social Ministry in Singapore; Chua Beng Huat, head, Social Research Unit, Housing and Development Board, Singapore; Nelson W.S. Chou, lecturer in social work, Chinese University of Hong Kong; Daw Aye, senior regional programer for Women's Programme, United Nations Economic and Social Commission for Asia and the Pacific, Bangkok, Thailand; Madeleen A. Schuringa, United Nations Educational, Scientific and Cultural Organization, Bangkok, Thailand; and V.J. Ram, chief, Social Development Division, Secretariat, United Nations Economic and Social Commission for Asia and the Pacific, Bangkok, Thailand.

These observations are in agreement with a number of scholarly studies and reports from those involved in development work. For example, see Mary Racelis Hollnsteiner, "Government Strategies for Urban Areas and Community Participation," *Assignment Children* 57-58 (1982):43-64; Coralie Bryant, *Participation, Planners, and Administrative Development in Urban Development Programs* (Washington, D.C.: Agency for International Development, 1976); Mayra Buvinić and Nadia H. Youssef, with Barbara Von Elm, *Women-Headed Households: The Ignored Factor in Development Planning* (Washington, D.C.: International Center for Research on Women, 1978).

    2. Social Education Bureau, *Women and Education in Japan* (Japan: Ministry of Education, 1974), p. 2.

    3. Interview with Dr. Chua Beng Huat, head, Social Research Unit, Housing and Development Board, National Development Building, July 1981, Singapore.

    4. Hong Kong Housing Authority, *Annual Report 1979-1980* (Hong Kong: Hong Kong Housing Authority, n.d.), p. 8.

    5. Interview with Huat.

    6. Buvinić and Youssef, *Women-Headed Households*, pp. 1, 5; Asian and Pacific Centre for Women and Development, *Environmental Issues Affecting Women with Particular Reference to Housing and Human Settlements* (Bangkok: APCWD, 1980), p. iii; U.N. Economic and Social Commission for Asia and the Pacific, *Report of the Regional Seminar/Workshop on the Role of Young Women in Social Progress and Development, Especially in Industries* (Singapore: U.N. Economic and Social Commission for Asia and the Pacific, 1980).

    7. Buvinić and Youssef, *Women-Headed Households*, pp. 5, 6, 20.

    8. Ibid., p. ii.

9. Interview with Yukiko Kada, Kyoto, Japan, April 1981.

10. For example, Janice E. Perlman, *The Myth of Marginality* (Chicago: University of Chicago Press, 1976); Kenneth Little, *West African Urbanization* (Cambridge: Cambridge University Press, 1965); Marc H. Ross, *The Political Integration of Urban Squatters* (Evanston, Ill.: Northwestern University Press, 1973); Joan N. Nelson, *Access to Power: Politics and the Urban Poor in Developing Nations* (Princeton, N.J.: Princeton University Press, 1979).

11. Nelson, *Access to Power,* pp. 97-99, 239-240, 247-248.

12. Ibid., pp. 292-307.

Bibliography

Abrams, Philip. "Statement of Philip Abrams, General Deputy Assistant Secretary for Housing-Federal Housing Commissioner before Subcommittee on Housing and Consumer Interest of the Select Committee on Aging." Washington, D.C.: Department of Housing and Urban Development, 1981.

Action. "Youth Community Service: Nontraditional Projects and Tasks for Volunteers." Washington, D.C.: Action, 1978.

Addams, Jane. *Twenty Years at Hull House.* New York: Macmillan, 1910.

Advisory Commission on Intergovernmental Relations. *Citizen Participation in the American Federal System.* Washington, D.C.: Government Printing Office, 1979.

Ahlbrandt, Roger S. Jr., and Cunningham, James V. *A New Public Policy for Neighborhood Preservation.* New York: Praeger, 1979.

Alinsky, Saul. *Reveille for Radicals.* Chicago: University of Chicago Press, 1946.

———. *Rules for Radicals.* New York: Random House, 1971.

Allan, Carole, and Brotman, Herman, comps. *Chartbook on Aging in America.* Washington, D.C.: 1981 White House Conference on Aging, 1981.

Allan, Graham A. *A Sociology of Friendship and Kinship.* London: George Allen and Unwin, 1979.

Allinson, Gary. "Revising Social Contracts in Postwar Japan." Paper presented at the Japanologist Conference on Technology Transfer, Transformation, and Development: The Japanese Experience, The United Nations University, Tokyo, April 20–23, 1981.

Altman, Irwin. *The Environment and Social Behavior.* Monterey, Calif.: Brooks-Cole Publishing Company, 1975.

———. "Privacy as an Interpersonal Boundary Process." Address presented to the American Psychological Association, San Francisco, 1977.

———. "Privacy Regulation: Culturally Universal or Culturally Specific?" Salt Lake: University of Utah, 1977.

Appleyard, Donald, with Gerson, M. Sue, and Lintell, Mark. *Liveable Urban Streets: Managing Auto Traffic in Neighborhoods.* Final Report dot-fh-ll-8026. Washington, D.C.: Federal Highway Administration, 1976.

Arensberg, Conrad M., and Kimball, Solon T. *Culture and Community.* New York: Harcourt, Brace & World, 1965.

Arnstein, Sherry R. "A Ladder of Citizen Participation." *Journal of American Institute of Planners* 35 (July 1969):216-224.

Asian and Pacific Center for Women and Development. "Environmental Issues Affecting Women with Particular Reference to Housing and Human Settlements." Papers prepared for APCWD Workshops held in collaboration with National Building Organization, New Delhi, April-June 1980.

Atchley, Robert C., and Byerts, Thomas O., eds. *Rural Environment and Aging.* Washington, D.C.: Gerontological Society, 1975.

Baldassare, Mark. *Residential Crowding in Urban America.* Berkeley: University of California Press, 1979.

Bane, Mary Jo; Lein, Laura; O'Donnell, Lydia; Stueve, C. Ann; and Wells, Barbara. "Child-Care Arrangements of Working Parents." In *Young Workers and Families: A Special Section.* Special Labor Force Report 233. Washington, D.C.: Department of Labor, Bureau of Labor Statistics.

Barnekov, Timothy K., and Callahan, Mary Helen, eds. *Neighborhoods: Changing Perspectives and Policies.* Newark: University of Delaware, 1980.

Barnes, J.A. "Networks and Political Process." In *Social Networks in Urban Situations.* Edited by J. Clyde Mitchell. Manchester: Manchester University Press, 1969.

Batten, T.R. *Communities and Their Development.* London: Oxford University Press, 1957.

Bayor, Ronald H. *Neighborhoods in Urban America.* Port Washington, N.Y.: Kennikat Press, 1982.

Beach, Mark. *Desegregated Housing and Interracial Neighborhoods: A Bibliographic Guide.* Philadelphia: National Neighbors, 1975.

———. *Interracial Neighborhoods in American Cities.* Monticello, Ill.: Vance Bibliographies, 1979.

Beach, Mark, and Beach, Oralee S. *Interracial Neighborhoods in the Urban Community.* Manuscript, 1978.

Bell, Colin, and Newby, Howard. *Community Studies: An Introduction to the Sociology of the Local Community.* New York: Praeger, 1972.

Bender, Thomas. *Community and Social Change in America.* New Brunswick, N.J.: Rutgers University Press, 1978.

Ben-Zadok, Efraim. "Economic and Racial Integration in a New Town." Ph.D. dissertation, New York University, 1980.

Berghorn, Forrest J.; Schafer, Donna E.; Steere, Goeffrey H.; and Wiseman, Robert F. *The Urban Elderly: A Study of Life Satisfaction.* Montclair, N.J.: Allenhead, Osman & Co., 1978.

Bibliography

Berghorn, Forrest J., and Schafer, Donna E. "Support Networks and the 'Frail' Elderly." Paper presented at the Thirty-second Annual Scientific Meeting of the Gerontological Society, Washington, D.C., November 1979.

Berheide, Catherine White, and Banner, Mae G. "Making Room for Employed Women at Home and at Work." *Housing and Society,* no. 4 (1981):153-163.

Bernard, Jessie. *The Sociology of Community.* Glenview, Ill.: Scott, Foresman, 1973.

───. *The Female World.* New York: Free Press, 1981.

Berry, Daniel E. "Investment in Central City Neighborhoods: A New Focus." n.d.

Biddle, W.W. *The Community Development Process: The Rediscovery of Local Initiative.* New York: Holt, Rinehart and Winston, 1968.

Binstock, Robert H., and Shanas, Ethel, eds. *Handbook of Aging and the Social Sciences.* New York: Van Nostrand Reinhold, 1976.

Bish, Musa; Bullock, Jean; and Milgram, Jean. *Racial Steering: The Dual Housing Market and Multiracial Neighborhoods.* Philadelphia: National Neighbors, 1973.

Black, Dean K., and Bengtson, Vern L. "Implications of Telecommunications Technology for Old People, Families, and Bureaucracies." In *Family Bureaucracy and the Elderly,* edited by Ethel Shanas, and Marvin B. Sussman. Durham, N.C.: Duke University Press, 1977.

Blau, Peter. *Bureaucracy in Modern Society.* New York: Random House, 1956.

Boissevain, Jeremy. *Friends of Friends: Networks, Manipulators and Coalitions.* Oxford: Basil Blackwell, 1974.

Bornsdarff, Lillian Gottfarb V. "Preventive Mental Health Work in Mother-Child Care Centres in Sweden and a Model of Parent Education." In *The Child and the City.* Edited by National Institute for Research Advancement. Tokyo, Japan: National Institute for Research Advancement, 1982.

Bott, Elizabeth. *Family and Social Network.* 2d ed. London: Tavistock, 1971.

Bowles, Elinor. "Older Persons as Providers of Services: Three Federal Programs." *Social Policy* 12 (1976):81-88.

Boyte, Harry C. *The Backyard Revolution: Understanding the New Citizen Movement.* Philadelphia: Temple University Press, 1980.

Brackett, Jean C. "New BLS Budgets Provide Yardsticks for Measuring Family Living Costs." *Monthly Labor Review* 92 (April 1969):3-16.

Bratt, Rachael G.; Byrel, Janet M.; and Hollister, Robert M., "The Private Sector and Neighborhood Preservation," mimeographed. Cambridge, Mass.: Neighborhood Policy Research, 1983.

Breckenfeld, Owney. *Columbia and the New Cities.* New York: Ives Washburn, 1971.
Breslow, Ruth W. "Suburban Maryland Experiment in Group Living for the Elderly Proves Successful." *Challenge* 10 (August 1979):22–23.
Brill, William, Associates. *Victimization, Fear of Crime and Altered Behavior: A Profile of the Crime Problems in Murphy Homes, Baltimore, Maryland.* Washington, D.C.: Department of Housing and Urban Development, 1977.
Brody, Elaine M. "Women's Changing Roles, and Care of the Aging Family." In *Aging: Agenda for the Eighties.* Edited by Julienne Pineau Hubbard. Washington, D.C.: Government Research Corporation, 1979.
Brooks, Richard O. "New Towns and Citizen Participation: A Policy Analysis." *Journal of Community Development Society* 2 (Fall 1971):70–84.
———. *New Town and Communal Values: A Case Study of Columbia, Maryland.* New York: Praeger, 1974.
Bryant, Coralie; with Colarulli, Guy C.; White, Louise G.; and Satterthwaite, George. *Participation, Planning, and Administrative Development in Urban Development Programs.* Washington, D.C.: Agency for International Development, 1976.
Burby, Raymond J. III; and Weiss, Shirley F., with Donnelly, Thomas G.; Kaiser, Edward J.; Zehner, Robert B.; Lewis, David F.; Loewenthal, Norman H.; McCalla, Mary Ellen; Rodgers, Barbara G.; and Smookler, Helene V. *New Communities U.S.A.* Lexington, Mass.: Lexington Books, D.C. Heath and Company, 1976.
Burkhart, Lynne Connolly. "Hidden Frontiers in a New Town: The Politics of Race and Class in Columbia, Maryland." Ph.D. dissertation, Johns Hopkins University, 1975.
———. *Old Values in a New Town: The Politics of Race and Class in Columbia, Maryland.* New York: Praeger, 1981.
Buvinić, Mayra; with Adams, Cheri S.; Edgcomb, Gabrielle S.; and Koch-Weser, Maritta. *Women and World Development: An Annotated Bibliography.* Washington, D.C.: Overseas Development Council, 1976.
Buvinić, Mayra, and Youssef, Nadia H., with Von Elm, Barbara. "Women-Headed Households: The Ignored Factor in Development Planning." Washington, D.C.: International Center for Research on Women, 1978.
Byerts, Thomas O. *Environmental Research and Aging.* Report from an Interdisciplinary Research Development Conference in St. Louis, Missouri, May 1973. Washington, D.C.: Gerontological Society, 1974.
Byerts, Thomas O.; Howell, Sandra C.; and Pastalan, Leon A. *Environmental Context of Aging: Lifestyles, Environmental Quality and Living Arrangements.* New York: Garland STPM Press, 1979.

Cahn, Edgar S., and Passett, Barry A., eds. *Citizen Participation: Effecting Community Change.* New York: Praeger, 1971.

Cahnman, Werner J. *Ferdinand Tönnies: A New Evaluation.* Leiden: E.J. Brill, 1973.

Cahnman, Werner J., and Rudolf, Heberle, eds. *Ferdinand Tönnies: On Sociology: Pure, Applied and Empirical.* Chicago: University of Chicago Press, 1971.

Cantor, Marjorie H. "Life Space and Social Support." In *Environmental Context of Aging: Life-Styles, Environmental Quality and Living Arrangements.* Edited by Thomas O. Byerts, Sandra C. Howell, and Leon A. Pastalan. New York: Garland STPM Press, 1979.

Carto, Pat. "Background History of Issues during the 1974-1975 Oakland Mills Village Board." Columbia, Md.: Oakland Village Board Files, 1975.

Cary, Lee J., ed. *Community Development as a Process.* Columbia: University of Missouri Press, 1970.

Center for Community Change. "Beyond the Numbers: The Failure of the Official Measure of Poverty." Washington, D.C.: Center for Community Change, 1979.

Central Mortgage and Housing Corporation. "Setting Up an Adventure Playground." Ottawa: Central Mortgage and Housing Corporation, 1977.

———. "Play Spaces for Preschoolers: Design Guidelines for the Development of Preschool Play Spaces in Residential Environments." Ottawa: Central Mortgage and Housing Corporation, 1978.

———. "Design Guidelines: Play Opportunities for School Age Children, 6 to 14 years." Ottawa: Central Mortgage and Housing Corporation, 1979.

Chadwick, Terry Brainerd. "Displacement: Consequences of Urban Revitalization for the Elderly." School of Urban Affairs, Portland State University, n.d.

Chambers, Clarke. *Seedtime of Reform: American Social Service and Social Action, 1918-1933.* Westport, Conn.: Greenwood, 1980.

Chapman, Ruth H.; Doucette, John F.; and Egan-McKenna, Gini. "Warren Village Program Evaluation: Task Two Report." Cambridge, Mass.: Abt Associates, 1980.

Chavis, David M.; Stucky, Paul E.; and Wandersman, Abraham. "Returning Basic Research to the Community: A Relationship between Scientist and Citizen." *American Psychologist* 38 (April 1983):424-434.

Checkoway, Barry, and Van Til, Jon. "What Do We Know about Citizen Participation? A Selective Review of Research." In *Citizen Participation in America: Essays on the State of the Art.* Edited by Stuart Langton. Lexington, Mass.: Lexington Books, D.C. Heath and Company, 1978.

Chelsvig, Kathleen. "Family Support Systems and the Aging: A Policy Report." Paper prepared by the National Retired Teachers Association, American Association of Retired Persons, and Wakefield Washington Associates. Washington, D.C., 1980.

Cherlin, Andrew J. *Marriage, Divorce, Remarriage.* Cambridge: Harvard University Press, 1981.

Childhood Resources. "A Model for the Nation: Child Care and Early Learning at Columbia." Washington, D.C.: Childhood Resources, 1971.

Christenson, James A., and Robinson, Jerry W. Jr., eds. *Community Development in America.* Ames: Iowa State University Press, 1980.

Churchman, Arza. "Children in Urban Environments: The Israeli Experience." Paper delivered at the MAB International Symposium on Managing Urban Space in the Interest of Children, Toronto, Canada, June 1979.

Citizen Participation 3, 3 (January, February 1982).

Citizens Planning and Housing Association. "CPHA's Baltimore Neighborhood: Self Help Handbook." Baltimore, Md: Citizens Planning and Housing Association, 1982.

Clinard, Marshall B. *Slums and Community Development: Experiments in Self-Help.* New York: Free Press, 1966.

Coalition on Women and the Budget. "Inequality of Sacrifice: The Impact of the Reagan Budget on Women." Washington, D.C.: Coalition on Women and the Budget, 1983.

Cochran, Moncrieff, and Henderson, Charles R., Jr., eds. "The Ecology of Urban Family Life: A Summary Report to the National Institute of Education." Ithaca: Comparative Ecology of Human Development Project, Cornell University, 1982.

Columbia Association. "The Briefing Book 1974: Background Materials on the Columbia Association and the Village Associations of Columbia." Columbia, Md., 1974.

———. "A Profile of Columbia Residents Living in Subsidized Housing." Office of Planning and Evaluation, 1974.

Cooley, Charles Horton. *Social Organization.* New York: Schocken, 1962.

Cooper, Clare C. *Easter Hill Village: Some Social Implications of Design.* New York: Free Press, 1975.

Coser, Lewis A. *Masters of Sociological Thought: Ideas in Historical and Social Context.* New York: Harcourt Brace Jovanovich, 1971.

Cox, Frances M., with Ndung'u Mberia. *Aging in a Changing Village Society: A Kenyan Experience.* Washington, D.C.: International Federation on Ageing, 1977.

Cox, Fred M.; Erlich, John L.; Rothman, Jack; and Tropman, John E. *Strategies of Community Organization: A Book of Readings.* Hasca, Ill.: F.E. Peacock, 1970.

Cox, Kevin R. "Social Change, Turf Politics, and Concepts of Turf Politics." Paper prepared for a Symposium on Public Provision and Urban Development, Washington, D.C., June 1-3, 1982.
Cranz, Galen. *The Politics of Park Design: A History of Urban Parks in America.* Cambridge: MIT Press, 1982.
Craven, P., and Wellman, B. "The Network City." In *The Community: Approaches and Applications.* Edited by Marcia Pelly Effrat. New York: Free Press, 1974.
Crump, Barry N. "The Portability of Urban Ties." Paper presented to the American Sociological Meeting, Chicago, 1977.
Dahrendorf, Ralf. *Essays in the Theory of Society.* Stanford: Stanford University Press, 1968.
Dannenberg, George; Gioglio, Gerald; and Fuccello, Elizabeth. "The Utilization of the Elderly in Child Welfare Services." Paper presented at the Thirty-second Annual Scientific Meeting of the Gerontological Society, Washington, D.C., November 1979.
David, Allen Freeman. "Spearheads for Reform—The Social Settlements and the Progressive Movement, 1890-1914." Ph.D. dissertation, University of Wisconsin, 1959.
Day-Lower, Dennis. "Testimony before the Select Committee on Aging, Subcommittee on Housing and Consumer Interests." Philadelphia: Shared Housing Resource Center, 1981.
Dear, Michael, and Scott, Allen J., eds. *Urbanization and Urban Planning in Capitalist Society.* London and New York: Methuen, 1981.
Director of Physical Development. Jakarta Capital City Government and Kip Implementation Unit. "Jakarta's Kampung Improvement Programme: In the Context of City Settlement Problem." Jakarta: Jakarta Capital City Government, 1976.
Dono, John E.; Falbe Cecilia M.; Kail, Barbara L.; Litwak, Eugene; Sherman, Roger H.; and Siegel, David. "The Structure and Function of Primary Groups in Old Age." Paper presented at the American Sociological Association, San Francisco, August 1978.
Dube, Leela. "Studies on Women in Southeast Asia." Bangkok, Thailand: UNESCO Regional Office for Education in Asia and Oceania, 1980.
Durkheim, Emile. *The Division of Labor in Society.* Translated by George Simpson. New York: Free Press, 1964.
Effrat, Marcia Pelly. "Approaches to Community: Conflicts and Complementarities." *Sociological Inquiry* 43 (1973):1-32.
———, ed. *The Community: Approaches and Applications.* New York: Free Press, 1974.
Ehrlich, Phyllis. *Mutual Help for Community Elderly: Mutual Help Model.* 2 vols. (Final Report and Handbook) Carbondale: Southern Illinois University, 1979.
———. "Service Delivery for the Community Elderly: The Mutual Help

Model." *Journal of Gerontological Social Work* 2 (winter 1979):125-135.

———. "Elderly Health Advocacy Group Handbook of Organizing Principles." Carbondale: Southern Illinois University, 1980.

Eichler, Edwin, and Kaplan, Marshall. *The Community Builders.* Berkeley: University of California Press, 1967.

Esbensen, Steen B. "An International Inventory and Comparative Study of Legislation and Guidelines for Children's Play Spaces in the Residential Environment." Ottawa, Canada: Mortgage and Housing Corporation, 1979.

Etzioni, Amitai. *A Sociological Reader on Complex Organizations.* 2d ed. New York: Holt, Rinehart and Winston, 1969.

Fainstein, Norman I., and Fainstein, Susan S., eds. *Urban Policy Under Capitalism.* Beverly Hills: Sage, 1982.

Fava, Sylvia F. "Women's Place in the New Suburbia." In *New Space for Women.* Edited by Gerda R. Wekerle. Boulder, Col.: Westview Press, 1980.

Fava, Sylvia F., and Desena, Judith. "The Chosen Apple: Young Suburban Migrants." In *The Apple Sliced: Sociological Studies of New York City.* Edited by Vernon Boggs, Gerald Handel, and Sylvia F. Fava. South Hadley, Mass.: Bergin and Garvey, 1983.

Fellin, Philip, and Litwak, Eugene. "Neighborhood Cohesion under Conditions of Mobility." *American Sociological Review* 28 (February-June 1983):364-376.

Fischer, Claude S. *The Urban Experience.* New York: Harcourt Brace Jovanovich, 1976.

———. "The Spatial Dimension of Social Support: New Data from Northern California." Paper presented at the Metro Seminar Series of the Center for Studies of Metropolitan Problems, NIMH, Rockville, Maryland, December 14, 1978.

———. "The Public and Private Worlds of City Life." *American Sociological Review* 46 (June 1981):306-316.

———. *To Dwell among Friends: Personal Networks in Town and City.* Chicago: University of Chicago Press, 1982.

Fischer, Claude S.; Jackson, Robert Max; Stueve, C. Ann; Gerson, Kathleen; and Jones, Lynne McCallister; with Baldassare, Mark. *Networks and Places: Social Relations in the Urban Setting.* New York: Free Press, 1977.

Fischer, Claude S., and Phillips, Susan L. "Who Is Alone? Social Characteristics of People with Small Networks." Working Paper 310. Berkeley: Institute of Urban and Regional Development, University of California, October 1979.

Fischer, Claude S., with Stacey Oliver. "Friendship, Sex, and the Life Cycle." Berkeley: Institute of Urban and Regional Development, University of California, March 1980.

Fisher, Julie. "Creating Communities: Squatter Neighborhood Associations in Latin America." *Grassroots Development* 6 (1982):13-17.

Fisher, Robert, and Romanofsky, Peter, eds. *Community Organization for Urban Social Change: A Historical Perspective.* Westport, Conn.: Greenwood Press, 1981.

Fly, Jerry; Reinhart, George; and Hamby, Russell. "Leisure Activity, Life Satisfaction, and Alienation in Retirement." Birmingham: University of Alabama, n.d.

Foer, Albert A. "Democracy in the New Towns: The Limits of Private Government." *University of Chicago Review* 36 (winter 1969):379-412.

Folkman, Daniel V., ed. *Urban Community Development: Case Studies in Neighborhood Survival.* Milwaukee: Community Development Society of America and the University of Wisconsin-Extension, Center for Urban Community Development, 1978.

Frankfather, Dwight. *The Aged in the Community: Managing Senility and Deviance.* New York: Praeger, 1977.

Fried, Marc. "Grieving for a Lost Home." In *The Urban Condition: People and Policy in the Metropolis.* Edited by Leonard J. Duhl, with the assistance of John Powell. New York: Basic Books, 1963.

Galbraith, John K. *The Affluent Society.* 3d rev. ed. New York: New American Library, 1978.

Gans, Herbert J. *The Urban Villagers: Group and Class in the Life of Italian-Americans.* New York: Free Press, 1962.

———. *The Levittowners: Ways of Life and Politics in a New Suburban Community.* New York: Vintage Books, 1967.

———. *People and Plans.* New York: Basic Books, 1968.

———. "The Possibility of Class and Racial Integration in American New Towns: A Policy-oriented Analysis." In *New Towns: Why and For Whom?* Edited by Harvey S. Perloff and Neil C. Sandberg. New York: Praeger, 1973.

Gartner, Alan; Greer, Colin; and Riessman, Frank, eds. *What Reagan Is Doing to Us.* New York: Harper and Row, 1982.

Gary, Lawrence E. "Support Systems in Black Communities: Implications for Mental Health Services for Children and Youth." UAR Occasional Paper 3, no. 4. Washington, D.C.: Institute for Urban Affairs and Research, Howard University, 1978.

Gelfand, Donald E., and Gelfand, Judy R. "Senior Centers and Support Networks." Baltimore: School of Social Work and Community Planning, University of Maryland, n.d.

Gelwicks, Louis E., and Newcomer, Robert J. *Planning Housing Environments for the Elderly.* Washington, D.C.: National Council on Aging, 1974.

Giele, Janet Zollinger. *Women and the Future: Changing Sex Roles in Modern America.* New York: Free Press, 1978.

Gittell, Marilyn; with Hoffacker, Bruce; Rollins, Eleanor; Foster, Samuel; and Hoffacker, Mark. *Limits to Citizen Participation: The Decline of Community Organizations.* Beverly Hills: Sage Publications, 1980.

Gladson, Laura Hayes. "Child Abuse: It Happens in the Best of Homes." *These Times,* August 1, 1979.

Glaser, Barney G., and Strauss, Anselm L. *The Discovery of Grounded Theory: Strategies for Qualitative Research.* Chicago: Aldine, 1967.

Glick, Paul C. "Living Arrangements of Children and Young Adults." *Journal of Comparative Family Studies* 7, no. 2 (Summer 1976):321–333.

Godschalk, David. "New Communities or Company Towns? An Analysis of Resident Participation in New Towns." In *New Towns: Why and for Whom?* Edited by Harvey S. Perloff and Neil C. Sandberg. New York: Praeger, 1973.

Goetze, Rolf. *Understanding Neighborhood Change: The Role of Expectations in Urban Revitalization.* Cambridge, Mass.: Ballinger, 1979.

Gonder, John, and Gordon, Steve. "The Housing Needs of 'Non-Traditional' Households." Washington, D.C.: Government Printing Office, 1979.

Gouldner, Alvin W. *The Coming Crisis of Western Sociology.* New York: Avon Books, 1970.

Granovetter, Mark. "The Strength of Weak Ties." *American Journal of Sociology* 78 (1973):1360–1380.

———. *Getting a Job.* Cambridge: Harvard University Press, 1974.

Gutkin, Janet. "RSVP Volunteers and Crime Prevention: A Program Assistance Paper for RSVP Directors." Washington, D.C.: ACTION, 1983.

Gutowski, Michael, and Feild, Tracey. *The Graying of Suburbia.* Washington, D.C.: Urban Institute, 1979.

Haddon, William, Jr., and Baker, Susan P. "Injury Control." In *Preventive and Community Medicine,* 2d ed. Edited by Duncan Clark and Brian MacMahon. Boston: Little, Brown, 1981.

Hafkin, Nancy J., and Bay, Edna G., eds. *Women in Africa: Studies in Social and Economic Change.* Stanford: Stanford University Press, 1976.

Hagoel, Lea. "Friendship Values and Intimacy Patterns in an Urban Community." Paper presented at the Seventy-fifth Annual Meeting of the American Sociological Association, New York, August 27–31, 1980.

Hallman, Howard W. "Neighborhood-Based Organizations: Reflections on Fifteen Years' Experience." Manuscript, n.d.

Bibliography

———. "Neighborhood Governance." Paper prepared for Department of Housing and Urban Development, 1983.

———. *Neighborhoods: Their Place in Urban Life.* Beverly Hills, Cal.: Sage Publications, 1984.

———. *The Organization and Operation of Neighborhood Councils: A Practical Guide.* New York: Praeger, 1977.

Hapgood, Karen, and Getzels, Judith. "Planning, Women, and Change." Report of the American Society of Planning Officials. *Planning Advisory Service* 301 (April 1974).

Hara, Hiroko. "The Childhood in Japanese Society during the Past 100 Years." Paper presented at Kolloquium "Kindheit, Familie und Poesie in Kulturvergleich," Goethe-Institut, Kyoto, Japan, May 21-24, 1980.

Hareven, Tamara K. "The Family as Process: The Historical Study of the Family Cycle." *Journal of Social History* 7 (Spring 1974):322-329.

Harre, David S. *Shared Housing for Older People: A New Approach: History and Lessons Learned.* Washington, D.C.: Richmond Fellowship of Metropolitan Washington, D.C., 1980.

Harris, Louis and Associates. *The Myth and Reality of Aging in America.* Washington, D.C.: National Council on the Aging, 1976.

Hendricks, Jon, and Hendricks, C. Davis. *Aging in Mass Society: Myths and Realities.* Cambridge, Mass.: Winthrop Publishers, 1977.

Henig, Jeffrey R. "Neighborhood Governance and Voluntarism." Manuscript. Department of Political Science, George Washington University, 1983.

Heritage Conservation and Recreation Service. *The Third Nationwide Outdoor Recreation Plan: Appendix 2, Survey Technical Report 3.* Washington, D.C.: Department of the Interior, 1979.

Hester, Randolph T., Jr. *Neighborhood Space.* Stroudsburg, Penn.: Dowden, Hutchinson and Ross, 1975.

Heumann, Leonard F. "Racial Integration in Residential Neighborhoods: Toward More Precise Measures and Analysis." *Evaluation Quarterly* 3 (1979):59-79.

Hill, Ann B., and Lane, Carol G. "Abstracts on Child Play Areas and Child Support Facilities." Milwaukee Community Design Center, 1978.

Hillery, George A. "Definitions of Community: Areas of Agreement." *Rural Sociology* (1955):111-23.

———. *Communal Organizations: A Study of Local Societies.* Chicago: University of Chicago Press, 1968.

Hing, Esther, and Cypress, Beulah K. *Use of Health Services by Women 65 Years of Age and Over: United States.* DHHS Publication (PHS) 81-1720. Hyattsville, Md.: Department of Health and Human Services, 1981.

Hochschild, Arlie Russell. *The Unexpected Community: Portrait of an Old Age Subculture.* Berkeley: University of California Press, 1973.

Hodgson, Susan. "Research and Progress Report: Intervening to Support Parents in High Risk Communities." The Child in the City Programme, University of Toronto, Toronto, Canada, 1982.

Hodgson, Susan; Lewis, Mary; McIntyre, Eileen; Meehan, Karen; Birnberg, Peggy; and Heyworth, Elspeth. "Towards Supportive Communities: The Need for a Continuum of Services and Its Implications." The Child in the City Programme, University of Toronto, Toronto, Canada, 1982.

Hollnsteiner, Mary Racelis. "Government Strategies for Urban Areas and Community Participation." *Assignment Children* 57-58 (1982):43-64.

"Hong Kong Housing Authority Annual Report 1979-80." Hong Kong: Fok Hing Co., 1980.

Hoppenfeld, Morton. "A Sketch of the Planning Building Process for Columbia, Maryland." *American Institute of Planners Journal* 33 (1967):398-409.

Howard, Ebenezer, ed. *Garden Cities of Tomorrow.* Cambridge: MIT Press, 1965.

Howell, Sandra C. *Designing for Aging: Patterns of Use.* Cambridge: MIT Press, 1980.

Hunter, Albert. *Symbolic Communities: The Persistence and Change of Chicago's Local Communities.* Chicago: University of Chicago Press, 1974.

———. "The Loss of Community: An Empirical Test through Replication." *American Sociological Review* 34 (1975):537-552.

Irwin, John. *Scenes.* Beverly Hills: Sage, 1977.

The Journal of Applied Behavioral Science 17 (1981). Special issue on citizen participation.

Karp, David A.; Stone, Gregory P.; and Yoels, William C. *Being Urban.* Lexington, Mass.: D.C. Heath and Company, 1977.

Keller, Suzanne. *The Urban Neighborhood: A Sociological Perspective.* New York: Random House, 1968.

———, ed. *Building for Women.* Lexington, Mass.: Lexington Books, D.C. Heath and Company, 1981.

Kershaw, Joseph Alexander, with the assistance of Courant, Paul N. *Government against Poverty.* Washington, D.C.: Brookings Institution, 1970.

Klein, Donald C., ed. *Psychology of the Planned Community: The New Town Experience.* New York: Human Sciences Press, 1978.

Kollias, Karen, with Naparstek, Arthur, and Haskell, Chester. *Neighborhood Reinvestment.* Washington, D.C.: National Center for Urban Ethnic Affairs, 1977.

Kramer, Ralph M., and Specht, Harry. *Readings in Community Organization.* Englewood Cliffs, N.J.: Prentice Hall, 1969.

La Gory, Mark. "Toward a Sociology of Space—The Constrained Choice

Model." Paper presented at the Seventy-fifth Annual Meeting of the American Sociological Association, New York, August 27-31, 1980.

Langley, Ann. "Abuse of the Elderly." Project Share Human Services Monograph Series 27. Rockville, Md.: Department of Health and Human Services, 1981.

Langton, Stuart. *Citizen Participation in America: Essays on the State of the Art.* Lexington, Mass.: Lexington Books, D.C. Heath and Company, 1978.

Lashley, Glen T. "The Aging Pedestrian." *Traffic Safety* (August 1960).

Laumann, Edward O. *Bonds of Pluralism: The Form and Substance of Urban Social Networks.* New York: Wiley, 1973.

Lawton, M. Powell. "How the Elderly Live." In *Environmental Context of Aging: Lifestyles, Environmental Quality and Living Arrangements.* Edited by Thomas O. Byerts, Sandra C. Howell, and Leon A. Pastalan. New York: Garland STP Press, 1979.

Lawton, M. Powell, and Nahemow, L. "Design Evaluation: The Social Uses of Elderly Housing." Final Report. Philadelphia: Geriatric Center, 1978.

Lawton, M Powell, and Byerts, Thomas O., eds. *Community Planning for the Elderly.* Washington, D.C.: Gerontological Society, 1973.

Lawton, M. Powell; Newcomer, Robert J.; and Byerts, Thomas O., eds. *Community Planning for an Aging Society: Designing Services and Facilities.* Stroudsburg, Penn.: Dowden, Hutchinson and Ross, 1976.

Lester, David. *The Elderly Victim of Crime.* Springfield, Ill.: Charles C. Thomas, 1981.

Levitan, Sar A. *The Great Society's Poor Law: A New Approach to Poverty.* Baltimore: Johns Hopkins Press, 1969.

———. *Programs in Aid of the Poor.* 3d ed. Baltimore: Johns Hopkins University Press, 1976.

Levitan, Sar A., and Taggart, Robert. *The Promise of Greatness.* Cambridge: Harvard University Press, 1976.

Liebert, Roland J., and Imershein, Allen W., eds. *Power, Paradigms, and Community Research.* Beverly Hills: Sage, 1977.

Little, Kenneth. *West African Urbanization: A Study of Voluntary Associations in Social Change.* London: Cambridge University Press, 1965.

Litwak, Eugene. "Geographic Mobility and Extended Family Cohesion." *American Sociological Review* 25 (1960):385-394.

———. "Extended Kin Relations in an Industrial Democratic Society." In *Social Structures and the Family Generational Relations.* Edited by E. Shanas and G. Streib. Englewood Cliffs, N.J.: Prentice-Hall, 1965.

Litwak, Eugene, and Szelenyi, Ivan. "Primary Group Structures and Their Functions: Kin, Neighbors and Friends." *American Sociological Review* 34 (1969):465-481.

Lopata, Helena Znaniecka. *Women as Widows: Support Systems.* New York: Elsevier, 1979.

Lynch, Kevin, ed. *Growing Up in Cities: Studies of the Spatial Environment of Adolescence in Cracow, Melbourne, Mexico City, Salta, Toluca and Warszawa.* Cambridge: MIT Press, 1977.

Marcus, Clare Cooper. "Children in Residential Areas: Guidelines for Designers." *Landscape Architecture* 64 (October 1974):372-377.

Marris, Peter, and Rein, Martin. *Dilemmas of Social Reform: Poverty and Community Action in the United States.* New York: Atherton Press, 1967.

Marshall, Patricia, ed. *Citizen Participation Certification for Community Development: A Reader on the Citizen Participation Process.* Washington, D.C.: National Association of Housing and Redevelopment Officials, 1977.

Marx, Karl, and Engels, Frederick. *Selected Works.* Revised ed. New York: International Publishers, 1969.

Mayer, Neil S., with Black, Jennifer L. *Keys to the Growth of Neighborhood Development Organizations.* Washington, D.C.: Urban Institute Press, 1981.

Merton, Robert K. *On Theoretical Sociology: Five Essays Old and New.* New York: Free Press, 1952.

Michelson, William. *Man and His Urban Environment: A Sociological Approach.* Rev. ed. Reading, Mass.: Addison-Wesley, 1970.

———. "Spatial and Temporal Dimensions of Child Care." *Signs: Journal of Women in Culture and Society* 5, no. 3, suppl. (1980):5242-5247.

Michelson, William; Levine, Saul V.; and Spina, Anna Rose. *The Child in the City: Changes and Challenges.* Toronto: University of Toronto Press, 1979.

Michelson, William, and Michelson, Ellen, eds. *Managing Urban Space in the Interest of Children.* MAB Report, 14. The Child in the City Programme, University of Toronto, Toronto, Canada, October 1980.

Michigan State Housing Development Authority. *Housing for the Elderly Development Process.* Lansing: Michigan State Housing Development Authority, 1974.

Mindick, Burton, and Boyd, Eulas. "A Multi-Level, Bipolar View of the Urban Residential Environment: Local Community vs. Mass Societal Forces." *Population and Environment,* 5, no, 4 (1984):221-241.

Mitchell, J. Clyde. *Social Networks in Urban Situations.* Manchester, England: Manchester University Press, 1969.

Moore, Robin, and Young, Donald. "Childhood Outdoors: Toward a Social Ecology of the Landscape." In *Children and the Environment.* Edited by Irwin Altman and Joachim F. Wohlwil. New York: Plenum, 1978.

Morgan, S. Philip, and Hirosimi, Kiyosi. "The Persistence of Extended Family Residence in Japan: Anachronism or Alternative Strategy?" *American Sociological Review* 48 (April 1983):269-281.
Moynihan, Daniel P. *Maximum Feasible Misunderstanding.* New York: Free Press, 1969.
Muller, Thomas; Soble, Carol; and Dujack, Susan. "The Urban Household in the 1980's—A Demographic and Economic Perspective." Washington, D.C.: Department of Housing and Urban Development, 1980.
Naisbitt, John. *Megatrends: Ten New Directions Transforming Our Lives.* New York: Warner Books, 1982.
Naparstek, Arthur J.; and Biegel, David. "Community Support Systems: An Alternative to Human Service Delivery." Washington, D.C.: University of Southern California, Washington Public Affairs Center, 1980.
Naparstek, Arthur J.; Biegel, David; and Spiro, Herzl R. *Neighborhood Networks for Humane Mental Health Care.* New York: Plenum Press, 1982.
National Commission on Neighborhoods. *People Building Neighborhoods: Final Report to the President and the Congress of the United States,* and *Case Study Appendixes,* vols. 1 and 2. Washington, D.C.: Government Printing Office, 1979.
National Institute for Research Advancement. International Pediatric Association, ed. *The Child and the City.* Tokyo: Nira, 1982.
National Safety Council. "Accident Facts." 1979 ed. Chicago: National Safety Council, 1979.
Neal, Sister Marie Augusta. *Values and Interests in Social Change.* Englewood Cliffs, N.J.: Prentice-Hall, 1965.
Nelson, Joan M. *Access to Power: Politics and the Urban Poor in Developing Nations.* Princeton, N.J.: Princeton University Press, 1979.
Newman, Oscar. *Defensible Space.* New York: Macmillan, 1972.
———. *Design Guidelines for Creating Defensible Space.* Washington, D.C.: National Institute of Law Enforcement and Criminal Justice, 1976.
Nisbet, Robert A. *The Sociological Tradition.* New York: Basic Books, 1966.
Norbeck, Edward. *Changing Japan.* New York: Holt, Rinehart and Winston, 1965.
Oakland Mills Village Board. "Oakland Mills Village Budget Recommendations for Fiscal Year 1976." Columbia, Md.: Oakland Mills Village Board Files, 1975.
Obenland, Robert James, and Blumenthal, Morton J. *A Guide to the Design and Development of Housing for the Elderly.* Concord, N.H.: New England Non-Profit Housing Development Corporation, 1978.

Olson, Philip. "Urban Neighborhood Research: Its Development and Current Focus." Paper presented at the Seventy-fifth Annual Meeting of the American Sociological Association, New York, August 27-31, 1980.

Parsons, Talcott, and Shils, Edward A., eds. *Towards a General Theory of Action*. New York: Harper and Row, 1962.

Pike, Mary L., comp. *Citizen Participation and Community Development*. Publication 571. Washington, D.C.: National Association of Housing and Redevelopment Officials, 1975.

Perlman, Janice E. *The Myth of Marginality: Urban Poverty and Politics in Rio de Janeiro*. Berkeley: University of California Press, 1976.

Perloff, Harvey S., and Sandberg, Neil C., eds. *New Towns: Why—and for Whom?* New York: Praeger, 1973.

Perry, Clarence Arthur. *Neighborhood and Community Planning. New York: Regional Plan of New York and Its Environs*. New York: Regional Plan of New York, 1929.

Peterson, Rebecca; Wekerle, Gerda R.; and Morley, David. "Women and Environments: An Overview of an Emerging Field." *Environment and Behavior* 10 (December 1978):511-534.

Pollowy, Anne-Marie. *The Urban Nest*. Stroudsburg, Penn.: Dowden, Hutchinson and Ross, 1977.

Radtke, Robert C., and Ehrlich, Phyllis. "A Mutual Help Model: Morale, Role Involvement and Informal Supports." Carbondale: Department of Psychology and Rehabilitation Institute, Southern Illinois University, n.d.

Raundalen, Magne, and Raundalen, Tora Synove. "Interviews with Four Thousand Norwegian Girls and Boys about Their Daily Life and the Future." Paper presented at the International Congress on The Child in the World of Tomorrow, Athens, Greece, July 1978.

Regnier, Victor A.; Murakami, E.; and Gordon, S. "The Relationship of Goods and Services Retrieval Patterns to the Perceived Neighborhood Context of Four Los Angeles Communities." Paper presented at the Seventh National Transportation Conference of Elderly Handicapped, Orlando, Florida, 1979.

Regnier, Victor A., and Rausch, Karen J. "Spatial and Temporal Neighborhood Use Patterns of Older Low-Income Central City Dwellers." Paper presented at the Environmental Design Research Association Annual Meeting, Charleston, South Carolina, 1980.

Reston Homeowners Association. "Design Book: A Guide for Reston Residents to the Planning and Design of Exterior Additions and Alterations." Reston, Va.: Reston Homeowners Association, 1975.

Rich, Richard C. "The Dynamics of Leadership in Neighborhood Organizations." *Social Science Quarterly* 60 (March 1980):570-587.

———. "A Political Economy Approach to the Study of Neighborhood Organizations." *American Journal of Political Science* 24 (November 1980):559-593.

———. "Interaction of the Voluntary and Governmental Sectors: Toward an Understanding of the Coproduction of Municipal Services." *Administration and Society* 13 (May 1981):59-76.

———. "The Political Economy of Public Services." In *Urban Policy under Capitalism*. Edited by Norman I. Fainstein and Susan S. Fainstein. Beverly Hills: Sage, 1982.

Rich, Richard C., ed. *The Politics of Urban Public Services*. Lexington, Mass.: Lexington Books, D.C. Heath and Company, 1982.

Rich, Richard C., and Rosenbaum, Walter A., eds. "Citizen Participation in Public Policy." *Journal of Applied Behavioral Science* 17 (1981).

Riesman, David; with Glazer, Nathan; and Denney, Reuel. *The Lonely Crowd: A Study of the Changing American Character*. Abridged ed. New Haven: Yale University Press, 1971.

Robins-Mowry, Dorothy. *The Hidden Sun: Women of Modern Japan*. Boulder, Colo.: Westview Press, 1983.

Robinson, Betsy, and Thurnher, Majda. "Taking Care of Aged Parents: A Family Cycle Transition." *Gerontologist* 19 (1979):586-593.

Rohe, William M., and Gates, Lauren B. "Neighborhood Planning: Promise and Product." *Urban and Social Change Review* 14 (1981).

Ross, Chris. "Residential Mobility in Female Headed Households." Paper presented at the Seventy-fourth Annual Meeting of the American Sociological Association, Boston, August 27-31, 1979.

Ross, Heather L., and Sawhill, Isabel V. *Time of Transition: The Growth of Families Headed by Women*. Washington, D.C.: Urban Institute, 1975.

Ross, Marc H. *The Political Integration of Urban Squatters*. Evanston, Ill.: Northwestern University Press, 1973.

Ross, Murray. *Community Organization: Theory and Principles*. New York: Harper and Row, 1955.

Rubin, Israel. "Function and Structure of Community: Conceptual and Theoretical Analysis." In *Perspectives on the American Community*. Edited by Roland L. Warren. Chicago: Rand McNally, 1966.

———. "Function and Structure of Community: Conceptual and Theoretical Analysis." *International Review of Community Development*, no. 21-22 (1969):111-119.

Sandberg, Neil C. "The Realities of Integration in New and Old Towns." In *New Towns: Why—and for Whom?* Edited by Harvey S. Perloff and Neil C. Sandberg. New York: Praeger, 1973.
Sandoz Pharmaceuticals. "Sensory Loss in the Elderly: An Overview." East Hanover, N.J.: Sandoz Pharmaceuticals, 1980.
Sarason, Seymour B. *The Psychological Sense of Community: Prospects for a Community Psychology.* San Francisco: Jossey-Bass, 1974.
Schindler-Rainman, Eva, and Lippitt, Ronald. *Building the Collaborative Community: Mobilizing Citizens for Action.* Riverside: University of California Extension, 1980.
Schlesinger, Arthur. *Age of Roosevelt: The Crisis of the Old Order.* Vol. 1. Boston: Houghton Mifflin, 1957.
Schoenberg, Sandra, and Dabrowski, Irene. "Factors Which Enhance the Participation of Women in Urban Neighborhood Social Life." Paper presented at the Seventy-third Annual Meeting of the American Sociological Association, San Francisco, September 5-8, 1978.
Schoenberg, Sandra Perlman, and Rosenbaum, Patricia. *Neighborhoods That Work: Sources for Viability in the Inner City.* New Brunswick, N.J.: Rutgers University Press, 1980.
Schreter, Carol. "House Sharing by Non-Frail Older Persons." In *Housing Options for the Community Resident Elderly: Policy Report of the Housing Choices of Older Americans Study.* Edited by Lloyd Turner, et al. Bryn Mawr, Penn.: Graduate School of Social Work and Social Research, 1982.
Sebstad, Jennefer. *Struggle and Development among Self Employed Women: A Report on the Self Employed Women's Association, Ahmedabad, India.* Washington, D.C.: Agency for International Development, 1982.
Self Employed Women's Association. "We, The Self-Employed." Ahmedabad, India: Embassy Printers, 1981.
Sennett, Richard, ed. *Classic Essays on the Culture of Cities.* New York: Appleton-Century-Crofts, 1969.
Seward, Rudy Ray. *The American Family: A Demographic History.* Beverly Hills: Sage, 1978.
Shabecoff, Alice, ed. *Neighborhoods: A Self-Help Sampler.* Washington, D.C.: Government Printing Office, 1979. Produced for U.S. Department of Housing and Urban Development.
Shanas, Ethel, and Sussman, Marvin B. *Family, Bureaucracy, and the Elderly.* Durham, N.C.: Duke University Press, 1977.
Sheppard, Harold L., and Herrick, Neal Q. *Where Have All the Robots Gone? Worker Dissatisfaction in the Seventies.* New York: Free Press, 1972.
Shy, Carl M.; Goldsmith, John R.; Hackney, Jack D.; Lebowitz, Michael D.; and Menzel, Daniel B. *Health Effects of Air Pollution.* New York: American Lung Association, 1978.

Bibliography

Simms, Margaret C. *Families and Housing Markets: Obstacles to Locating Suitable Housing.* Washington, D.C.: Government Printing Office, 1980.

Sinding, Monica K. "The Philosophic Basis for New Town Development in America." Chapel Hill: Center for Urban and Regional Studies, University of North Carolina, 1967.

Slidell, John B. "The Shape of Things to Come? An Evaluation of the Neighborhood Unit as an Organizing Scheme for American New Towns." Chapel Hill: Center for Urban and Regional Studies, University of North Carolina, 1972.

Smith, E., and Schimandle, W.J. "A Study of Emergency Response Systems for Housing for the Aged." Sacramento: Mentoris Company, 1973.

Smith, Linda S. "Kinkeeping in the Middle Generation: The Effects of Role Strain." Paper presented at the Annual Meeting of the Gerontological Society, Washington, D.C., November 1979.

Smith, Robert J. *Crime against the Elderly: Implications for Policy-Makers and Practitioners.* Washington, D.C.: International Federation on Ageing, 1979.

Smookler, Helene V. "Deconcentration of the Poor: Class Integration in New Communities." Ph.D. dissertation, University of California, 1975.

Sobal, Jeff. "Social Participation, Household Density, and Experienced Crowding." Paper presented at the Seventy-fifth Annual Meeting of the American Sociological Association, New York, August 27-31, 1980.

Social Education Bureau. *Women and Education in Japan.* Tokyo: Social Education Bureau, Ministry of Education, Japan, 1974

"Social Welfare and Human Settlements." Papers presented at a symposium held in conjunction with HABITAT, University of British Columbia, Vancouver, May 30-June 4, 1976.

Sommers, Tish. "Aging in America: Implications for Women." Washington, D.C.: National Council on the Aging, 1976.

Spiegel, Hans B.C. *Decentralization: Citizen Participation in Urban Development.* Vol. 3. Fairfax, Va.: Learning Resources Corporation/NTL, 1974.

Statutes at Large. Vol. 78. *Economic Opportunity Act of 1964.* Section 202(a)(3). 88th Congress, 1st session, 1964.

Stein, Maurice R. *The Eclipse of Community: An Interpretation of American Studies.* New York: Harper Torch Books, 1965.

Street, David. *Handbook of Contemporary Urban Life.* San Francisco: Jossey-Bass, 1978.

Stueve, Ann, and Fischer, Claude S. "Social Networks and Older Women." Working Paper 292. Prepared for the Workshop on Older Women, Washington, D.C., September 14-16, 1978.

Susskind, Lawrence. "Planning for New Towns: The Gap between Theory and Practice." *Sociological Inquiry* 43 (1973):291-310.

Susskind, Lawrence, and Elliott, Michael. Working papers presented at a symposium, "Citizen Participation in Western Europe," Washington, D.C., April 28-29, 1980.

Susskind, Lawrence, and Elliott, Michael; with Appleyard, Donald; Draisen, Marc; Godschalk, David; Hartman, Chester; Perlman, Janice; Spiegel, Hans; and Zeisel, John. "Learning from Public Participation in Western Europe." *Urban Innovation Abroad* (September 1980).

Sussman, Marvin B. "The Family Life of Old People." In *Handbook of Aging and the Social Sciences*. Edited by Robert H. Binstock and Ethel Shanas. New York: Van Nostrand Reinhold, 1976.

Suttles, Gerald D. *The Social Construction of Communities*. Chicago: University of Chicago Press, 1972.

Sweeney, Tadhg. "Performance Criteria for the Design of Housing for the Elderly in New England." Boston, Mass.: Brett Donham Architects, 1975.

Ten-Sun, Jan. "The Current Social Welfare Policy and Programs in the Republic of China." Paper presented at the Sino-American Conference on Social Welfare Development in the 1980s, Taipei, December 29-31, 1980.

Thorns, David C. *The Quest for Community*. New York: Wiley, 1976.

Thuillier, R.H. "Air Quality Considerations in Residential Planning." Vols. 1-3. Washington, D.C.: SRI International for U.S. Department of Housing and Urban Development, 1980.

Tiven, Marjorie Bloomberg. *Older Americans: Special Handling Required*. Washington, D.C.: National Council on the Aging, 1971.

Toffler, Alvin. *Future Shock*. New York: Random House, 1970.

Tönnies, Ferdinand. *Community and Society, Gemeinschaft und Gesellschaft*. Edited by Charles P. Loomis. New York: Harper and Row, 1963.

Transport and Road Research Laboratory. Department of the Environment. "Age Differences in Behavior of Pedestrians Crossing the Road." Crowthorne, England: Department of the Environment, 1972.

Turner, Lloyd; with Schreter, Carol; Zetrick, Bonnie; Weisbrod, Glen; and Pollakowski, Henry. *Housing Options for the Community Resident Elderly: Policy Report of the Housing Choices of Older Americans Study*. Washington, D.C.: Department of Health and Human Services, Administration on Aging, Office of Human Development Services, 1982.

UNESCO. Regional Office for Education in Asia and the Pacific. *Rural Families with Dislocated Males: Effects of Urban Male Migration on*

Female Members Left in the Village. Bangkok, Thailand: UNESCO Regional Office for Education in Asia and the Pacific, 1981.

Unger, Donald G., and Wandersman, Abraham. "Informal Social Relations among Neighbors and Their Interface with Neighborhood Organizations." Draft. University of South Carolina, n.d.

United Nations. Economic and Social Commission for Asia and the Pacific. "Report of the Expert Group Meeting on Women and Forest Industries." Bangkok, June 2-6, 1980.

———. Economic and Social Commission for Asia and the Pacific. "Report of the Regional Seminar/Workshop on 'The Role of Young Women in Social Progress and Development, Especially in Industries.'" Singapore, May 10-20, 1980.

———. Economic and Social Commission for Asia and the Pacific. "Progress, Proposals and Issues in Various Fields of Activity of ESCAP: Report of the Second Asian and Pacific Ministerial Conference on Social Welfare and Social Development." Thirty-seventh Session, Bangkok, March 10-21, 1981.

———. Department of Economic and Social Affairs. "The Social Impact of Housing: Goals, Standards, Social Indicators and Popular Participation: Report of an Interregional Seminar on the Social Aspects of Housing, Holte, Denmark, September 14-27, 1975." New York: United Nations, 1977.

———. "Programme of Action for the Second Half of the United Nations Decade for Women: Equality, Development and Peace." Paper presented at the World Conference of the United Nations Decade for Women, Copenhagen, Denmark, 1980.

U.S. Department of Commerce. Bureau of the Census. Current Population Reports, Series P-23, no. 49. *Population of the United States, Trends and Prospects: 1950-1990.* Washington, D.C.: Government Printing Office, 1974.

———. Department of Commerce. Bureau of the Census. Current Population Reports. Series P-20, No. 326. *Household and Family Characteristics: March 1977.* Washington, D.C.: Government Printing Office, 1978.

———. Department of Commerce. Bureau of the Census. Current Population Reports, Series P-20, No. 331. *Geographical Mobility: March 1975 to March 1978.* Washington, D.C.: Government Printing Office, 1978.

———. Department of Commerce. Bureau of the Census. Current Population Reports, Series P-23, No. 100. *A Statistical Portrait of Women in the United States: 1978.* Washington, D.C.: Government Printing Office, 1980.

———. Department of Commerce. Bureau of the Census. Current Population Reports, Series P-60, No. 129. *Money Income of Families and Persons in the United States: 1979.* Washington, D.C.: Government Printing Office, 1981.

———. Department of Commerce. Bureau of the Census. Current Population Reports. Series P-20, No. 380. *Marital Status and Living Arrangements: March 1982.* Washington, D.C.: Government Printing Office, 1982.

———. Department of Commerce. Bureau of the Census. Current Population Reports, Series P-20, No. 381. *Household and Family Characteristics: March 1982.* Washington, D.C.: Government Printing Office, 1983.

———. Department of Commerce. Bureau of the Census. Current Population Reports, Series P-60, No. 143. *Characteristics of Households and Persons Receiving Selected Noncash Benefits: 1982.* Washington, D.C.: Government Printing Office, 1984.

———. Department of Commerce. Bureau of the Census. Current Population Reports. Series P-60, No. 144. *Characteristics of the Population below the Poverty Level: 1982.* Washington, D.C.: Government Printing Office, 1984.

———. Department of Commerce. Bureau of the Census. "The Future of the American Family." Statement of Paul C. Glick before the Select Committee on Population, U.S. House of Representatives, May 1978.

———. Environmental Protection Agency. *Noise, a Health Problem.* Washington, D.C.: Environmental Protection Agency, Office of Noise Abatement and Control, 1978.

———. Department of Health, Education and Welfare. "Transportation Authorities in Federal Human Services Programs." Washington, D.C.: Department of Health, Education and Welfare, 1976.

———. Department of Health, Education and Welfare. *Health United States 1979.* Washington, D.C.: Government Printing Office, 1980.

———. Department of Health, Education and Welfare. *Healthy People: The Surgeon General's Report on Health Promotion and Disease Prevention.* Washington, D.C.: Government Printing Office, 1979.

———. Department of Health and Human Services. *The Need for Long Term Care: Information and Issues.* Washington, D.C.: Government Printing Office, 1981.

———. Department of Housing and Urban Development. Office of the Assistant Secretary for Fair Housing and Equal Opportunity. *Fair Housing: An American Right/Right for Americans.* Summary Report of Conference Proceedings. Washington, D.C.: Government Printing Office, 1978.

Bibliography

———. Department of Housing and Urban Development (HUD). *Occasional Papers in Housing and Community Affairs 1.* Washington, D.C.: Department of Housing and Urban Development, 1978.

———. HUD. Office of Policy Development and Research. "Housing for the Elderly and Handicapped (The Experience of the Section 202 Program from 1959 to 1977)." Washington, D.C.: Department of Housing and Urban Development, 1979.

———. HUD. *A Survey of Citizens Views and Concerns about Urban Life.* Washington, D.C.: Government Printing Office, 1979.

———. HUD. *Children in the Built Environment: A Bibliography.* Washington, D.C.: Government Printing Office, 1979.

———. HUD. Office of Policy Development and Research. "Housing Our Families." Washington, D.C.: Department of Housing and Urban Development, 1980.

———. HUD. *Neighborhood Planning Primer.* Washington, D.C.: Government Printing Office, 1980.

———. HUD. *Neighborhood Self-Help Case Studies: Abstracts of Reports on Revitalization Projects Funded by the Office of Neighborhood Self-Help Development.* Washington, D.C.: Government Printing Office, 1980.

———. HUD. *Residential Displacement—An Update: Report to Congress.* Washington, D.C.: HUD, 1981.

———. Department of Labor. "Autumn 1972 Urban Family Budgets and Comparative Indexes for Selected Urban Areas." *News,* June 15, 1973.

———. Department of Labor. Bureau of Labor Statistics. Special Labor Force Report 217. *Children of Working Mothers, March 1977.* Washington, D.C.: Government Printing Office, 1978.

———. Department of Labor. Bureau of Labor Statistics. *Monthly Labor Review* 102, no. 10 (October 1979).

———. Department of Labor. Bureau of Labor Statistics. *Marital and Family Characteristics of the Labor Force.* Washington, D.C.: Government Printing Office, 1981.

———. Department of Labor. *Worktime: The Traditional Workweek and Its Alternatives.* Reprint from the 1979 Employment and Training Report of the President. Washington, D.C.: Government Printing Office, 1979.

———. Department of Labor. Women's Bureau. "Employment Goals of the World Plan of Action: Developments and Issues in the United States." Washington, D.C.: Department of Labor, 1980.

———. Department of Labor. "Autumn 1981 Urban Family Budgets and

Comparative Indexes for Selected Urban Areas." *News,* April 16, 1982.

———. Office of Consumer Affairs. "People Power: What Communities Are Doing to Counter Inflation." Washington, D.C.: Office of Consumer Affairs.

———. Department of State. "United States Women: Issues and Progress in the UN Decade for Women 1976-1985." Preliminary Report. Washington, D.C.: Department of State, 1980.

———. Department of State. "Report on the United States Delegation to the World Conference of the United Nations Decade for Women: Equality, Development and Peace." Washington, D.C.: Government Printing Office, 1981.

———. Senate. Special Committee on Aging. *Developments in Aging (Part 1 and Part 2 Special Report).* Washington, D.C.: Government Printing Office, 1980.

———. Department of Transportation, Urban Mass Transportation Administration, Transportation System Center. *The Handicapped and Elderly Market for Urban Mass Transit.* Washington, D.C.: Department of Transportation, 1973.

Vance, Bill. "U.S. Adventure Playground Report." Los Angeles: American Adventure Play Association, 1978.

Wachs, Martin. *Transportation for the Elderly: Changing Life-styles, Changing Needs.* Berkeley: University of California Press, 1979.

Waldman, Elizabeth; Grossman, Allyson Sherman; Hayghe, Howard; and Johnson, Beverly L. "Working Mothers in the 1970's: A Look at the Statistics." *Monthly Labor Review* 102 (October 1979):39–49.

Warren, Donald I. *Black Neighborhoods: An Assessment of Community Power.* Ann Arbor: University of Michigan Press, 1975.

———. "Helping Networks, Neighborhood, and Community Patterns: Consequences for Personal Well-Being." Final Report. Washington, D.C.: National Institute of Mental Health, 1976.

———. "Social Bonds in the Metropolitan Community: A Conceptual Overview." Rochester, Mich.: Oakland University, 1977.

———. "Neighborhoods in Urban Areas." In John Turner ed., *Encyclopedia of Social Work,* 17th issue. Washington, D.C.: National Association of Social Workers, 1977.

———. *Helping Networks: How People Cope with Problems in the Urban Community.* Notre Dame, Ind.: University of Notre Dame Press, 1981.

Warren, Rachelle B., and Warren, Donald I. *The Neighborhood Organizer's Handbook.* Notre Dame, Ind.: University of Notre Dame Press, 1977.

Warren, Roland L. "Alternative Community Paradigms." Paper presented at an Eastern Sociological Society Seminar on Community Theory and Research, 1974.

———. *The Community in America*. Chicago: Rand McNally, 3d ed., 1978.
———. "The Good Community—What Would It Be?" *Journal of the Community Development Society* 1 (1970):14–23.
———, ed. *Perspectives on the American Community: A Book of Readings*. 2d ed. Chicago: Rand McNally, 1973.
———. *Social Change and Human Purpose: Toward Understanding and Action*. Chicago: Rand McNally, 1977.
———. *The Structure of Urban Reform*. Lexington, Mass.: Lexington Books, D.C. Heath and Company, 1974.
Warren Village, Inc. "The Annual Plan 1980–81." Denver, Colo.: Warren Village, 1980.
———. "The Annual Plan 1982–83." Denver, Colo.: Warren Village, 1982.
Webber, Melvin M. "Order in Diversity, Community without Propinquity." In *Neighborhood, City and Metropolis*. Edited by Robert Gutman and David Popenoe. New York: Random House, 1970.
Weber, Max. *The Theory of Social and Economic Organization*. Translated by Talcott Parsons. New York: Free Press, 1947.
Wekerle, Gerda R.; Peterson, Rebecca; and Morley, David. *New Space for Women*. Boulder, Col.: Westview Press, 1980.
Wellesley Editorial Committee. *Women and National Development: The Complexities of Change*. Chicago: University of Chicago Press, 1977.
Wellman, Barry. "The Community Question: The Intimate Networks of East Yorkers." *American Journal of Sociology* 84 (1979):1201–1231.
———. "The New East York Study: Strategy and Tactics." Working Paper 22. Toronto: Department of Sociology, University of Toronto, May 1981.
Wellman, Barry, and Whitaker, M., eds. "Community, Network, Communication: An Annotated Bibliography." 2d ed. Toronto: Centre for Urban and Community Studies, University of Toronto, 1974.
Wentowski, Gloria J. "Old Age in an Urban Setting: Coping Strategies, Reciprocity, and Personal Networks." N.d.
White House Conference on Aging. "Chartbook on Aging in America." Washington, D.C.: 1981 White House Conference on Aging, 1981.
———. "Executive Summary of Technical Committee on Family, Social Services and Other Support Systems." Washington, D.C.: 1981 White House Conference on Aging, 1981.
———. *Report of Technical Committee on Creating an Age Integrated Society: Implications for the Family*. Washington, D.C.: Government Printing Office, 1981.
———. *Report of the Mini-Conference on Euro-American Elderly*. Washington, D.C.: Government Printing Office, 1981.
———. *Report of the Mini-Conference on Intergenerational Cooperation*

and Exchange. Washington, D.C.: Government Printing Office, 1981.

———. *Report of the Mini-Conference on Self-Help and Senior Advocacy.* Washington, D.C.: Government Printing Office, 1981.

Wireman, Peggy. "Building Good Advisory Committees: Some Important Considerations." In Patricia Marshall, ed., *Citizen Participation Certification for Community Development: A Reader on the Citizen Participation Process.* Washington, D.C.: National Asociation of Housing and Redevelopment Officials, 1977.

———. "Community Development and Citizen Participation—Friend or Foe?" *Journal of the Community Development Society* 1 (Fall 1970): 54–62.

———. "Citizen Participation." In John Turner, ed., *Encyclopedia of Social Work.* 17th issue. Washington, D.C.: National Association of Social Workers, 1977.

———. "Making Neighborhoods Suitable for Children." In *The Child and the City.* Edited by National Institute for Research Advancement and International Pediatric Association. Tokyo: National Institute for Research Advancement, 1982.

———. "Some Nuances of Integration." Speech given at the Conference on Voluntary Programs and Concepts in Support of Fair Housing, Washington, D.C., June 1–3, 1977.

———. "Meanings of Community in Modern America: Some Implications from New Towns." Ph.D. dissertation, American University, 1977.

———. "The Functions of Intimate Secondary Relationships." Paper presented at the Ninth World Congress of Sociology, Uppsala, Sweden, August 1978.

———. "Intimate Secondary Relationships." Paper presented at the Seventy-third Annual Meeting of the American Sociological Association. San Francisco, September 4–8, 1978.

———. "But That's Where the Children Have to Live: Using Urban Social Fabric in Support of Children." In *Managing Urban Space in the Interest of Children.* Edited by William Michelson and Ellen Michelson. The Child in the City Programme, University of Toronto. Toronto: Canada/MAB Committee, 1980.

———. "How Can a Home for the Elderly Be More Like a Home?" Paper presented at the Thirty-second Annual Scientific Meeting of the Gerontological Society, Washington, D.C., November 1979.

———. "Adventure Playground." *Challenge* 11 (March 1980):8–12.

Wireman, Peggy, and Sebastian, Antoinette. "Important Considerations for Environmental Assessments of Housing Sites for the Elderly." In *Housing an Aging Society.* Edited by Thomas O. Byerts, M. Powell Lawton, and Robert J. Newcomer. New York: Van Nostrand Reinhold Co., forthcoming.

Wirth, Louis. "Urbanism as a Way of Life." *American Journal of Sociology* 44 (1938):1-24.
Wolff, Kurt H. *The Sociology of Georg Simmel*. London: Collier-Macmillan, 1950.
"Women and the American City." *Signs* 5 (Spring 1980).
Women's and Minors' Bureau. *The Status of Women in Japan*. Tokyo: Women's and Minors' Bureau, Ministry of Labor, 1977.
Yin, Robert K.; Lucas, William A.; Szanton, Peter L.; and Spindler, Andrew J. *Citizen Organizations: Increasing Client Control over Services*. Santa Monica, Calif.: Rand Corporation, 1973.
Young, Michael, and Wilmott, Peter. *Family and Kinship in East London*. London: Routledge and Kegan Paul, 1957.
Zukin, Sharon. "The Cutting Edge: A Decade of the New Urban Sociology." *Theory and Society* 9 (1980):575-601.
Zurcher, Louis A.; Green, Alvin E.; with Johnson, Edward; and Patton, Samuel. *From Dependency to Dignity: Individual and Social Consequences of a Neighborhood House*. New York: Behavioral Publications, 1969.

Index

Abt Associates, 124-125
Administration on Aging, 136, 138
Advisory Commission on Intergovernmental Relations, 63
Ahlbrandt, Roger S., Jr., and James V. Cunningham, 42, 60, 62-63, 66
Aid to Dependent Children, 124
Air pollution, 115
Alinsky, Saul, 66-67
Alternate housing, 122-125
Altman, Irwin, 9
Anomic neighborhoods, 41
"At risk," 15-17; households, 17-19; individuals, 19-23

Baltimore, Md., 111
Banks, 59
Beach, Mark, and Oralee S. Beach, 111-112
Bender, Thomas, 1, 113
Benton, Ill., 136-139
Bethnal Green, East London, 31
Beulah, Hazen, and Glenullin, N. Dak., 132
Black Fathers, 103-104
Black Focus, 107-108
Blacks, 92-93; "at risk," 20-22; and racial integration, 99-105; social organizations, 103-104, 107-108; teenagers, 101-102
Boston, xxiii; West End, 29-31
Bott, Elizabeth, 33
Brookings Institution, 59
Burkhart, Lynne C., 102, 104-106

Cable television, 61, 135
Carter administration, 68
Child support, 146-147
Children: and air/noise pollution, 115-117; Asian, 156; and grandparents, 121, 135; and lead poisoning, 117; and physical environment, 115-118; and play areas, 118, 156; and traffic dangers, 117-118
Citizen participation, 56-60
Class integration, 105-106
Cleveland Heights, Ohio, 111
Coincidence of boundaries, 37
Columbia, Md., 2, 87-97, 99-106
Communities, 29-50; institutional aspects of, 36-37; and population mobility, 9; psychological aspects of, 29-33; social network analysis of, 33-36; and Urban Gardening Program spillover effects, 79-80. See also Neighborhood(s) *entries*
Community Action Program, 54-55, 56, 57
Community and Social Change in America (Bender), 1
Community atmosphere, 119-120
Community design, 115-128
Community development, 53-55, 91-92, 149
Community Development Block Grant Program (CDBG), 56, 57, 59
Community integration, 12-13
Community newspapers, 61, 156-157
Community relationships, 120-122
Community supports for the elderly, 129-143
Community theory: "lost," "saved," and "liberated" communities, 29-33
Community-without-propinquity concept (Webber), 33
Comprehensive Employment Training Act (CETA), 56
Computers, 135
Conflict theory, 32
Cooley, Charles H., 2
Coping needs, 15-16
Coproduction, 64-66, 158
Core needs, 15

Crump, Barry N., 6

Developing countries, 53, 153–160
Diffuse neighborhoods, 41
Displaced homemakers, 62

East London, 31, 33
Ehrlich, Phyllis, 136
Elderly, the, 129–143; abuse of, 134–135; "at risk," 22; and children, 121, 135; as homemakers, 133; long-term care of, 134; meals for, 133, 134; physical environment of, 129–131; and telephones, cable TV, and computers, 135; and Urban Gardening Program, 78, 121; as volunteers/employees, 133–134
Encounter groups, 8
Ethnic communities, 29–31, 32, 40
Ethnic relations and Urban Gardening Program, 82–84
Extended families, 154–155; artificial, 121

Fairfax County, Va., 107
Families: extended, 121, 154–155; and intimate secondary relationships, 9–11; neighborhood support for, 44–46; and support networks, 23–25; three-generation, 153, 154; with children, 120–122
Family Services, 123
Female-headed households: and child support, 146–147; in developing countries, 155–156. *See also* Single-parent families
Fischer, Claude S., 17, 23, 24–25, 31–32, 34, 43, 59–60, 80
Food stamp program, 22
Foster Grandparents, 121
Fried, Marc, 31
Friendships, 31–32
Functionalism, 32
Funding, 149

Gans, Herbert J., 12, 29, 40
Gemeinschaft-Gesellschaft theory (Tönnies), 1, 2, 29

Goetze, Rolf, 63–64, 66
Grandparents/grandchildren, 121, 135
"Granny flats," 26
Granovetter, Mark, 33
Great Britain's colonial village development, 53
Green Lake housing project. *See* Reston, Va.
Group therapy, 8

Harre, David, 140
Heterogeneous populations, 11–12
Hispanics, 22
Hodgson, Susan, 15, 16
Hong Kong, 154
Horizontal-vertical integration, 36–37, 46
Households: "at risk," 17–19; neighbor-support of, 44–46; spillover effects of Urban Gardening Program, 77–79; support needs, 15–28; types of support, 23–25
Housing: alternate, 122–125; high-rise/low-rise, 154; shared, 139–141
Howard County, Md., 99
Hunter, Albert, 42, 43–44, 61–62, 67
Hyde Park-Kenwood, Chicago, 2, 54, 67

Individuals "at risk," 19–23; and spillover effects of Urban Gardening Program, 77–79
Indonesia, 61
Information flow, 60–64
Integral neighborhoods, 40
Integrated communities, 111–112. *See also* Columbia, Md.; Hyde Park-Kenwood, Chicago; Reston, Va.
Integration, 99–114. *See also* Class integration; Community integration; Horizontal-vertical integration; Pluralism; Racial integration
Intimate secondary relationships, xxi–xxii, 2–13
Irwin, John, 7
Italian community (Boston's West End), 29–31, 40

Index

Jack and Jill, 103, 107
Jakarta, Indonesia, 156, 157
Janowitz, Morris, 61
Japan, 61, 153, 156-157

Kinship systems, 154-155
Kyoto, Japan, 61

Lead poisoning, 117
Leadership development, 60, 80-81
Linkages outside neighborhood, 81-82
Litwak, Eugene, 11, 23-24, 132
Litwak, Eugene, and Ivan Szelenyi, 33

"Maximum feasible participation," 54-55
Meals on Wheels, 133
Megatrends (Naisbitt), xxiii
Men and child support, 146-147
Merton, Robert K., 1
Model Cities Program, 56, 59
Montgomery County, Md., 99
Mosaic neighborhoods, 41
Mothers, employed, 118-119
Mutual help program, 136-139

Naisbitt, John, xxiii
Naparstek, Arthur J., David E. Biegel, and Herzl R. Spiro, 148
National Commission on Neighborhoods, 68
National Institute of Mental Health, 61
National Science Foundation, 58
Neighborhood involvement, 42-44
Neighborhood organizations: co-option of, 147-148; in Japan, 156-157
Neighborhood Reinvestment Corporation, 64
Neighborhood support, 44-46
Neighborhoods, 38-41; functions of, 38-40; typology of, 40-41
New Delhi, India, 154
Newcomers, 9, 62
Newspapers, community, 61, 156-157
Nixon administration, 57
Noise pollution, 115-117
North Dakota, 132
Norway, 117

Oakland Mills Village. *See* Columbia, Md.

Parochial neighborhoods, 40
Physical environment: and children, 115-118; and the elderly, 129-131
Play areas, 118, 156
Pluralism, 82-84, 92-93, 99
Politics and power, 66-69
Pollution, 115-117
Population mobility, 9
Portland, Oreg., 111
Poverty index, 22
Primary relationships, 2. *See also* Intimate secondary relationships
Privacy, 9, 147
Program operation, 55-56
Project SENIOR, 134
Property values, 95

Race relations, 82-84, 92-93
Racial integration, 99-105
Rand Corporation, 58
Reagan administration, 56, 68
Resident involvement, 51-73
Respite care, 134
Reston, Va., 2, 107-111
Rich, Richard C., 65
Rich, Richard C., and Abraham Wanderman, 63
Richmond Fellowship of Metropolitan Washington, 139-141
Rohe, William, and Lauren Gates, 59, 60
Ross, Heather L., and Isabel V. Sawhill, 20
Rouse, James, 87, 99

"Scenes" (Irwin), 7-8
Schoenberg, Sandra, and Patricia Rosenbaum, 65, 95
Secondary relationships, 2. *See also* Intimate secondary relationships
Self-help, 51-53
SENIOR, 134
Senior centers, 134
Senior Companion Program, 133
Services and facilities: for the elderly,

130–131, 135; for families with children, 118–119
Shared functions, theory of (Litwak), 23–24
Shared housing, 139–141
Simmel, Georg, 1
Simon, Robert E., 107
Singapore, 154, 157, 158
Single-parent families: alternate housing for, 122–125; and Urban Gardening Program, 78. *See also* Female-headed households
Smookler, Helene, 100
Social environment for the elderly, 131–136
Social network analysis, 31, 32, 33–36
Social networks, 17, 23–25, 90–91
Spillover effects: coproduction, 64–66; information flow, 60–64; of Urban Gardening Program, 77–84
Stepping-stone neighborhoods, 41
Support networks, 17, 23–25
Surgeon-General's Report, The, 22
Suttles, Gerald, 32
Sweden, 61

Teenagers, 101–102
Telephones and the elderly, 135
Third World, 53, 153–160
Three-generation families, 153, 154
Tocqueville, Alexis de, xxii
Tönnies, Ferdinand, 1
Traffic safety, 117–118
Transitory neighborhoods, 41
Transportation for the elderly, 129–130

Understanding Neighborhood Change (Goetze), 63
United Nations, 53
United States Department of Agriculture, Cooperative Extension Service, 53. *See also* Urban Gardening Program
United States Department of Housing and Urban Development (HUD), 122; Office of Neighborhoods and Voluntary Action, 56, 57
Urban Gardening Program, 75–86, 121, 149
Urban renewal/revitalization, 31, 40, 56, 57, 63–64
Urban Villagers, The (Gans), 29

Volunteerism, xxii, 133–134

Wandersman, Abraham, 58
War on Poverty, 44, 54–55, 56, 57
Warren, Donald, 17, 34–35, 64
Warren, Rachelle, and Donald Warren, 40–41, 45
Warren, Roland, 36, 46
Warren Village, Denver, Colo., 122–125
Washington, D.C., 139–141
Weak ties concept (Granovetter), 33–34
Webber, Melvin, 33
Wellman, Barry, 29, 31
West Harlem Community Organization (New York City), 55–56
Winthrop, John, xxiii
Women: "at risk," 22; as displaced homemakers, 62; employed, 118–19. *See also* Female-headed households; Single-parent families

Young, Michael, and Peter Wilmott, 31

Zoning codes, 26

About the Author

Peggy Wireman has her Ph.D. in sociology, and has worked in the field of urban development and community involvement for over twenty years. She is a former grass-roots neighborhood organizer, has taught university courses on community development, and has lectured on social planning in the United States and Asia. She is a member of the American Institute of Certified Planners. Dr. Wireman has provided policy advice and program assistance on citizen participation, environmental management, and city, new town, and neighborhood development for the U.S. Department of Housing and Urban Development, where she currently is employed in the Office of Environment and Energy.